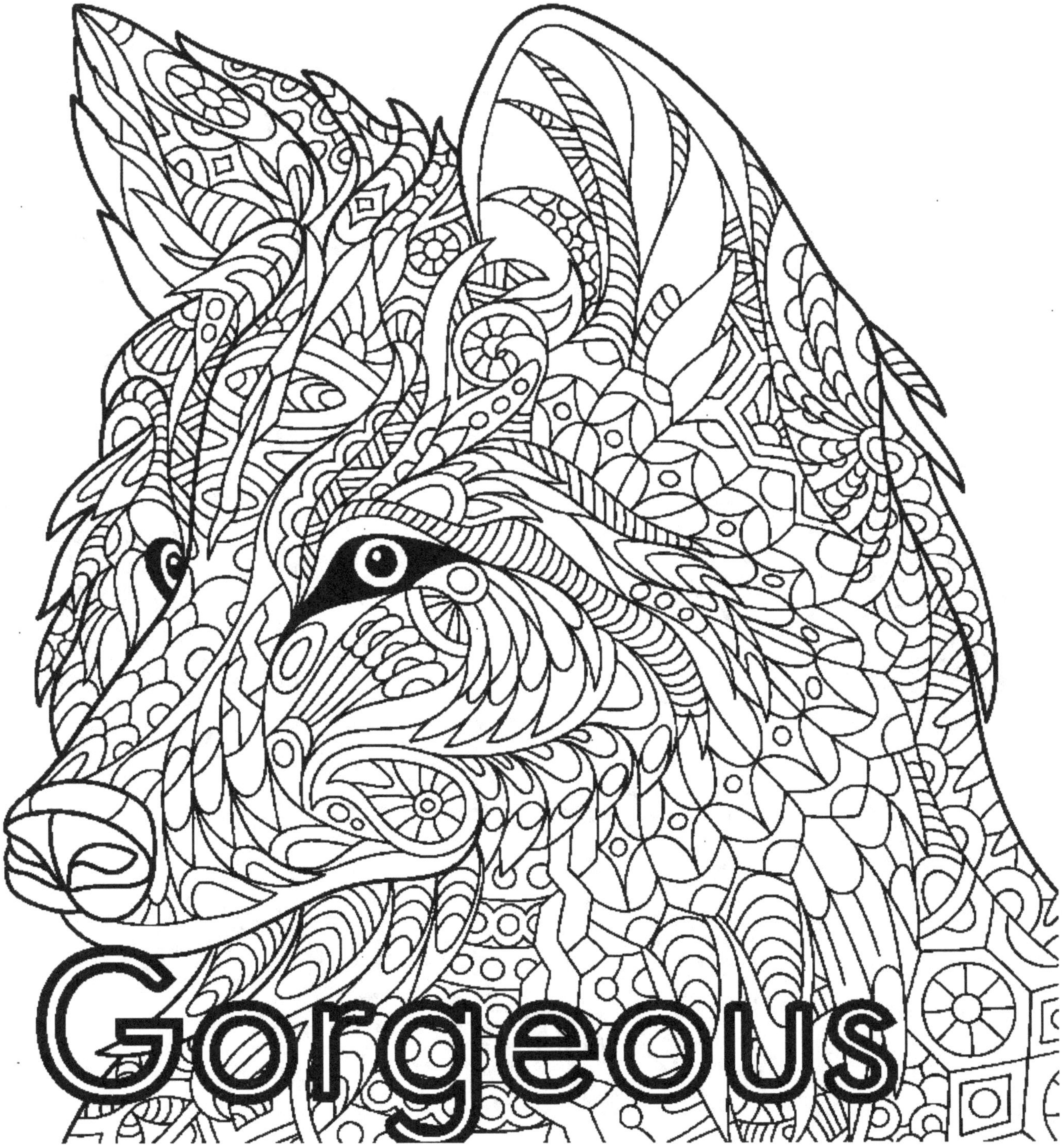
Gorgeous

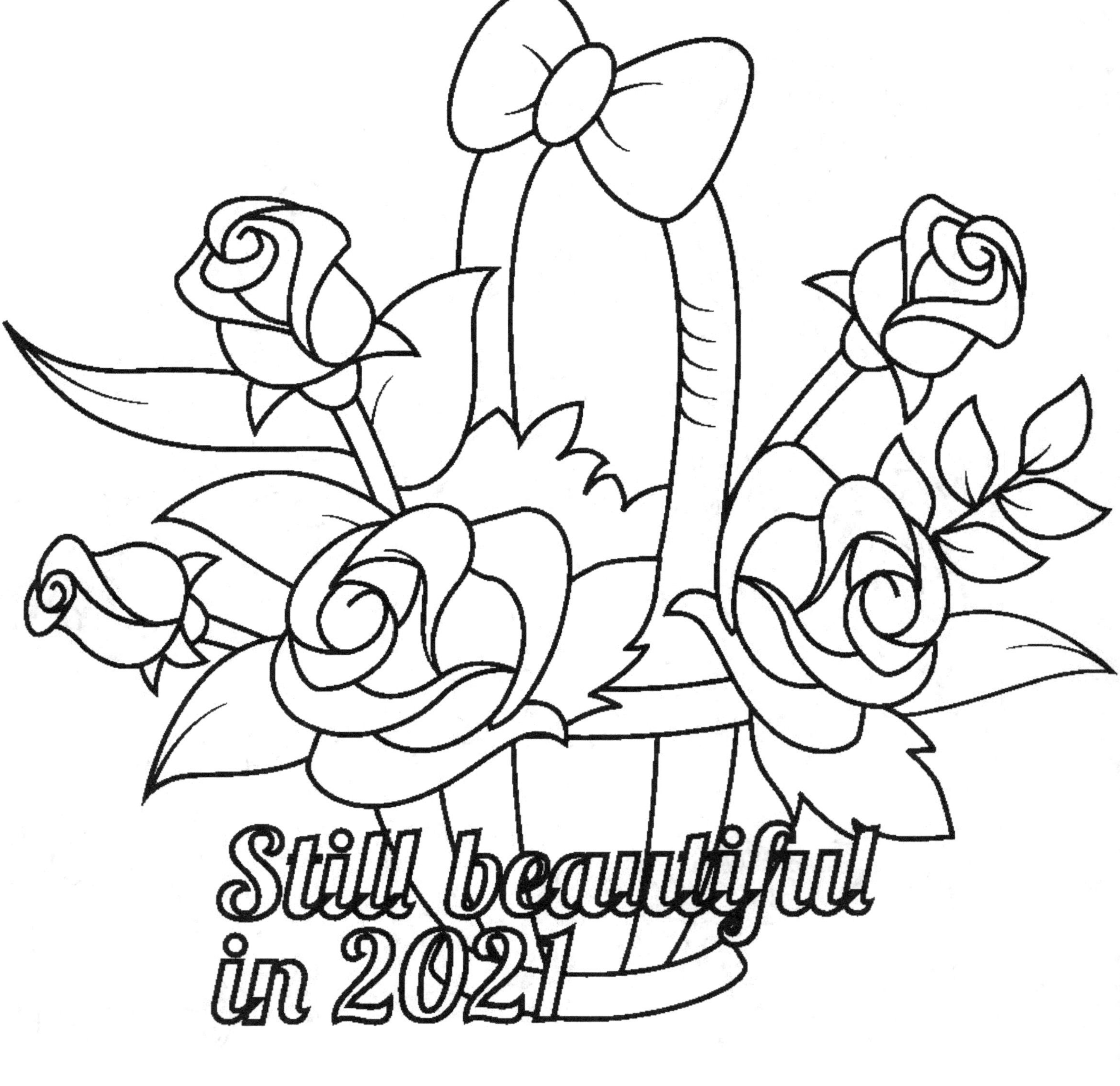
Still beautiful
in 2021

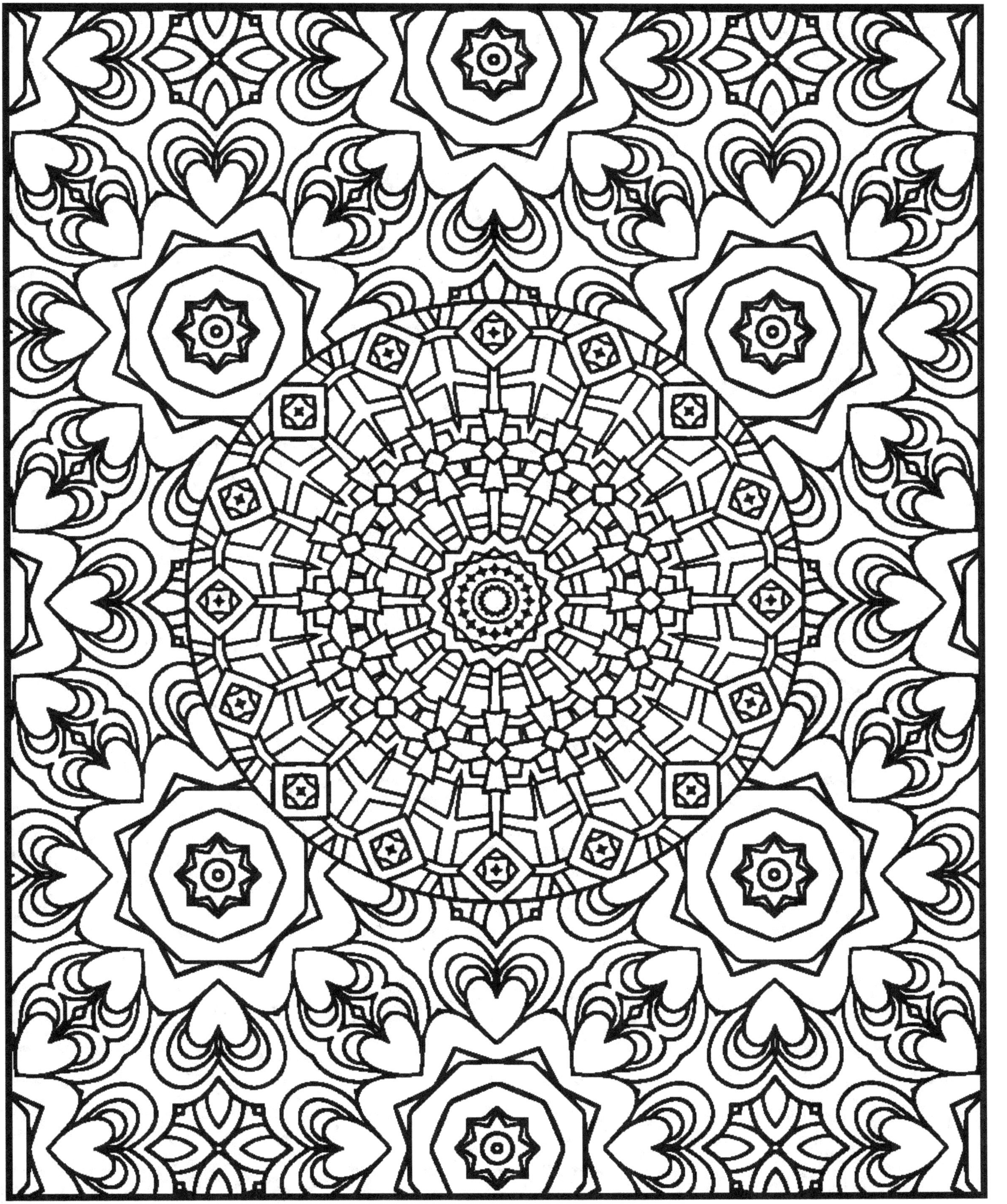

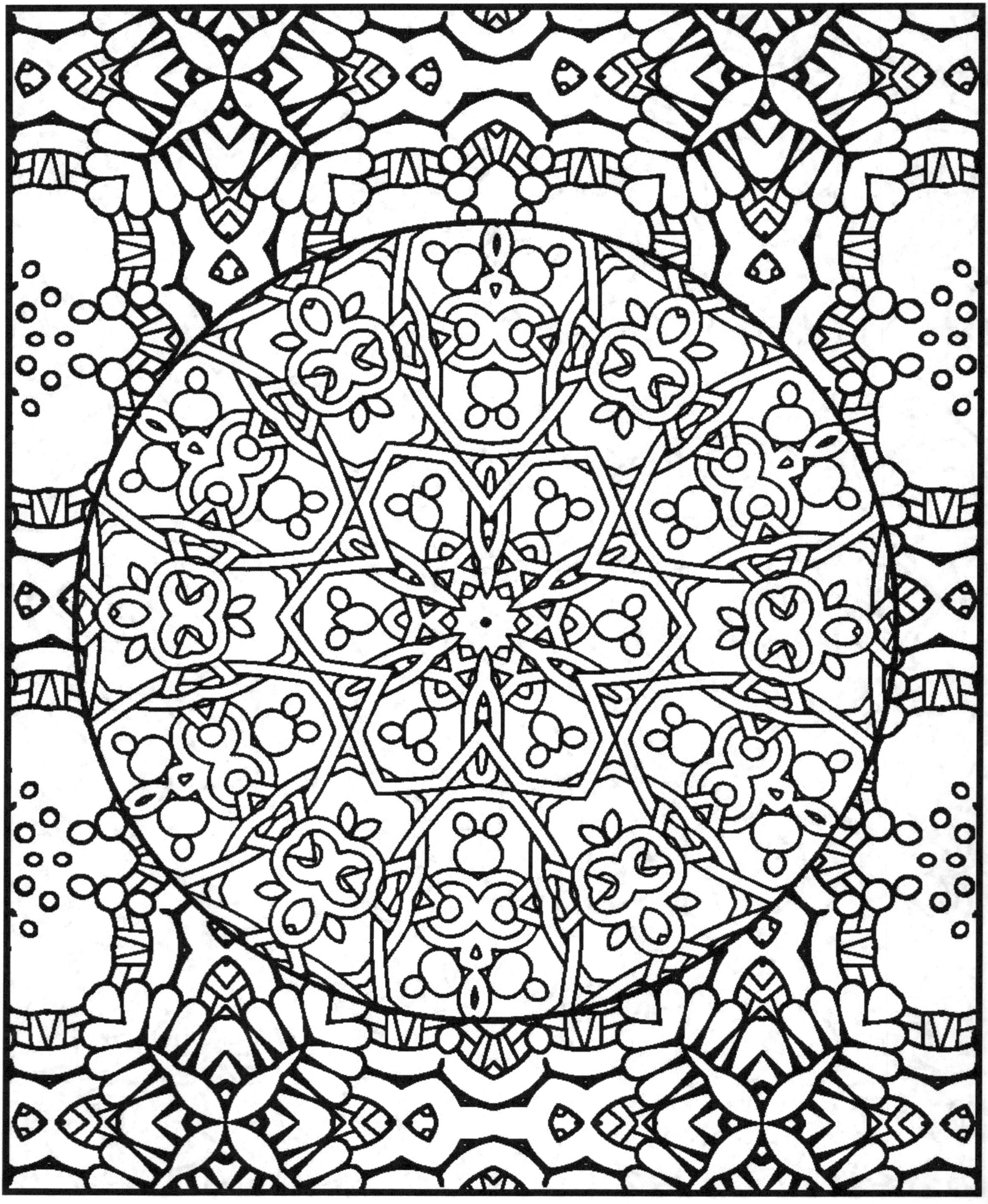

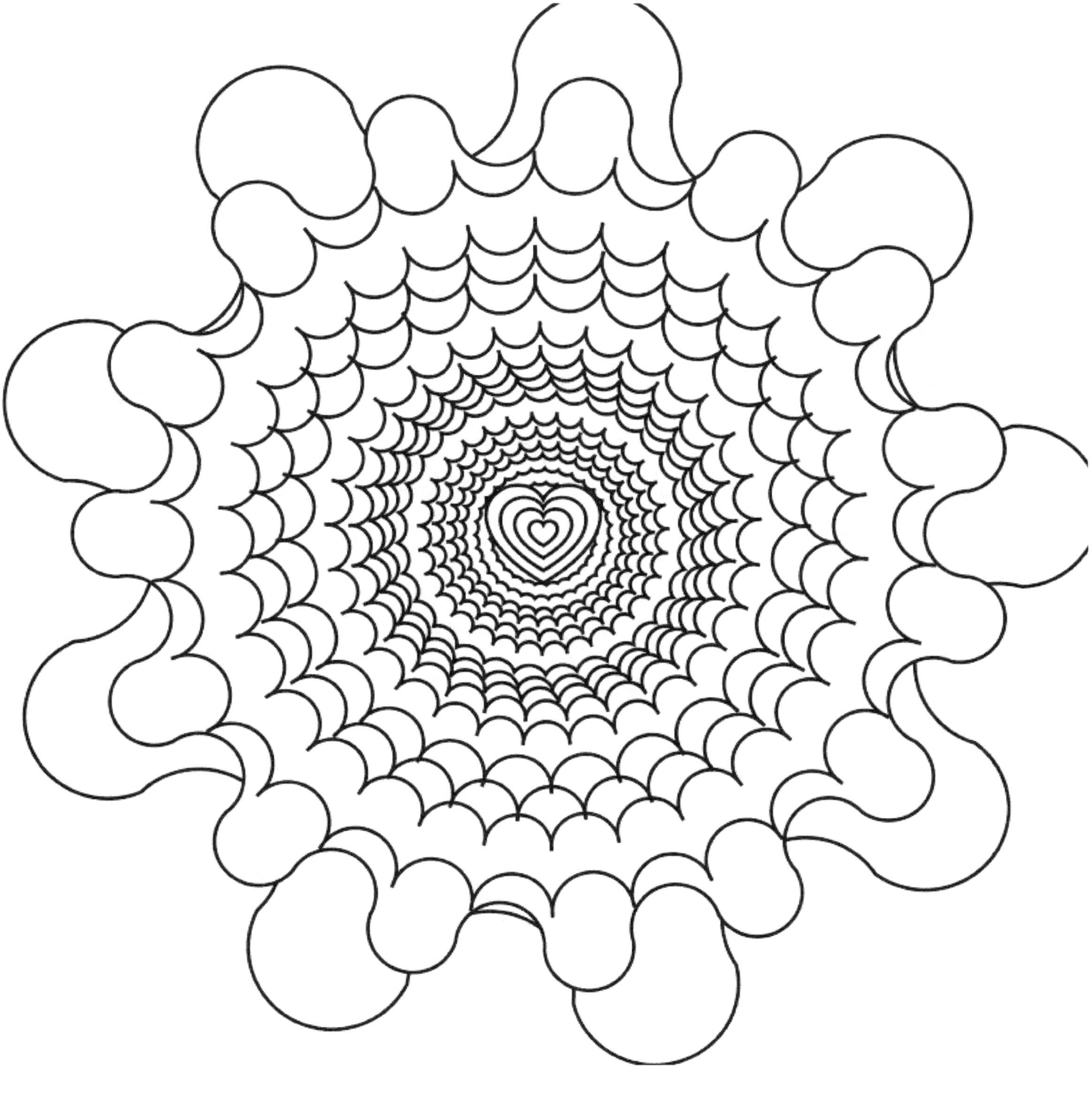

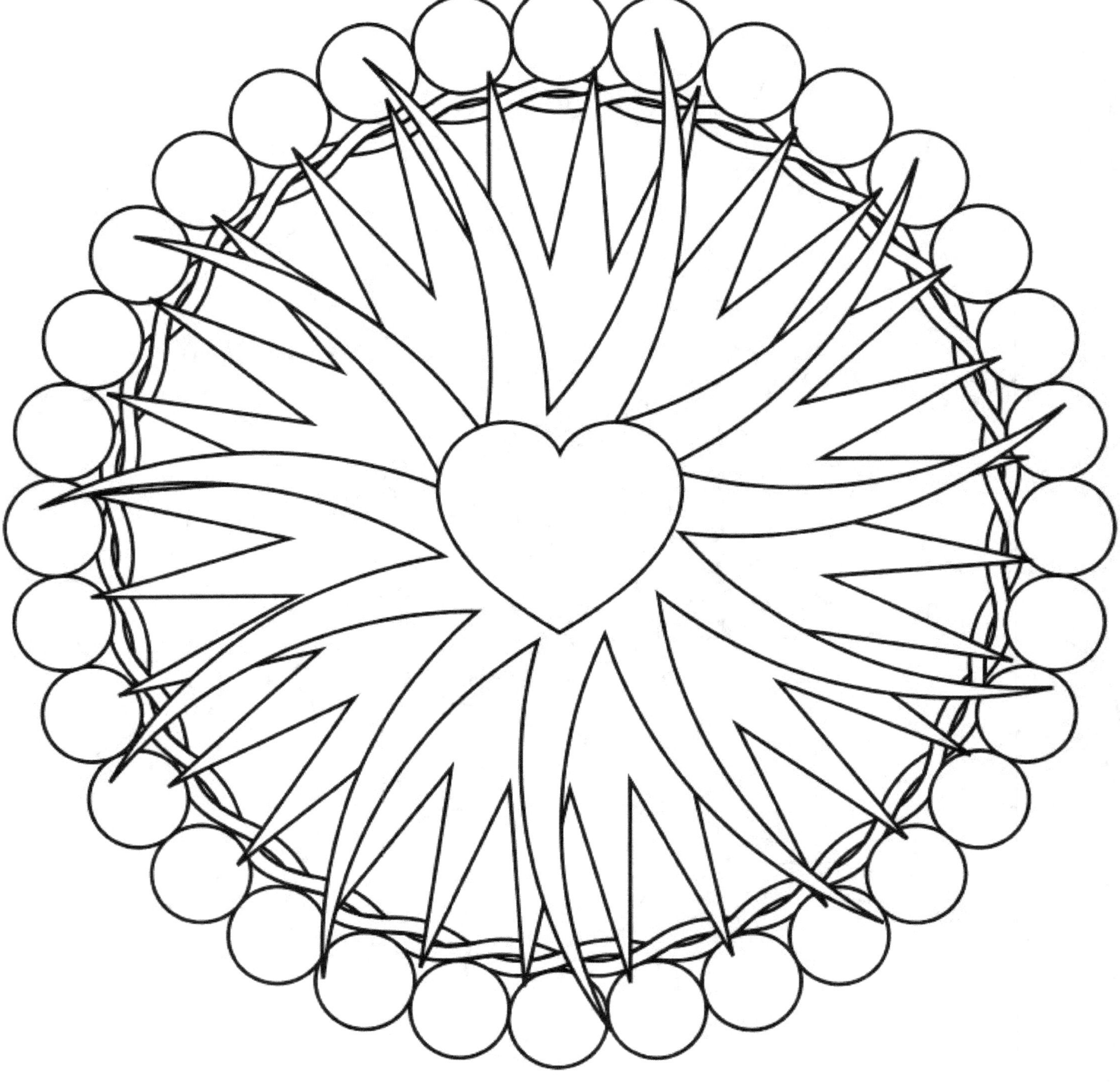

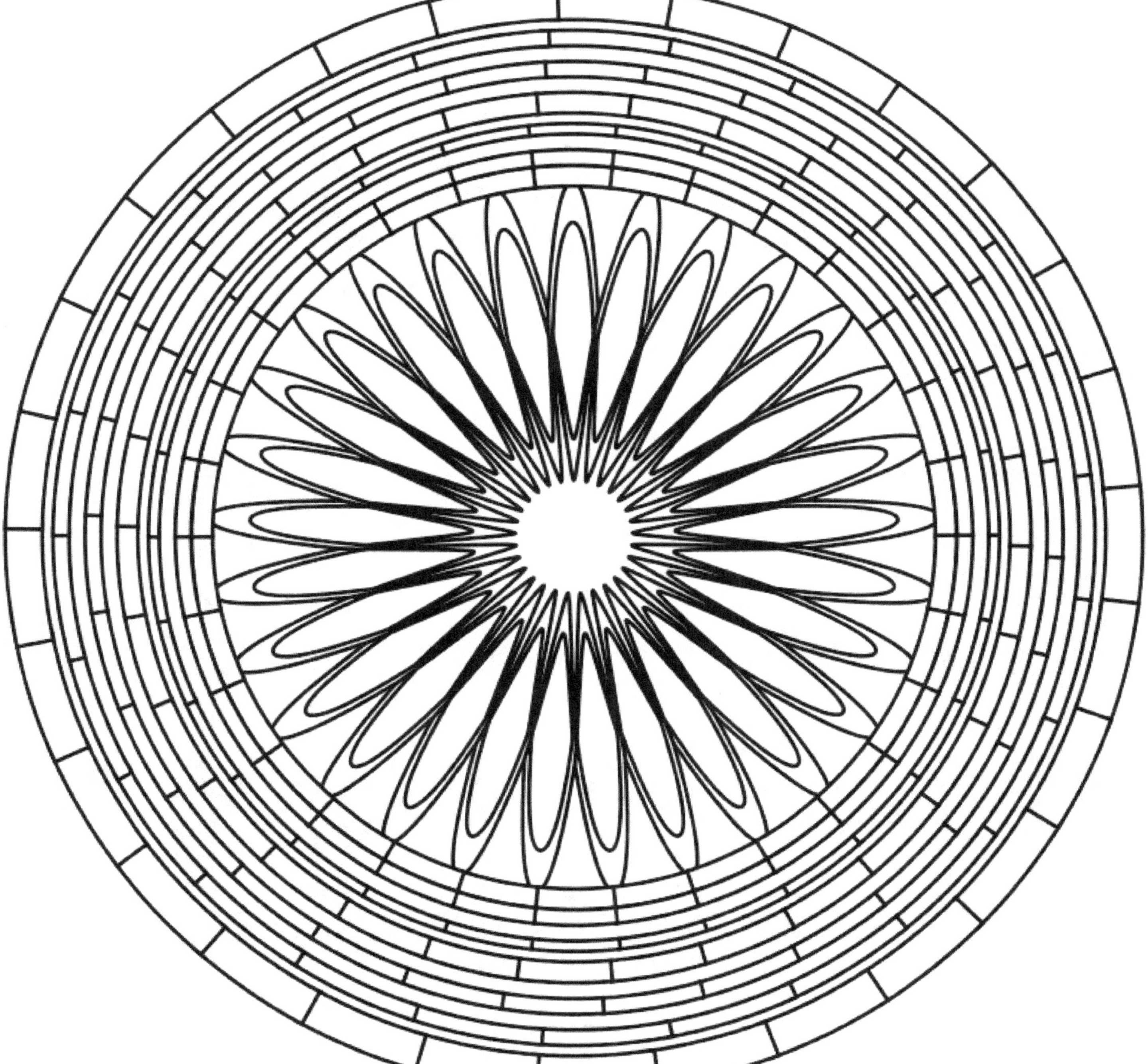

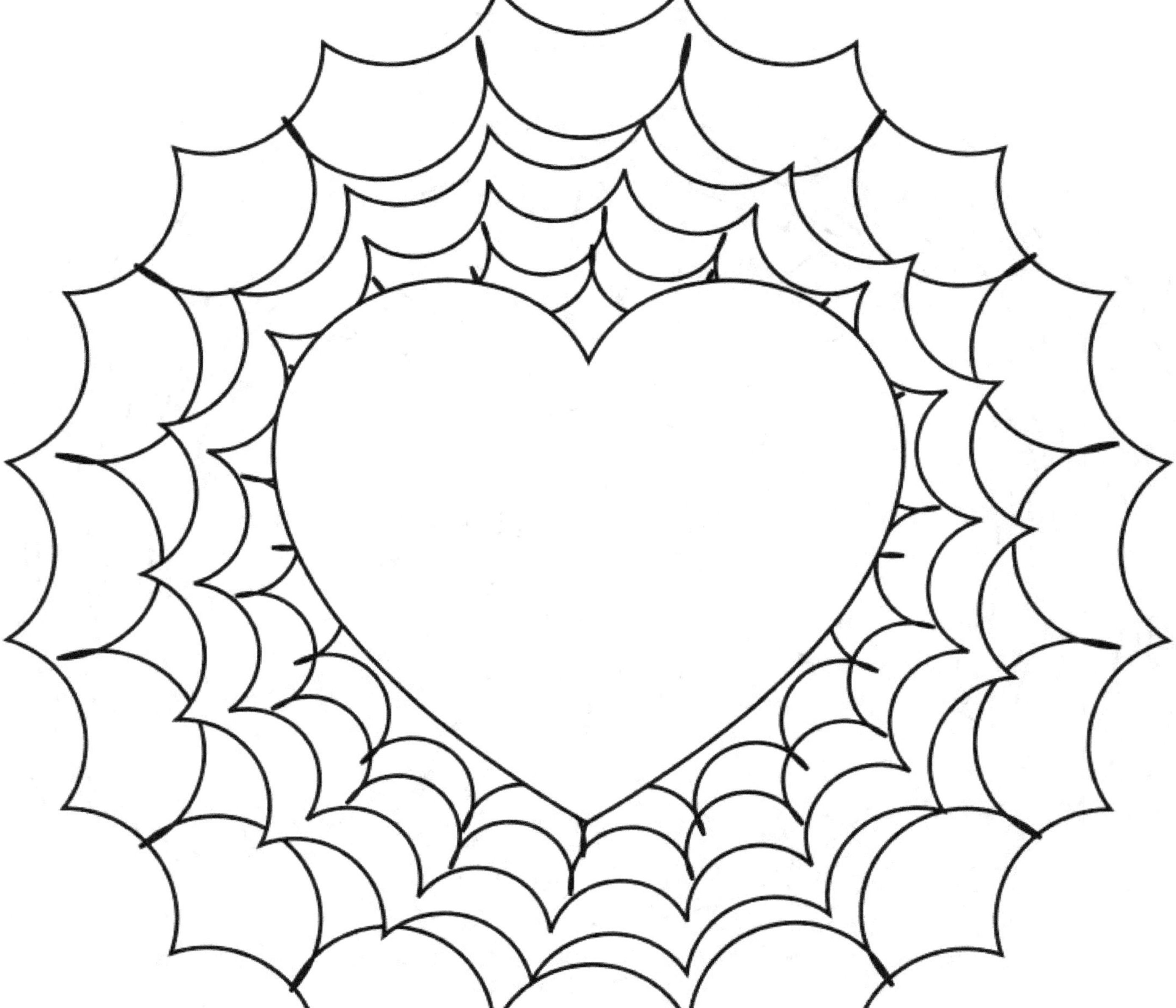

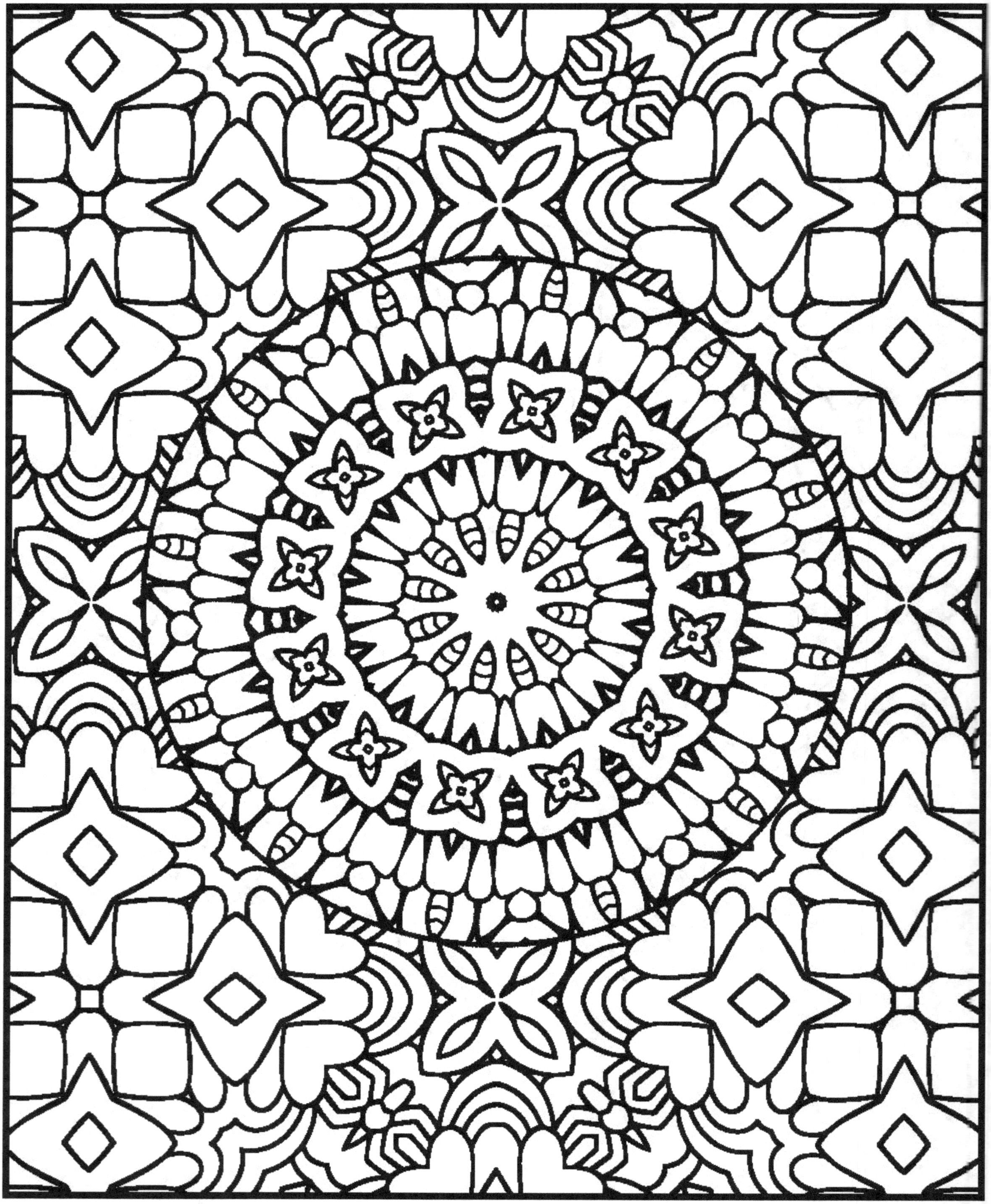

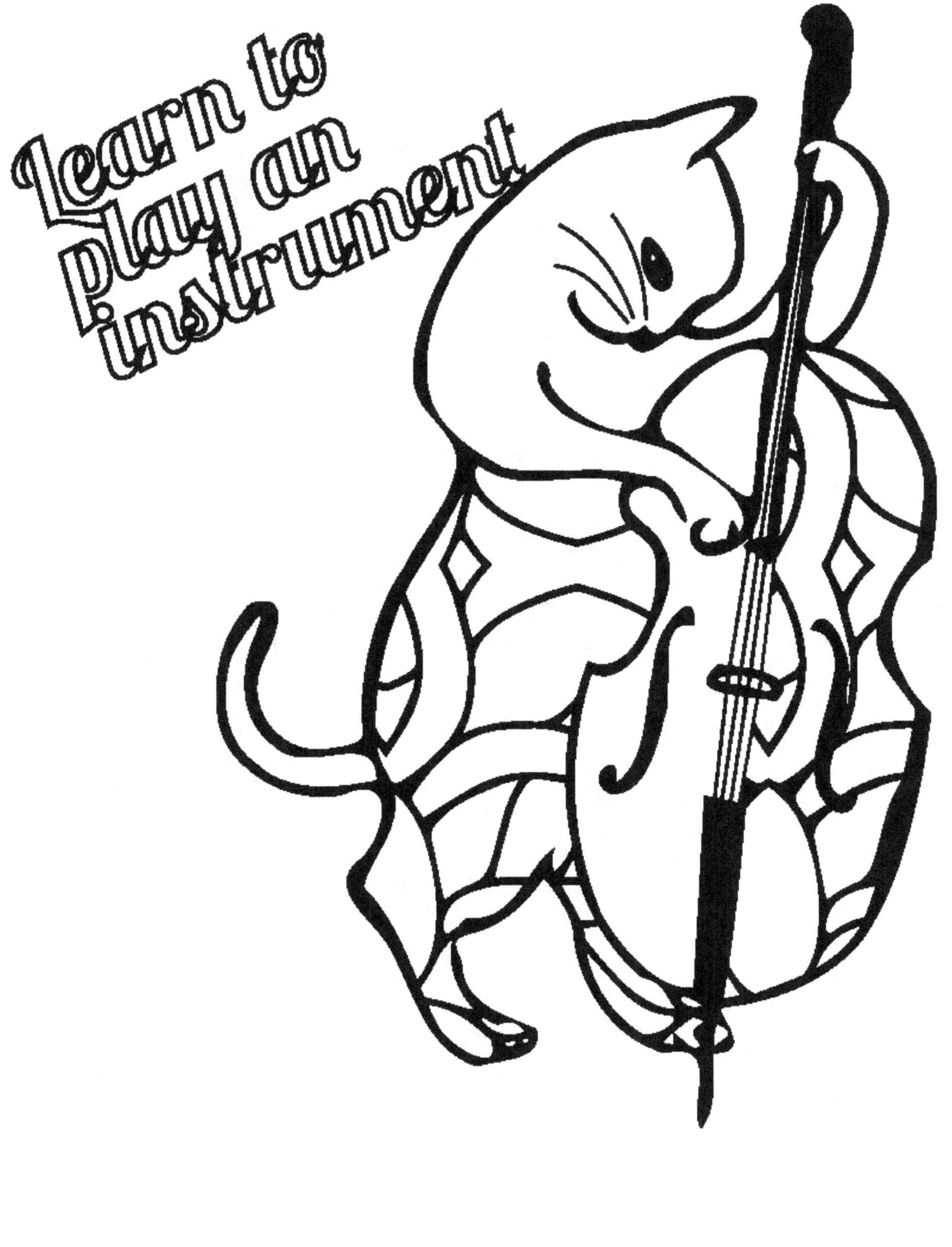
Learn to
play an
instrument

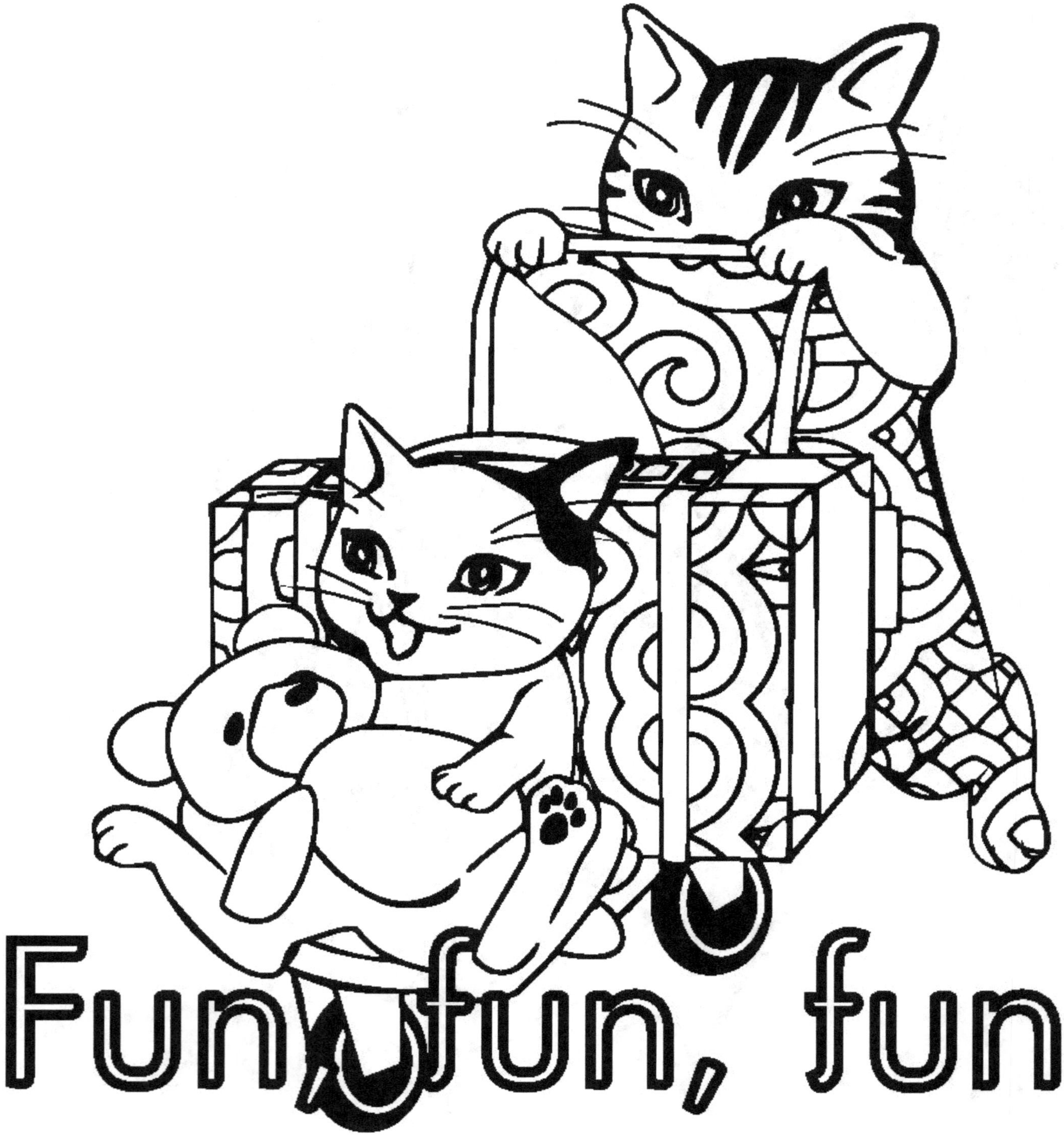
Fun, fun, fun

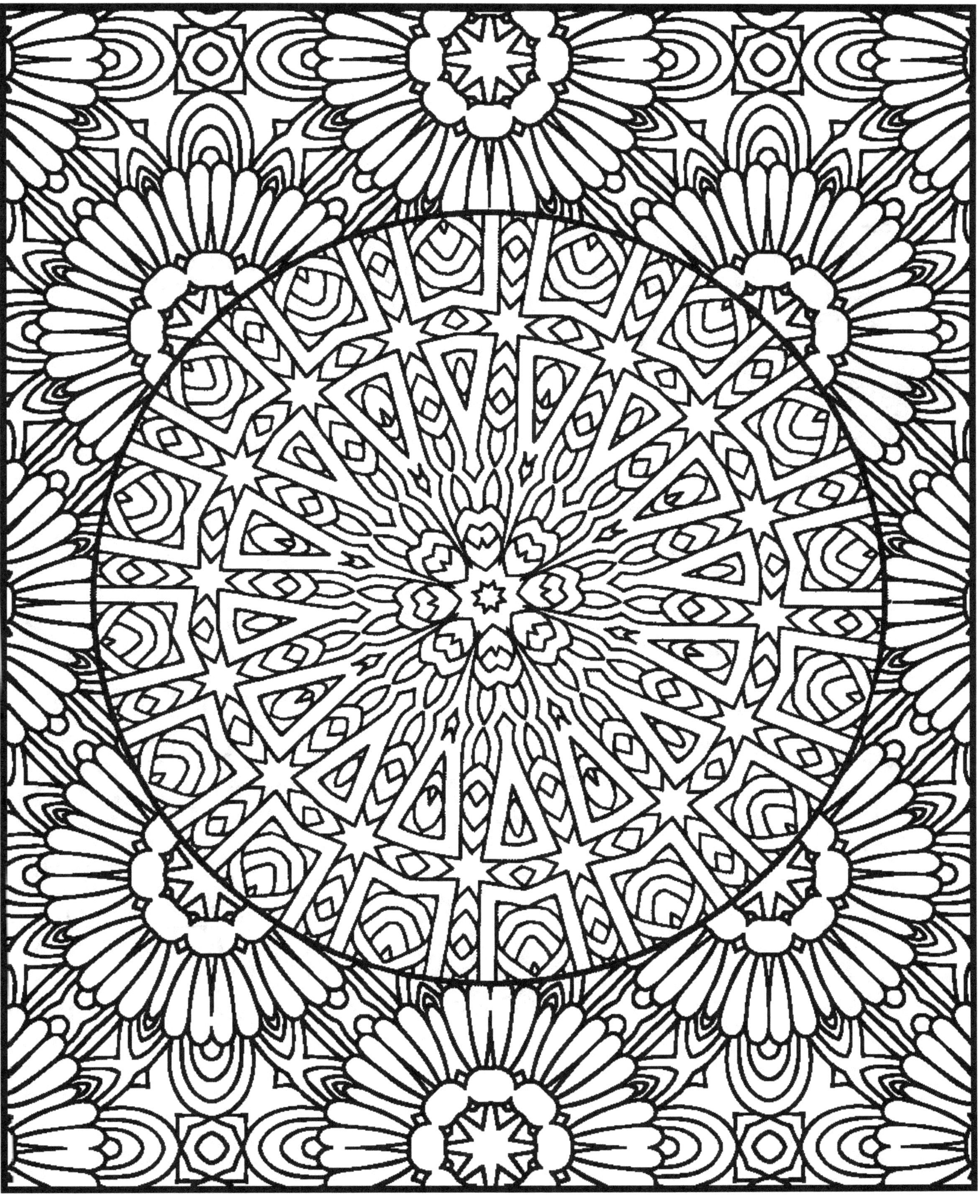

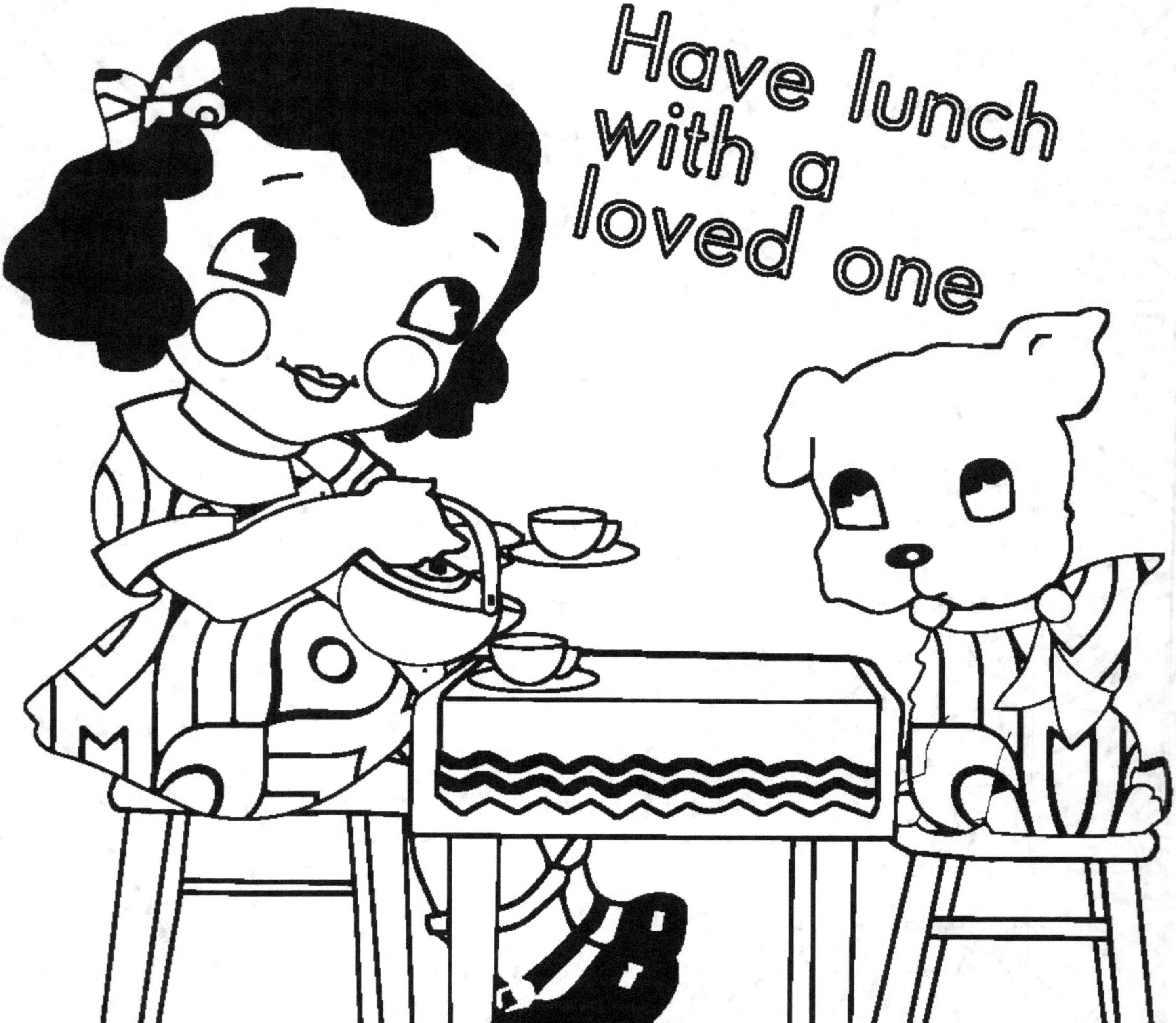
Have lunch
with a
loved one

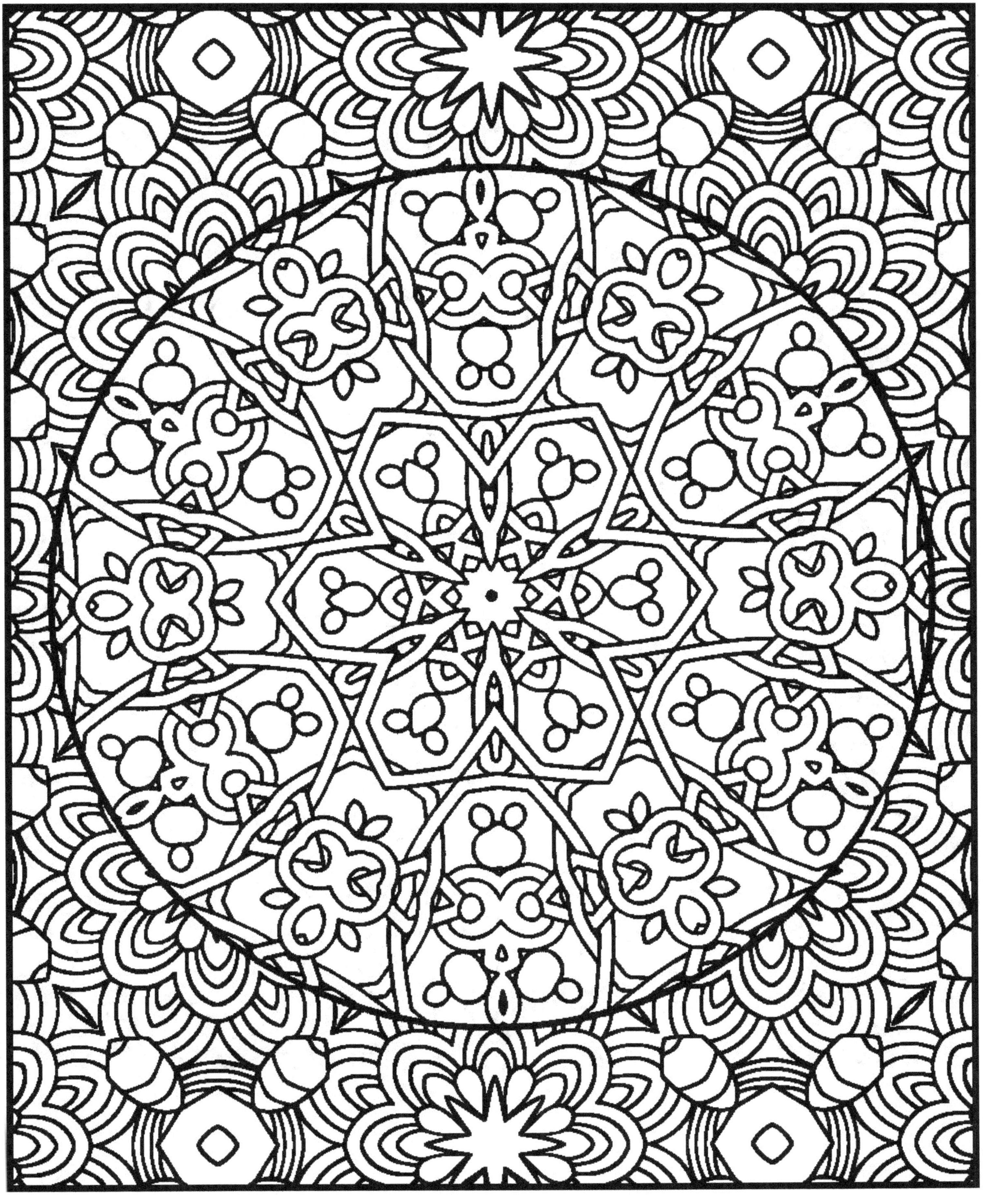

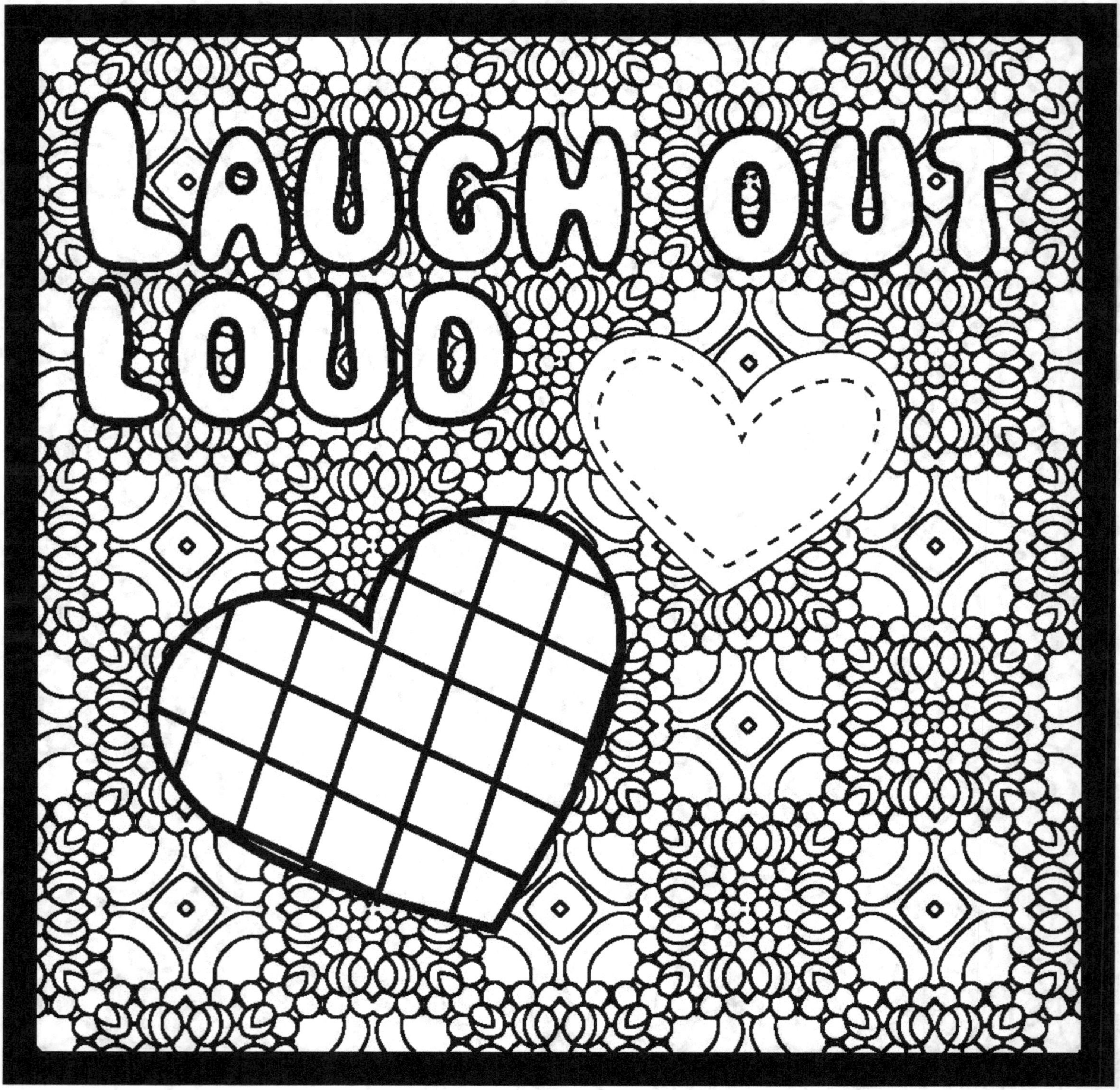
LAUGH OUT
LOUD

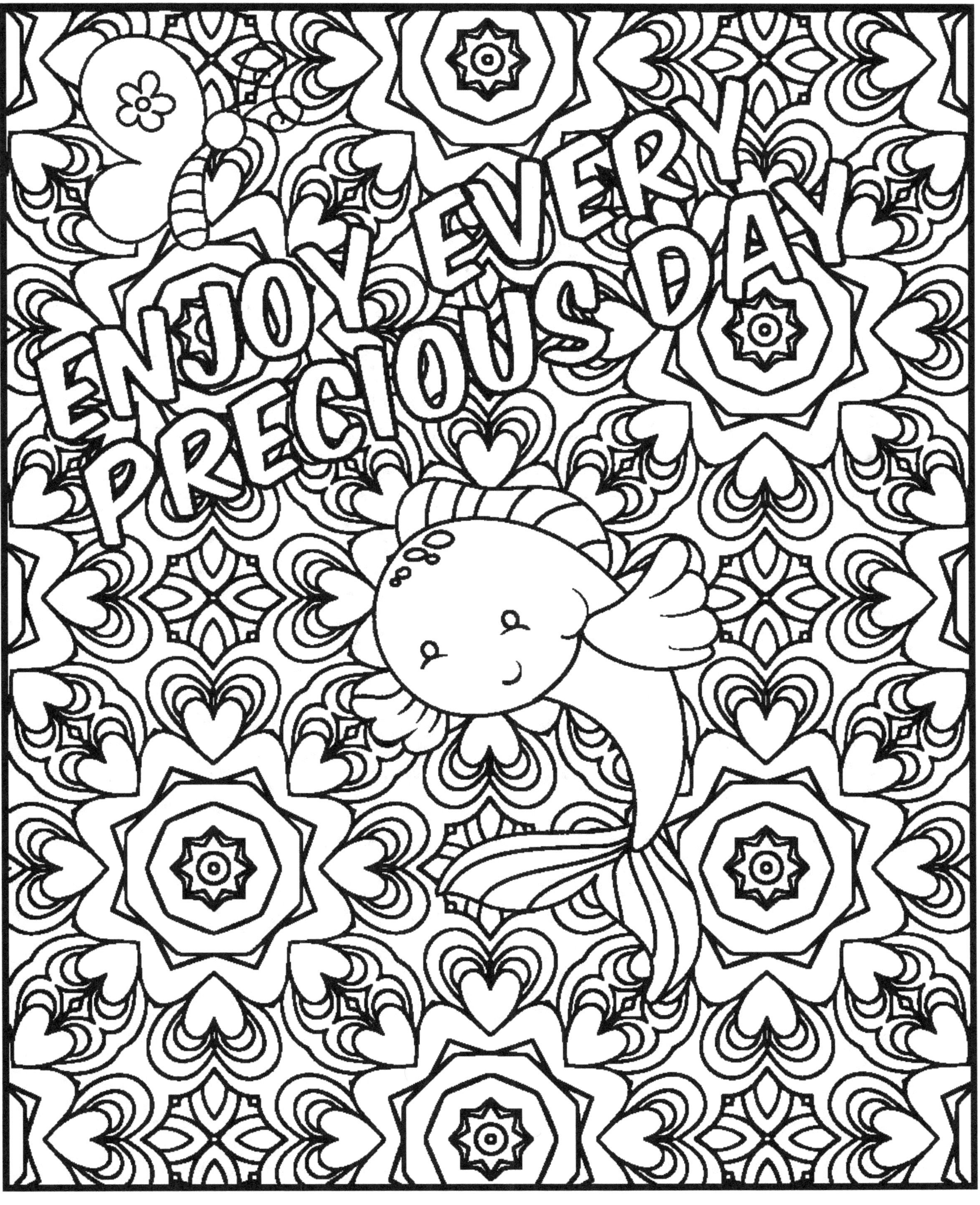

ENJOY EVERY
PRECIOUS DAY

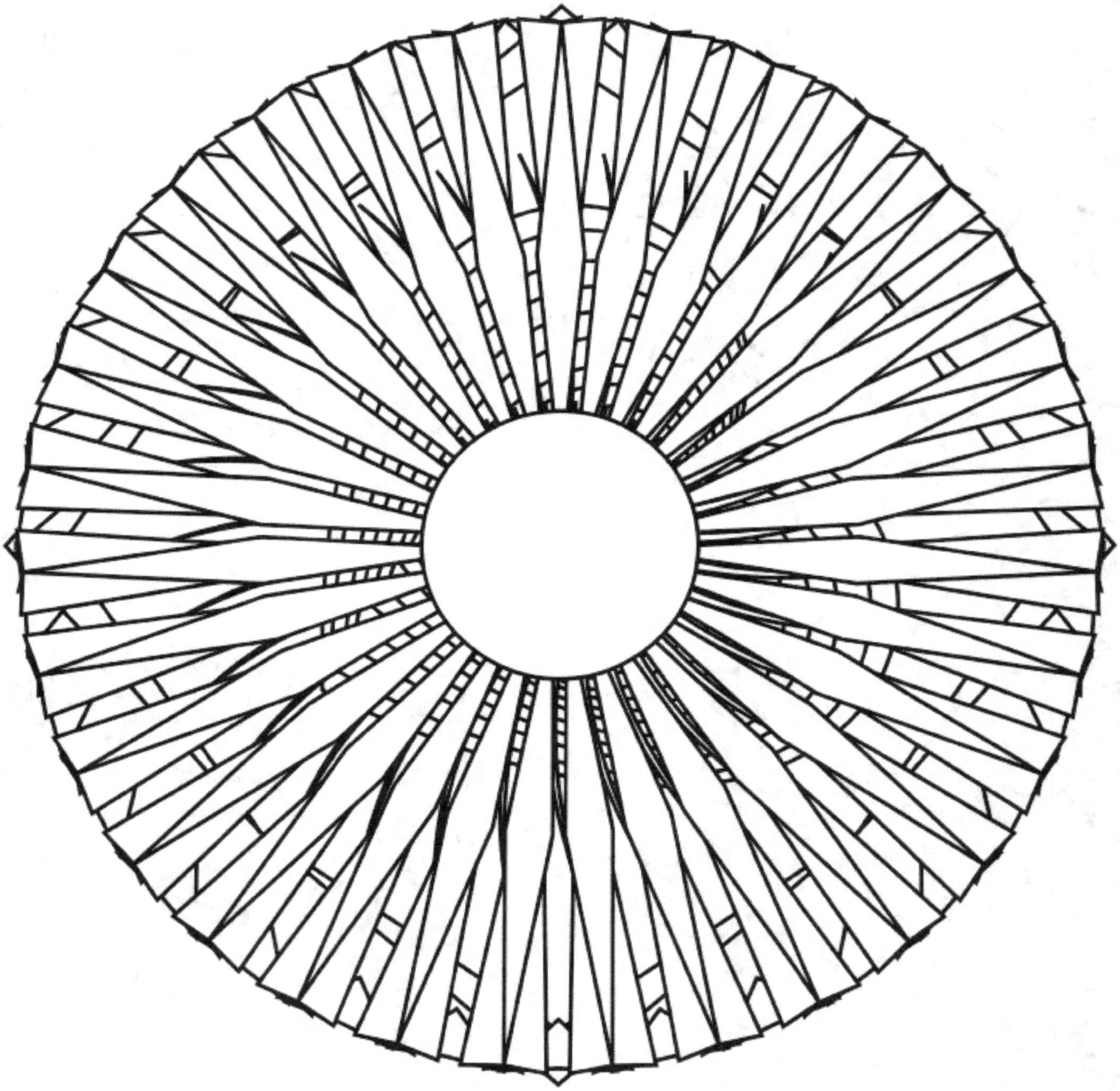

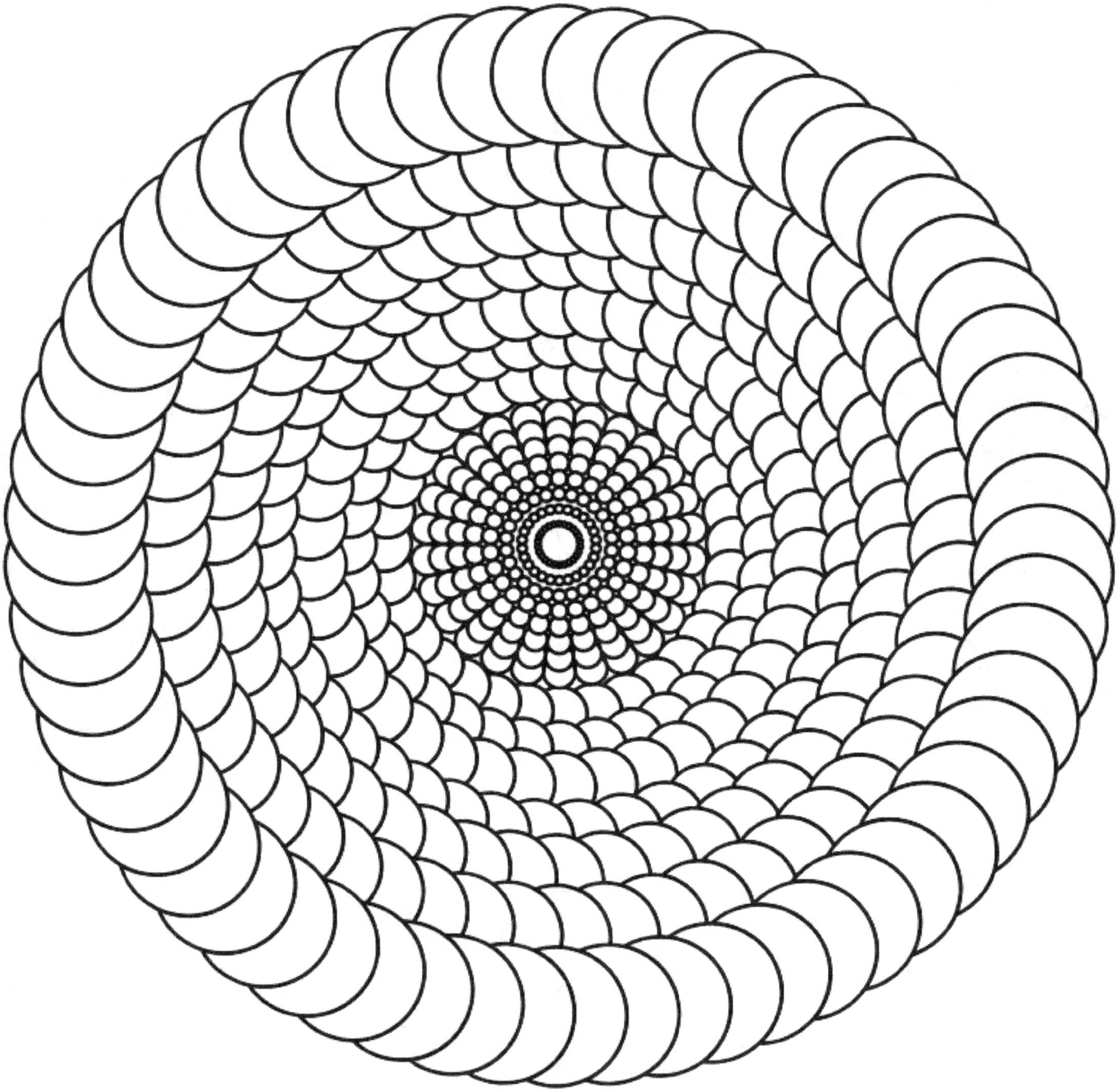

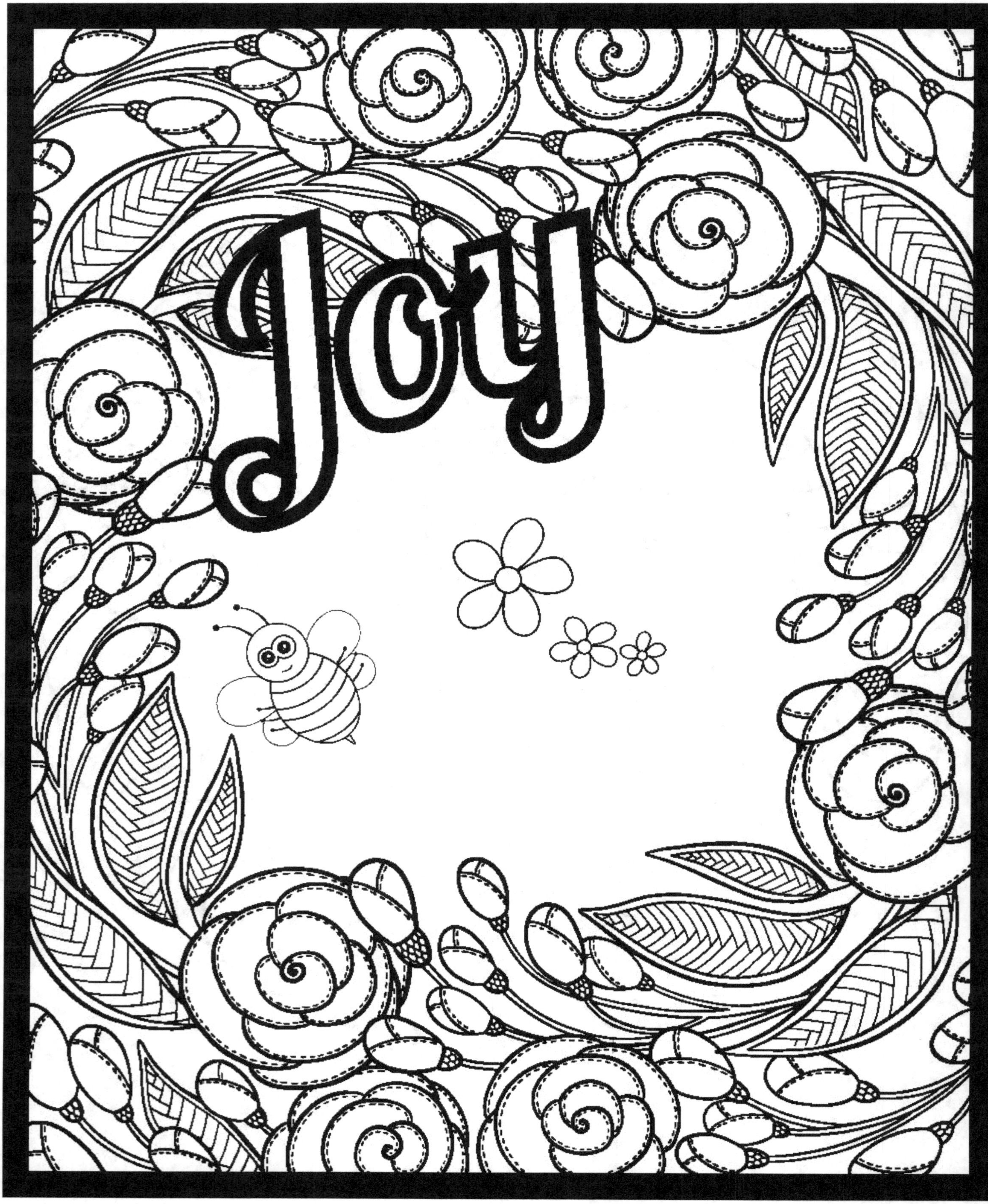
Joy

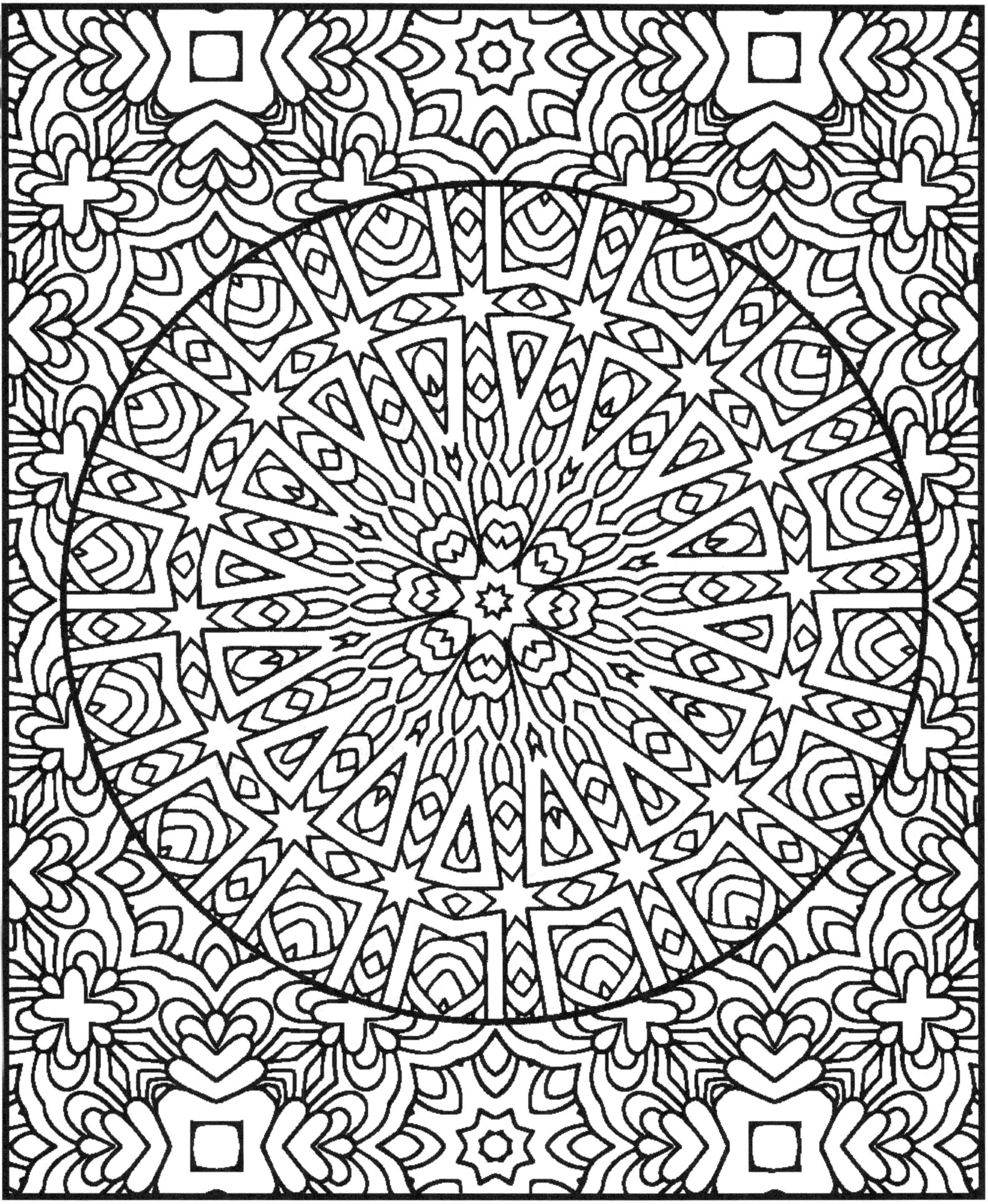

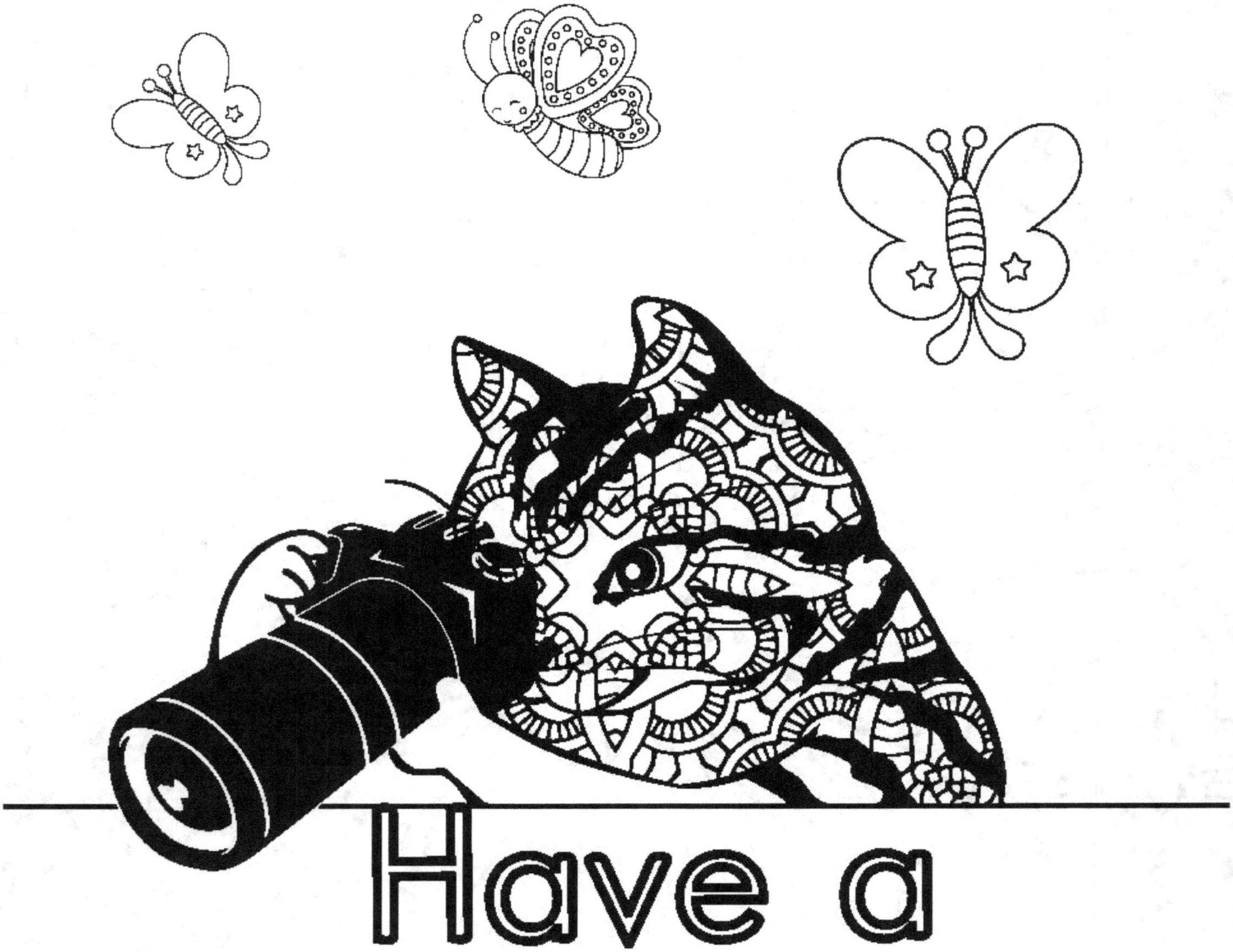

Have a hobby

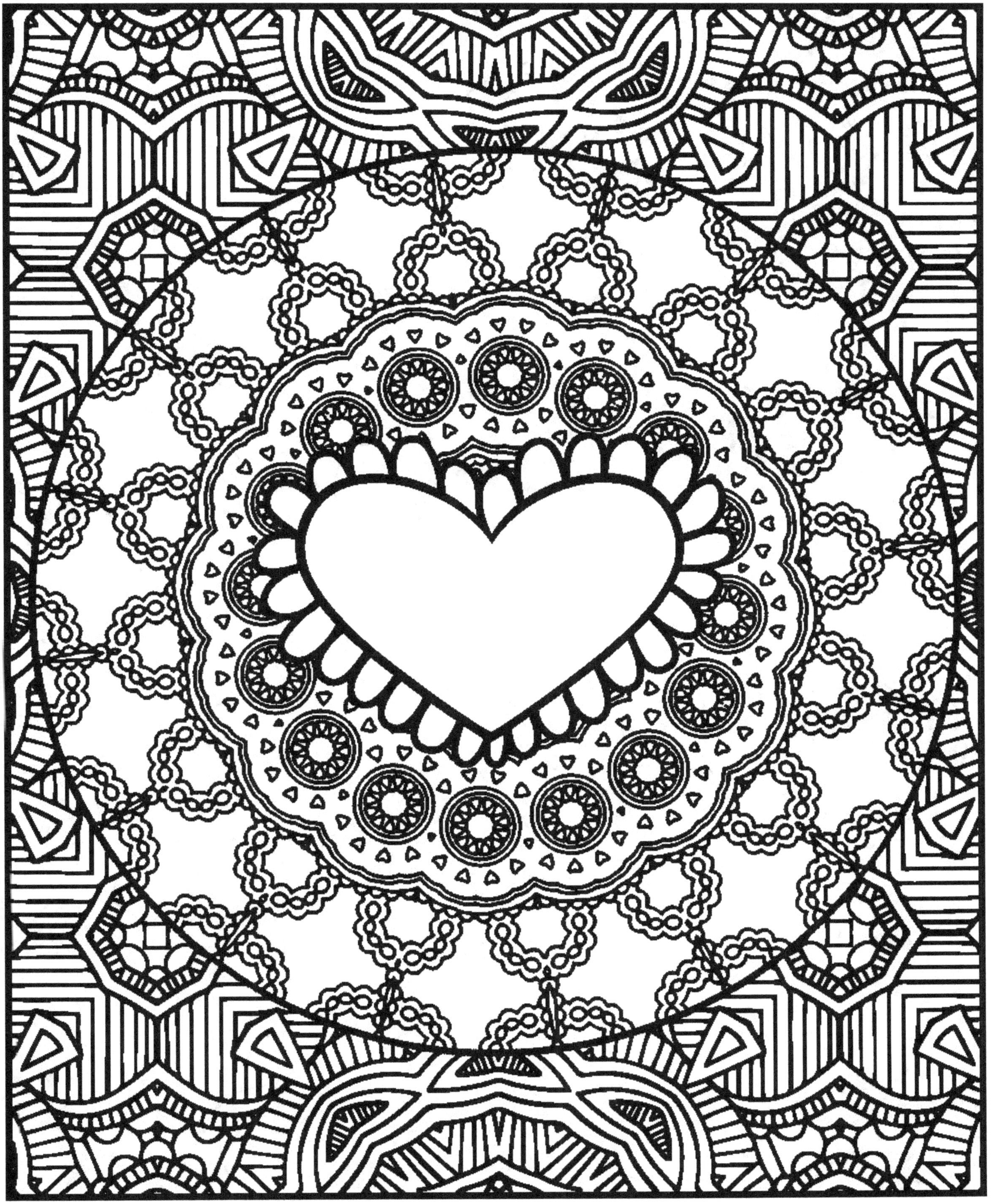

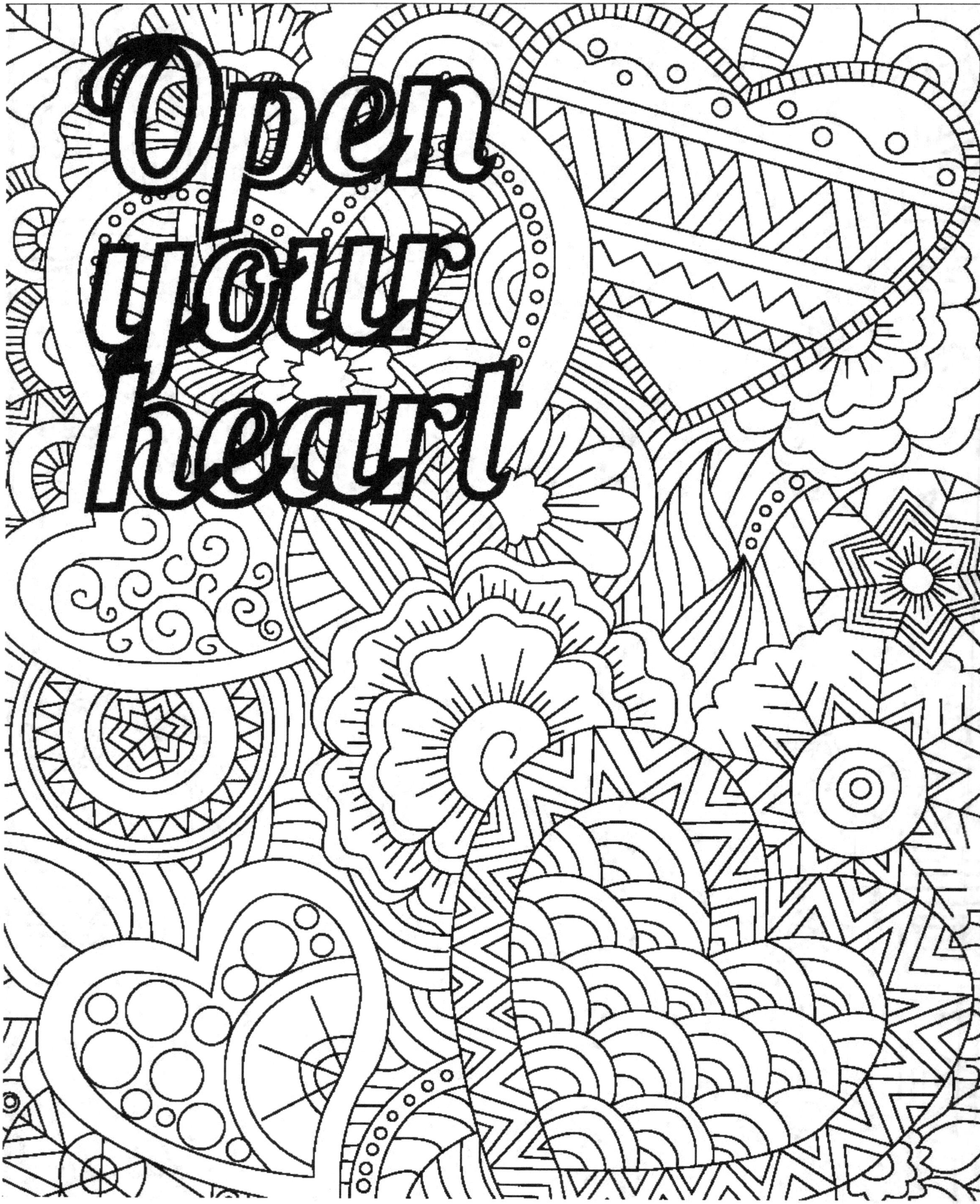
Open your heart

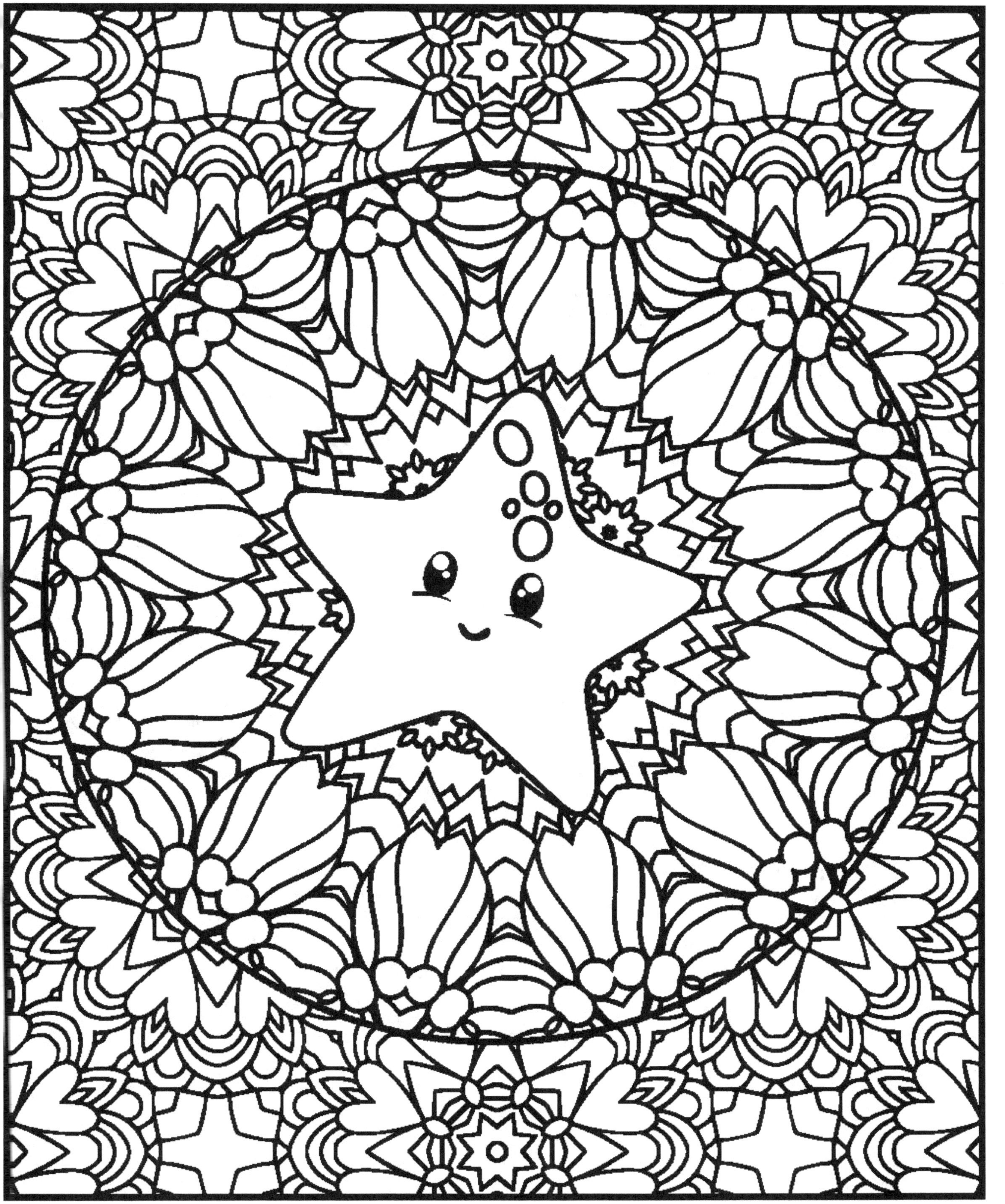

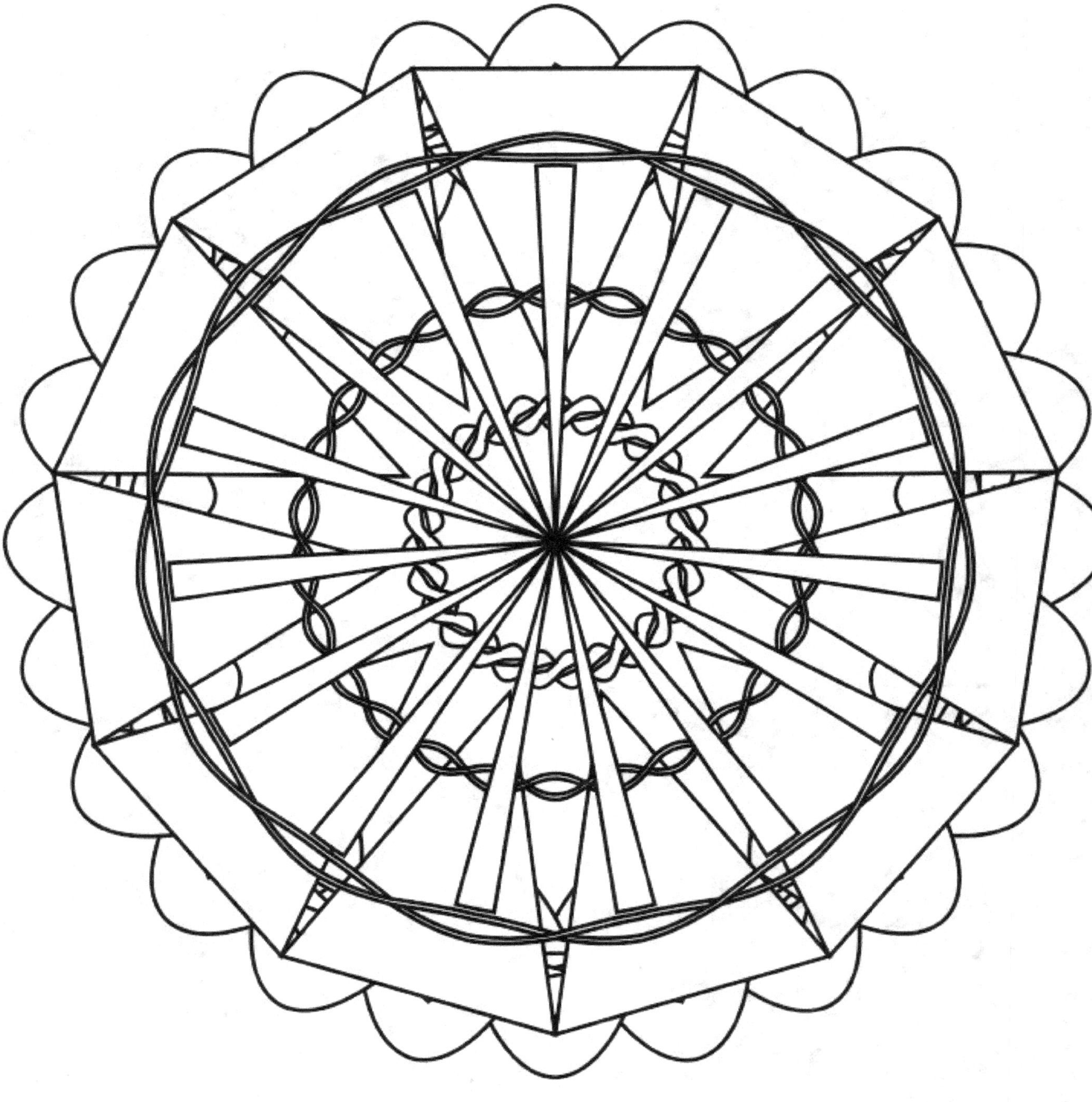

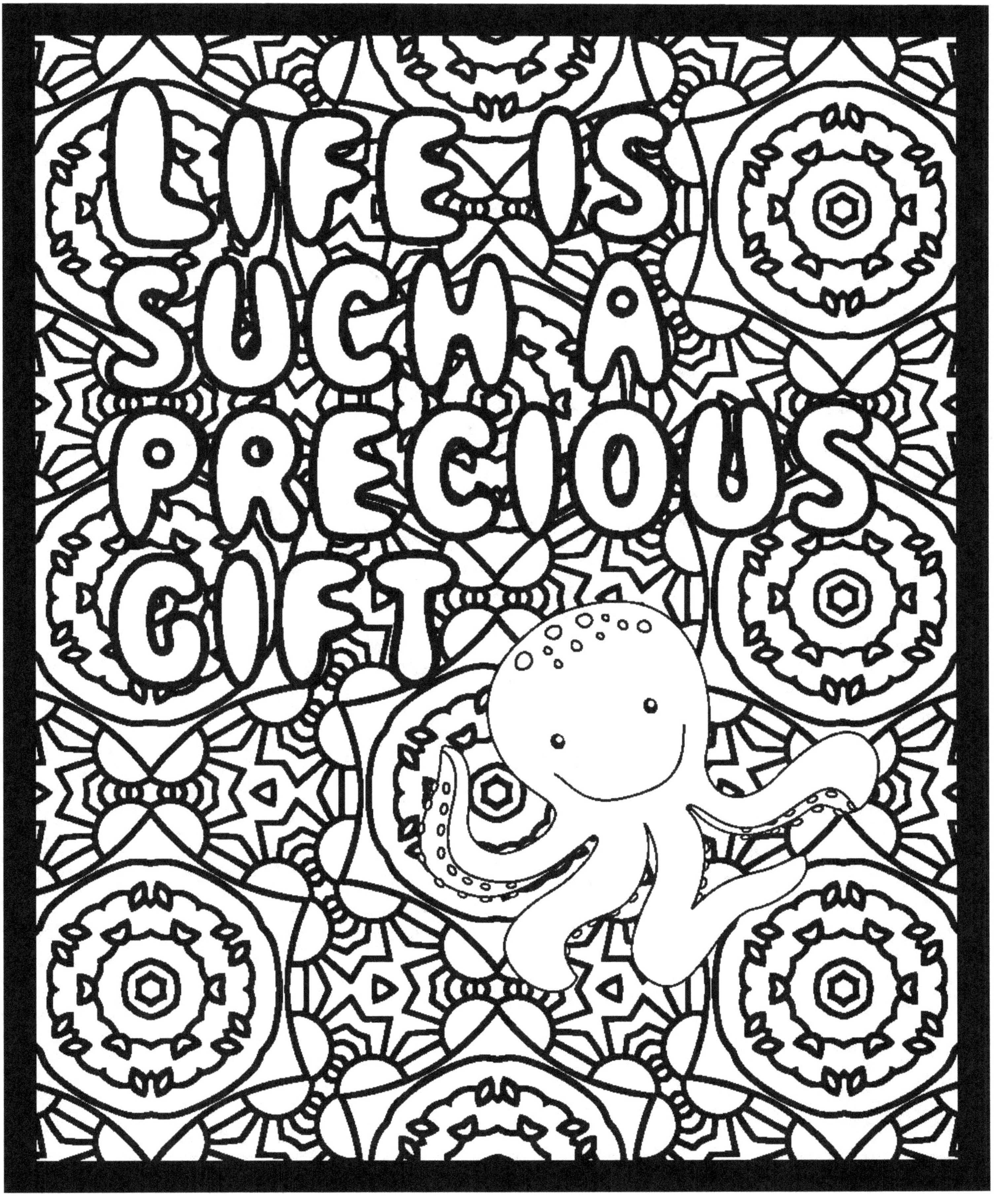
LIFE IS SUCH A PRECIOUS GIFT

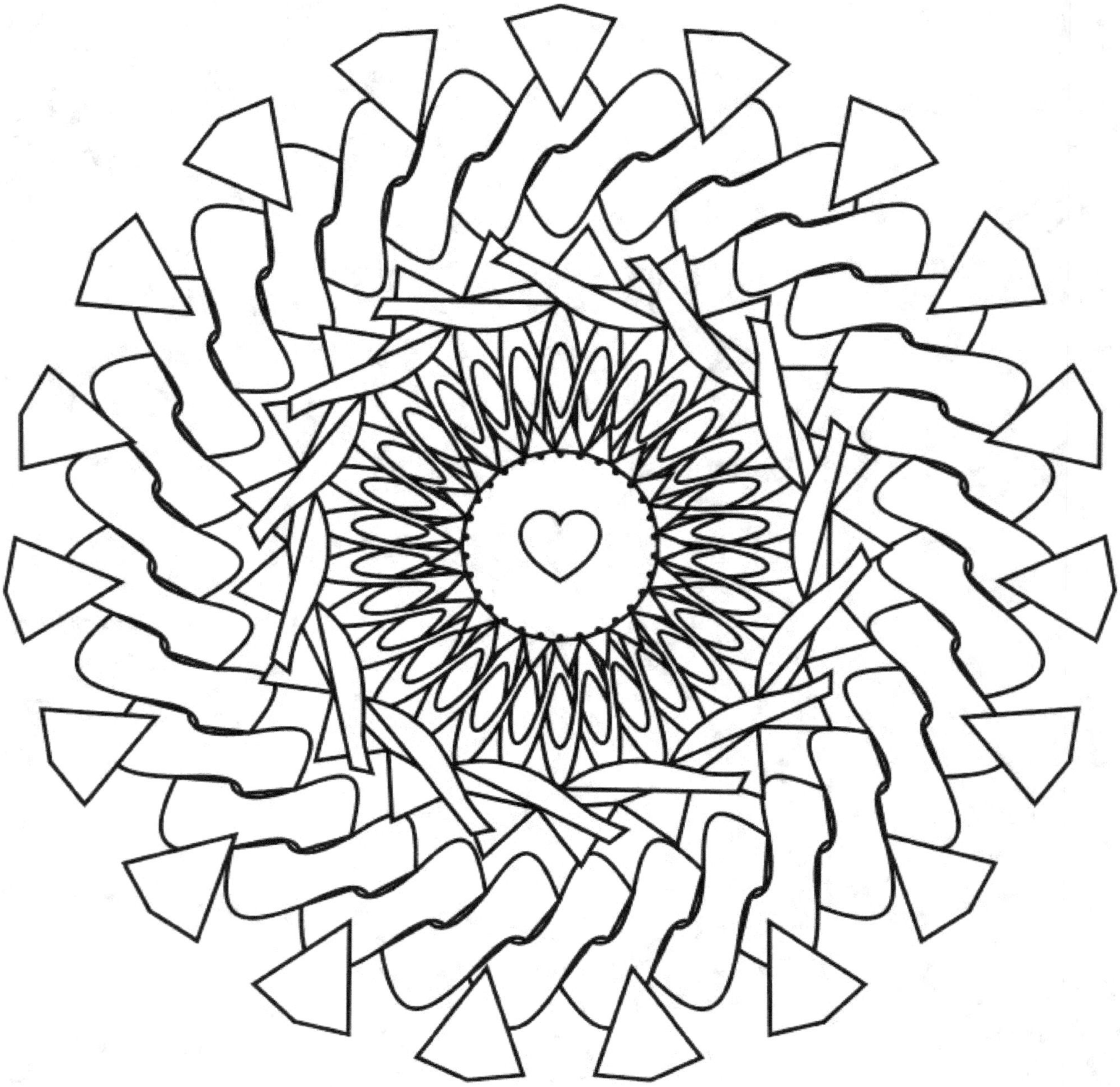

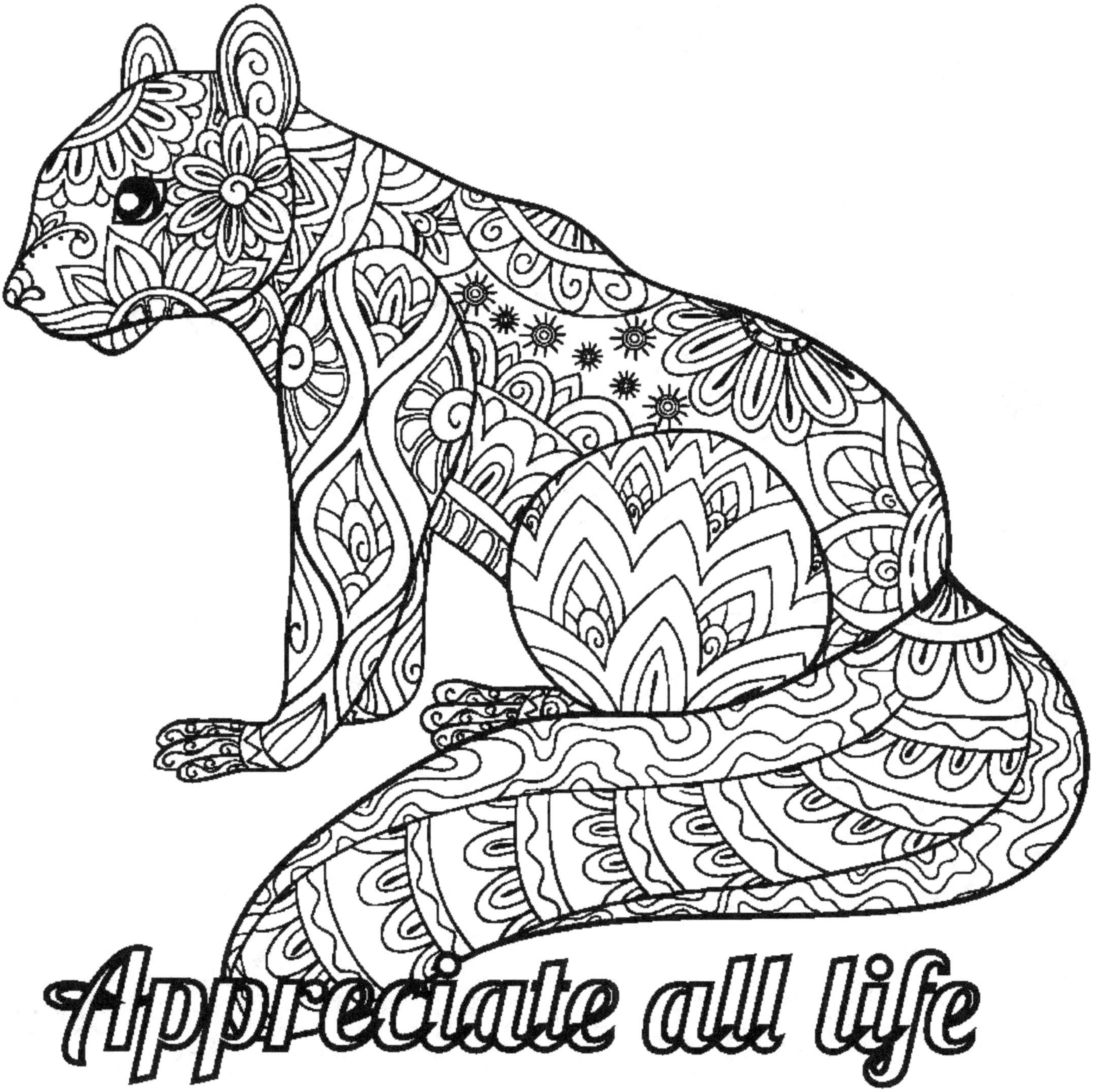

Appreciate all life

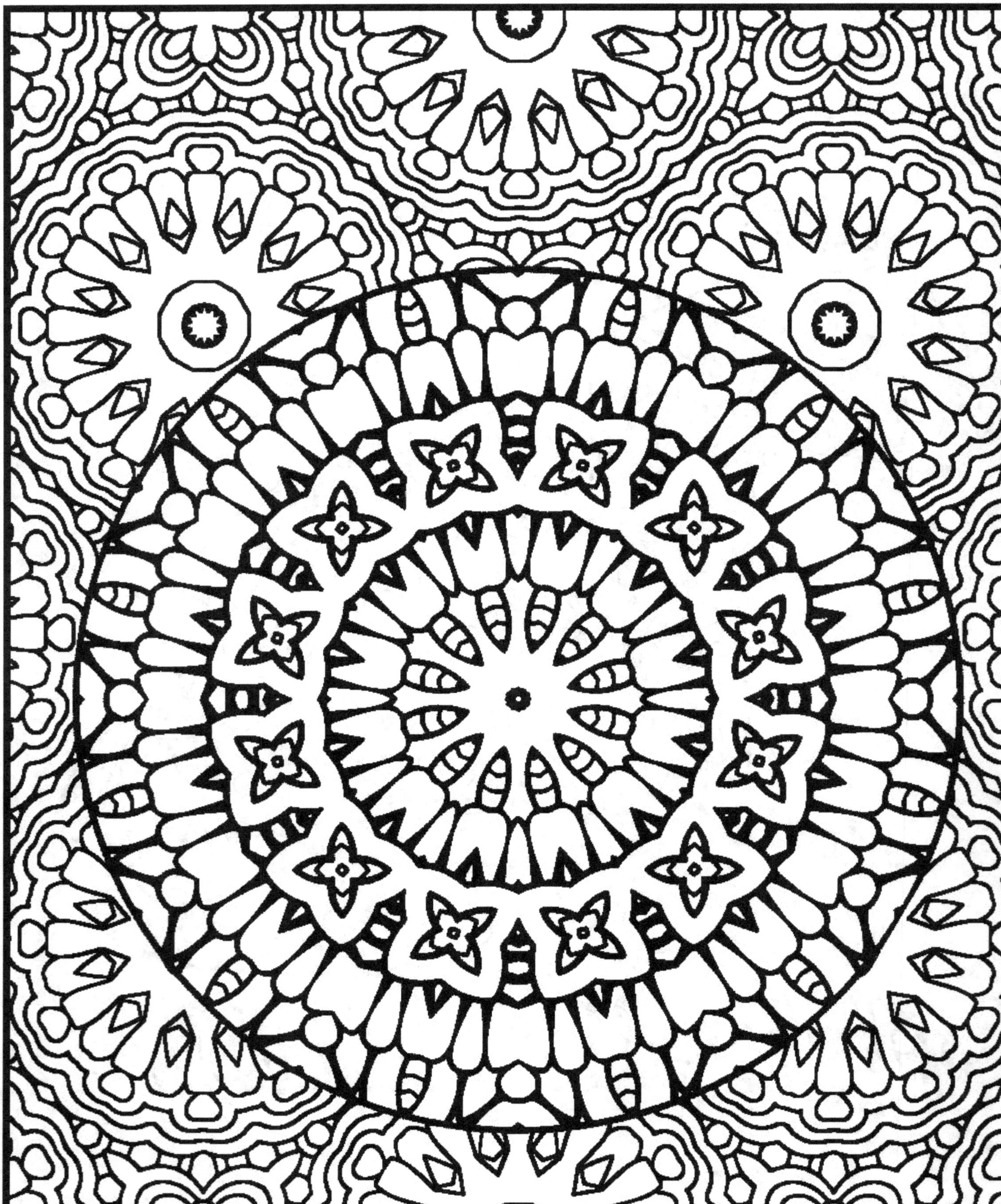

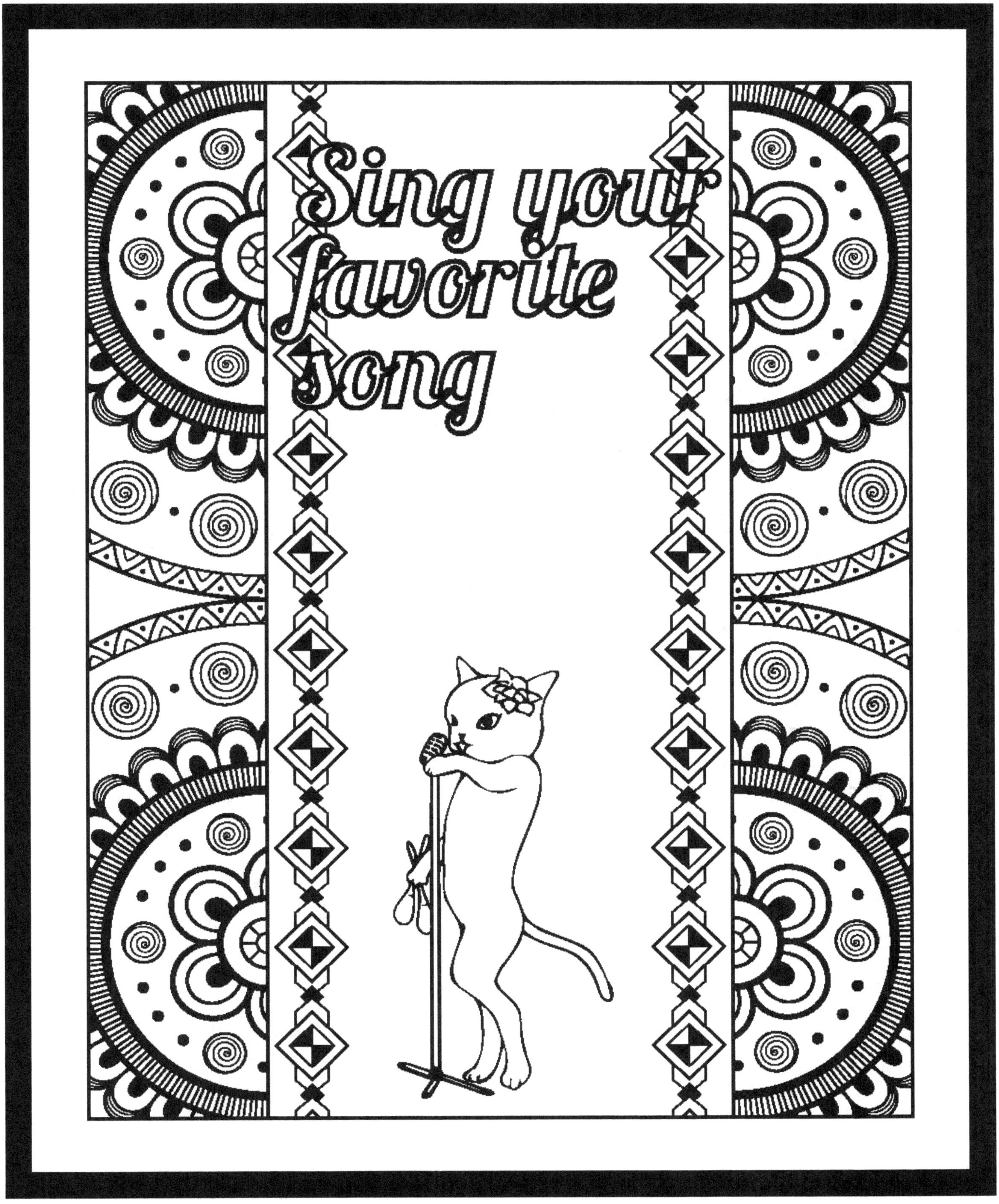
Sing your favorite song

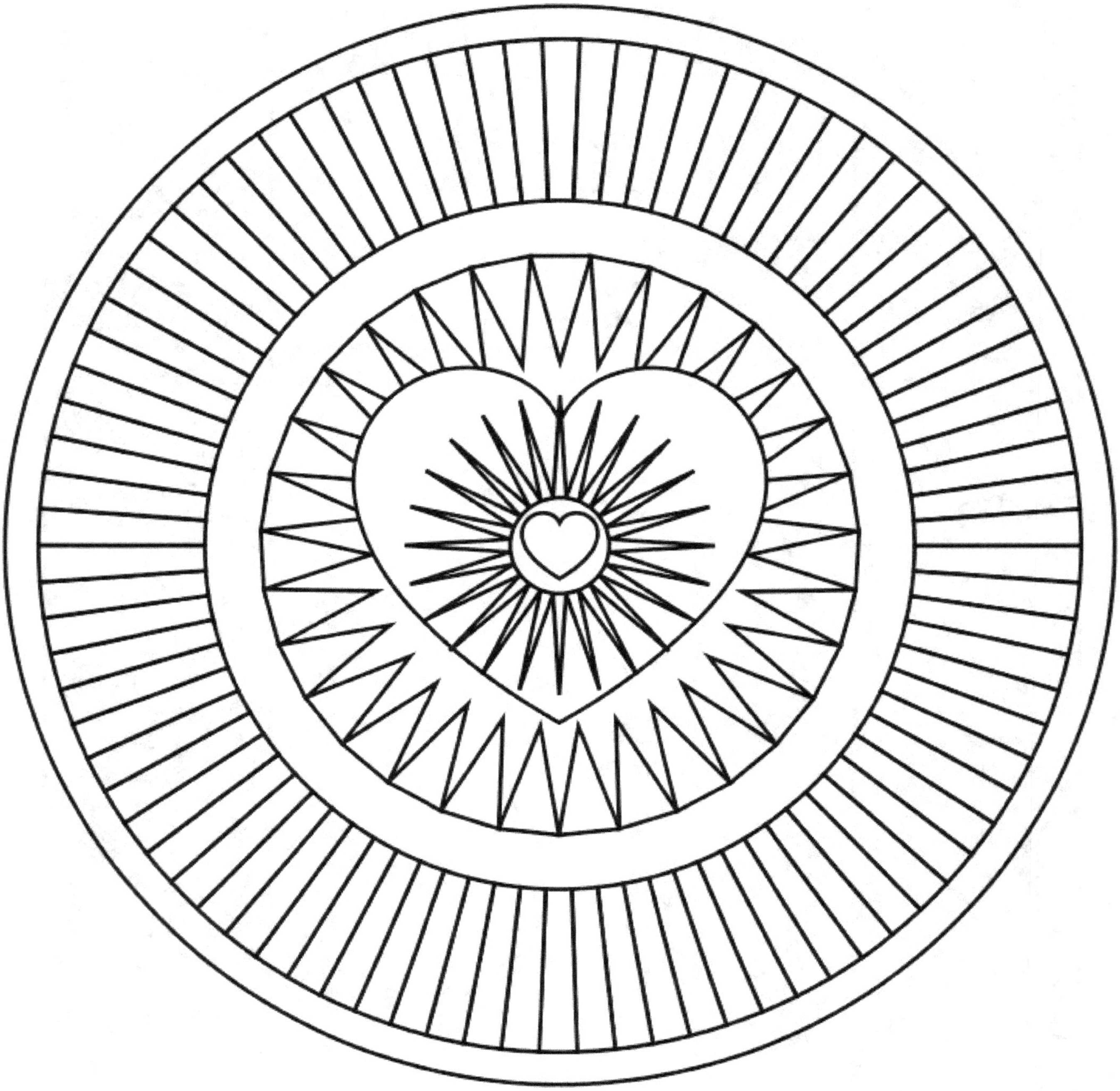

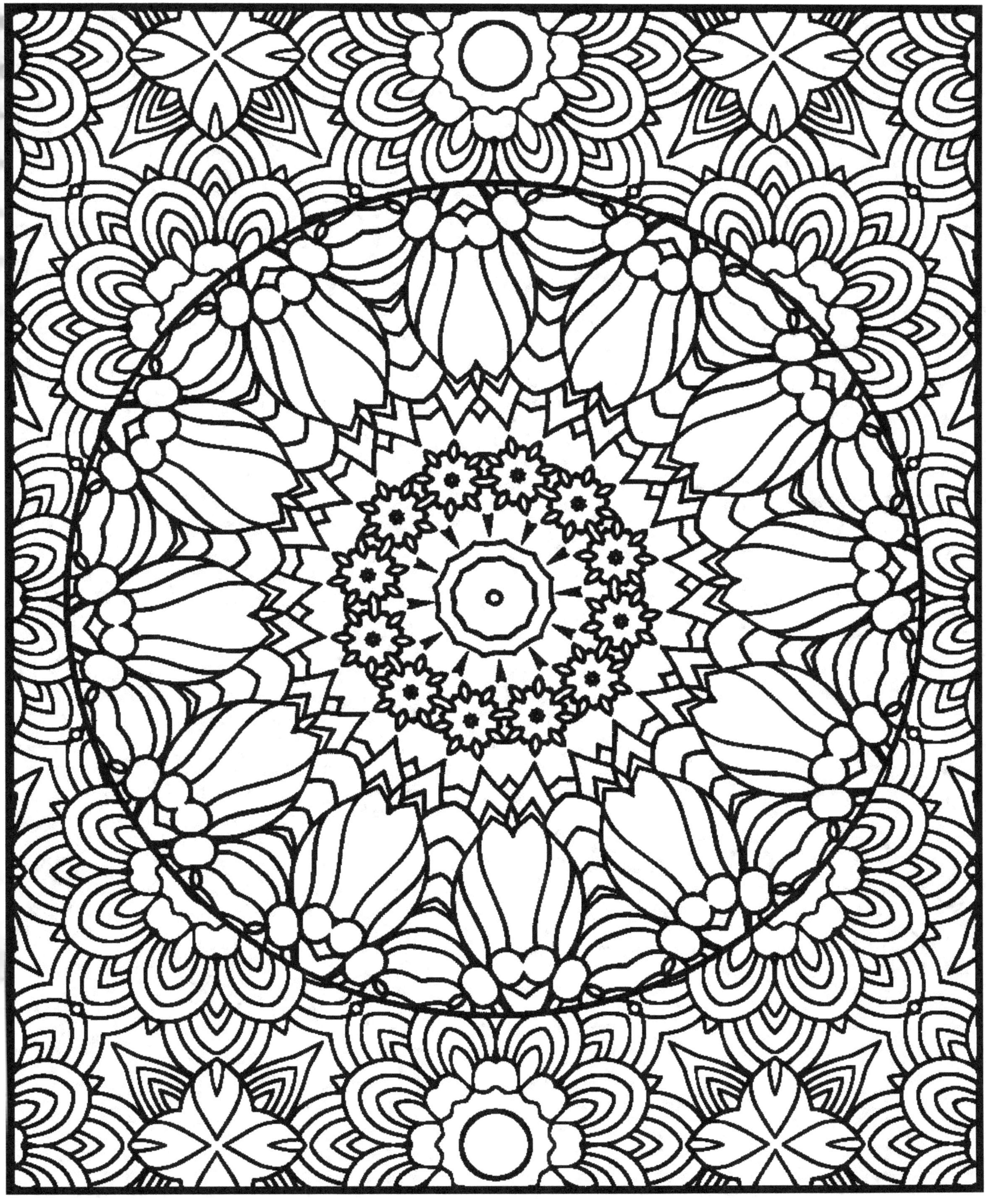

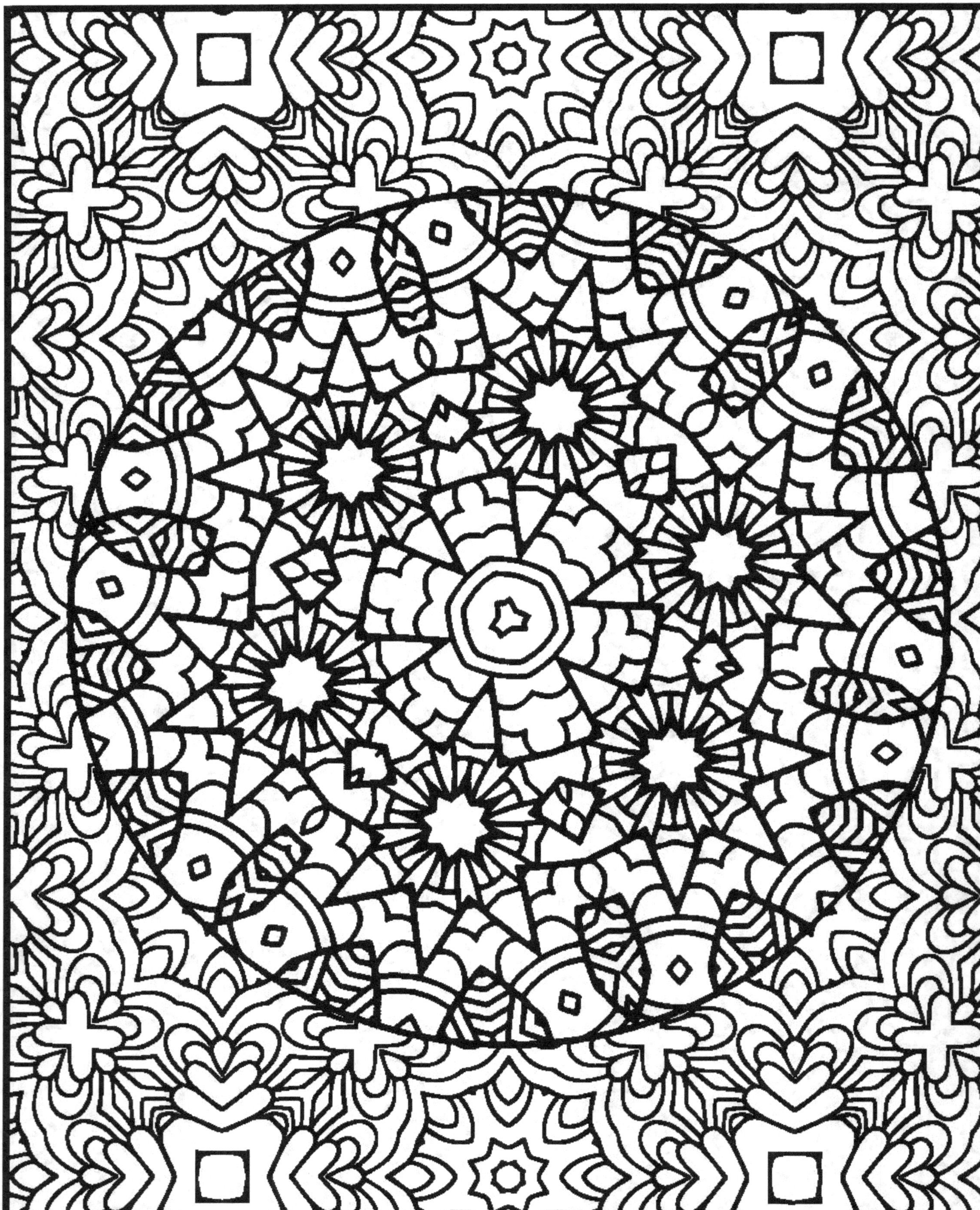

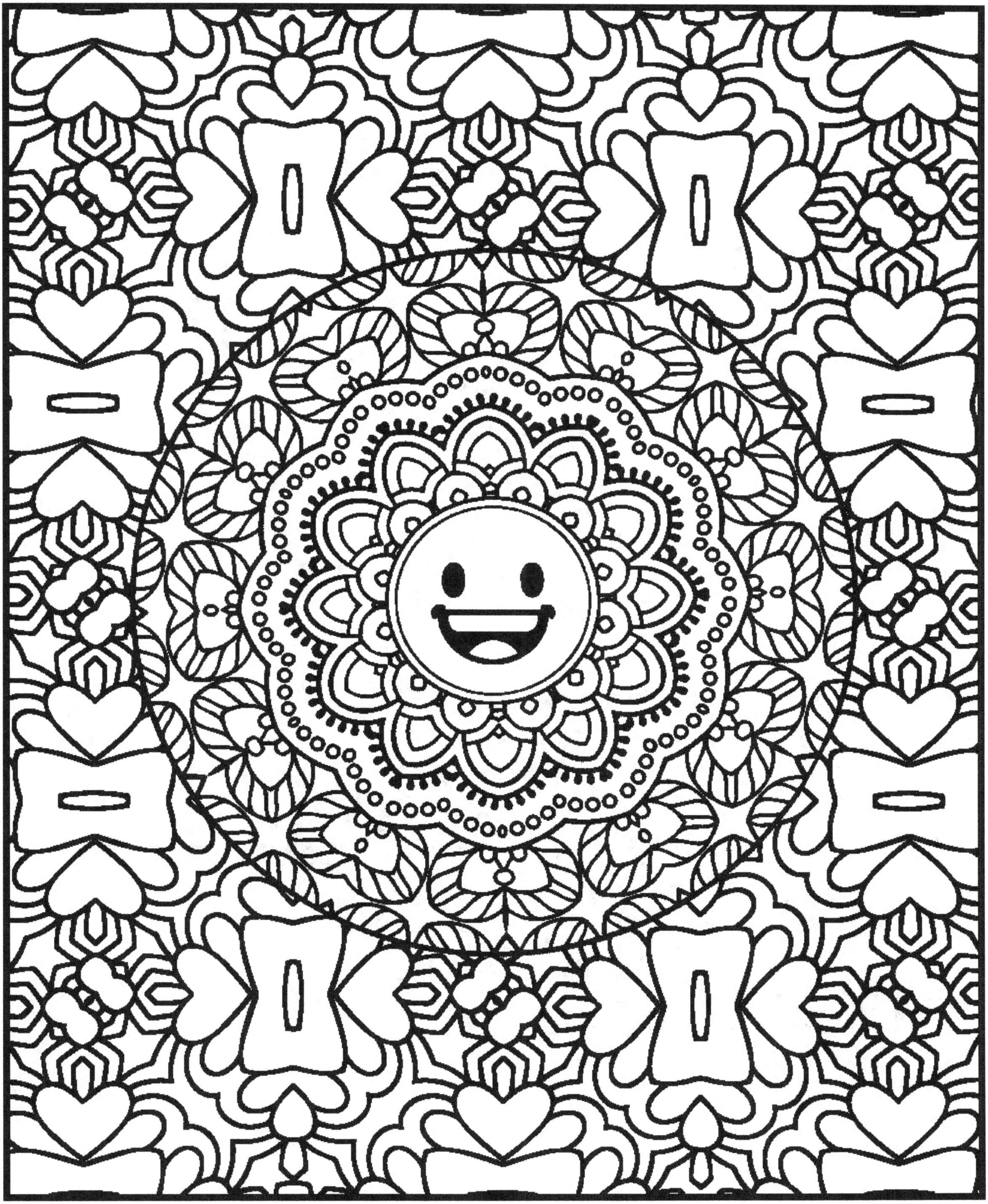

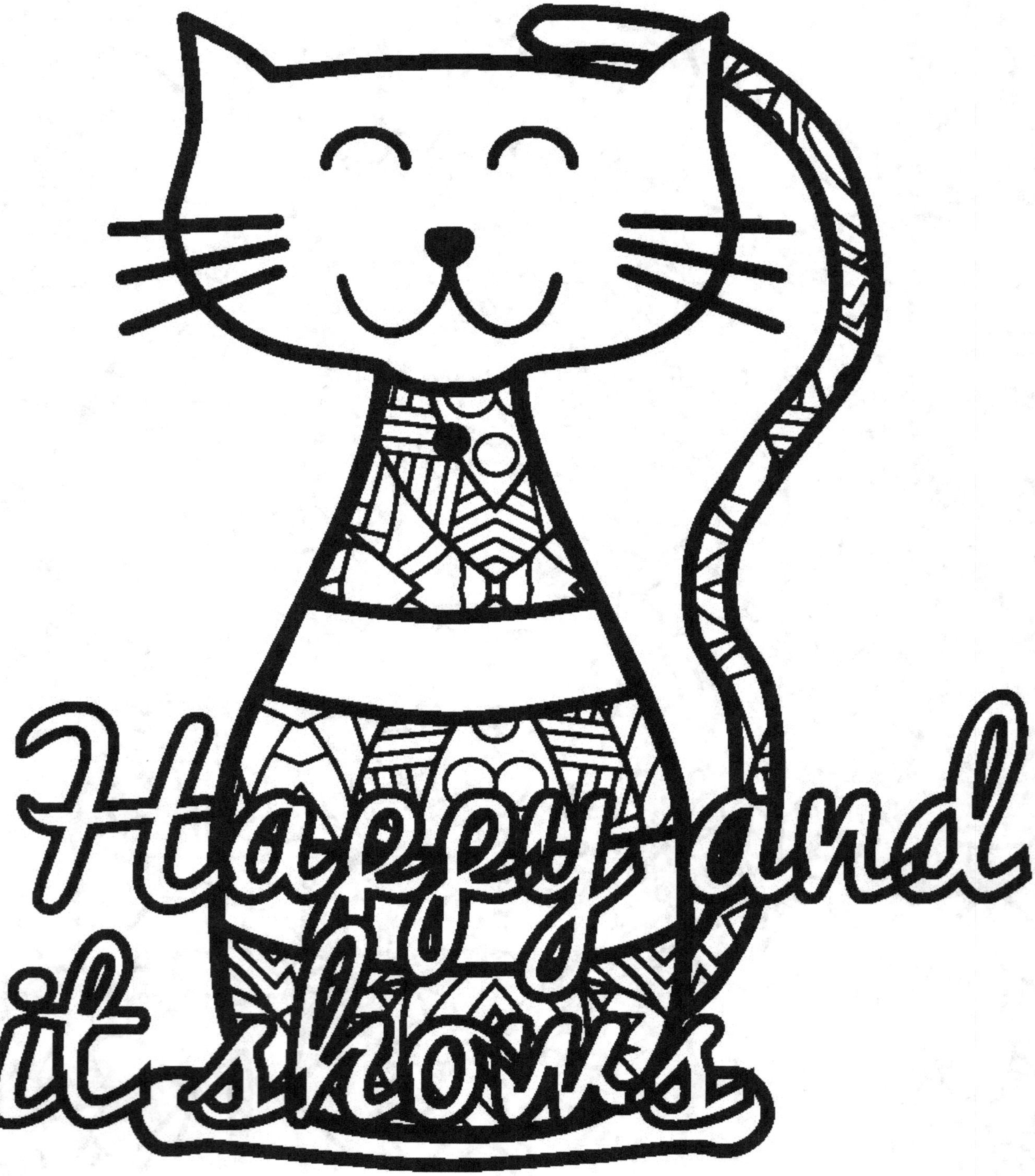
Happy and
it shows

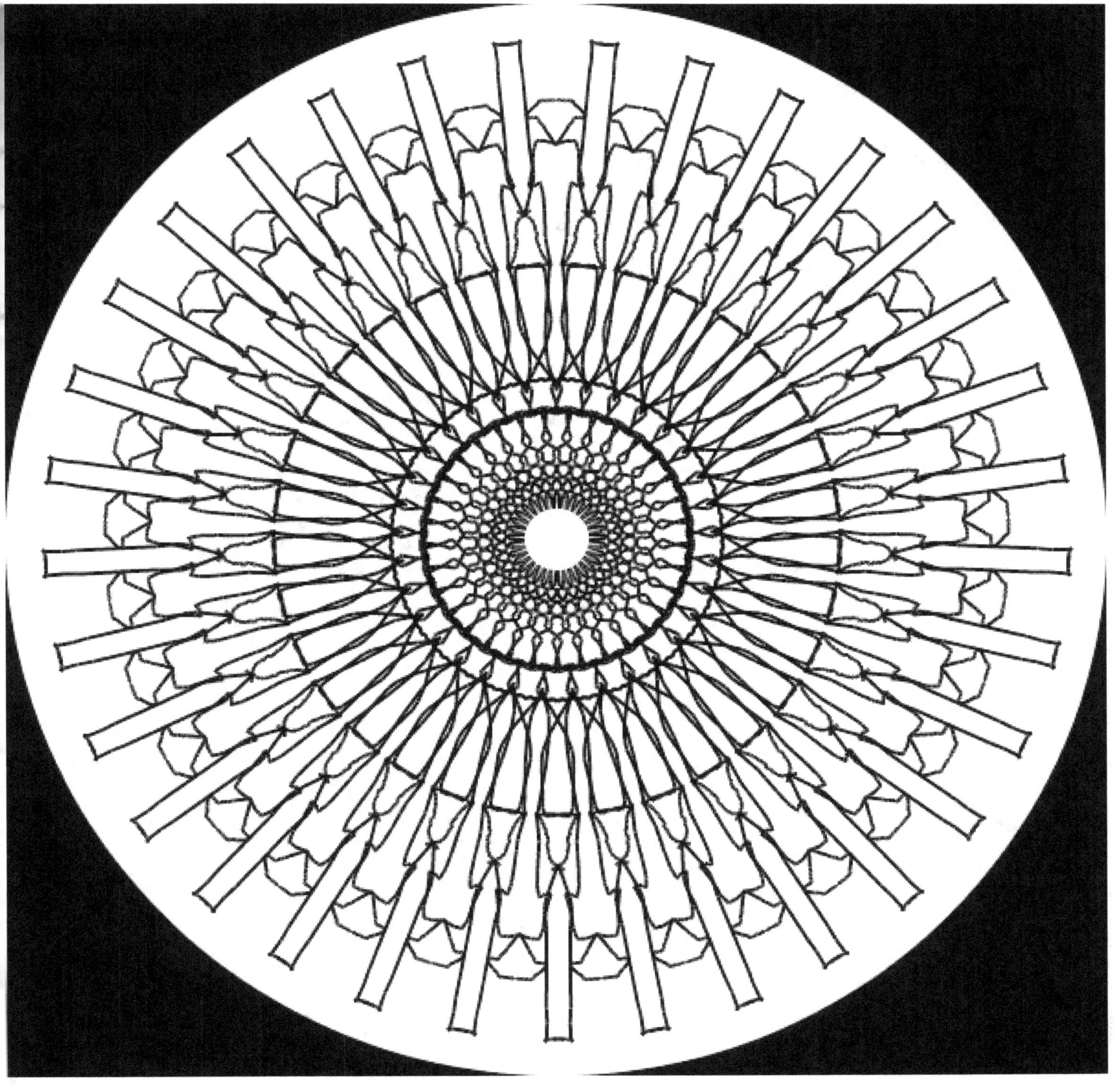

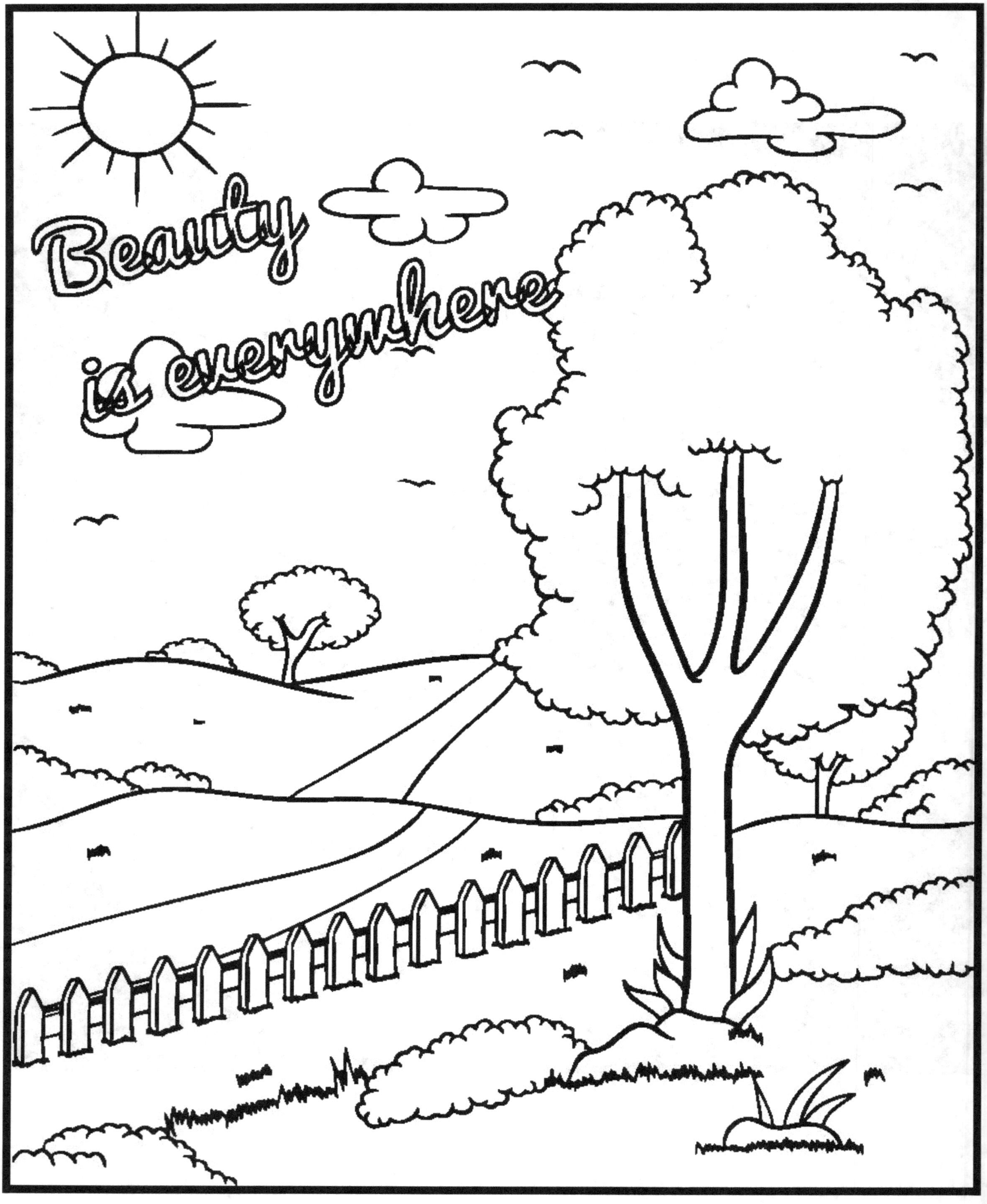
Beauty
is everywhere

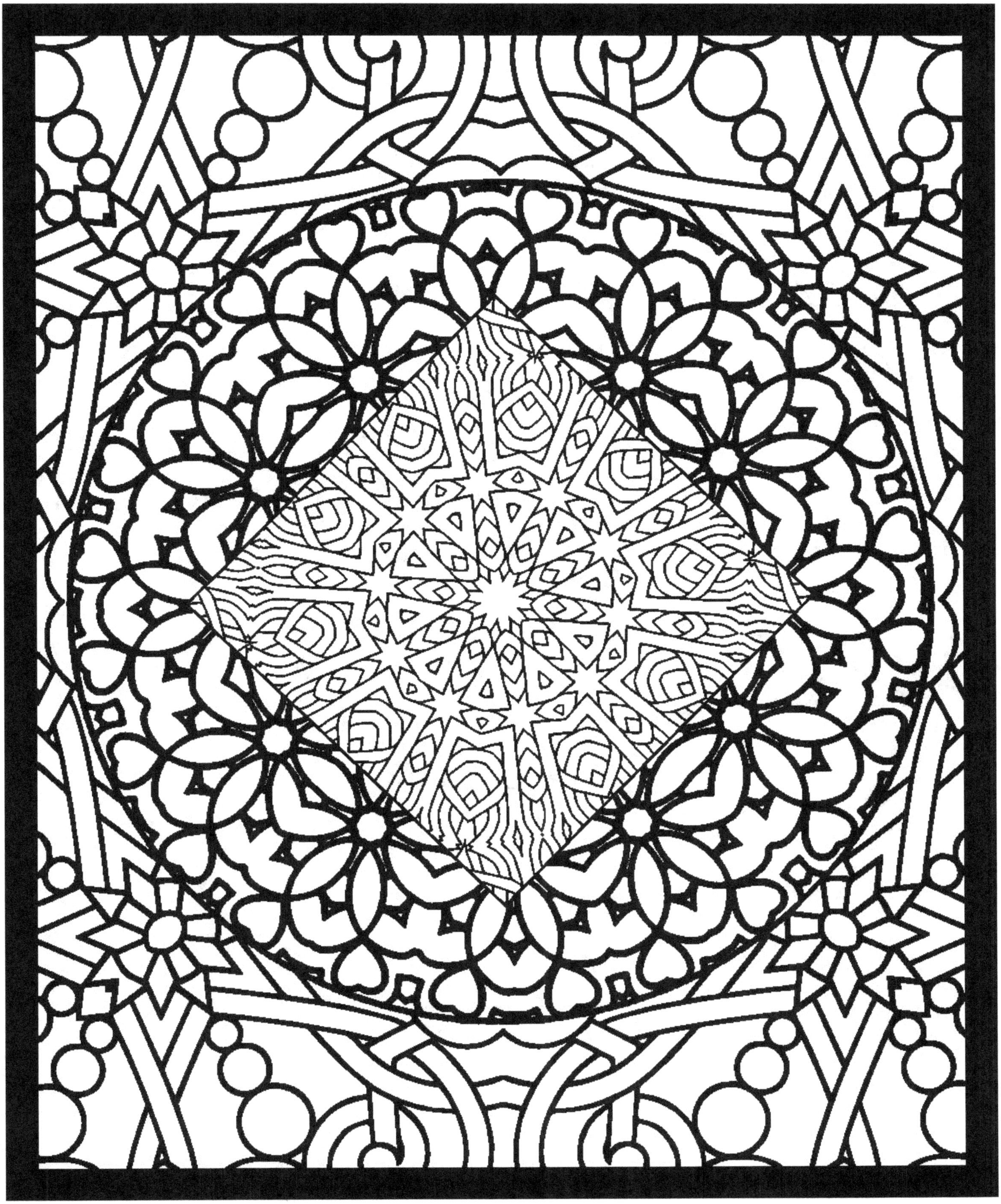

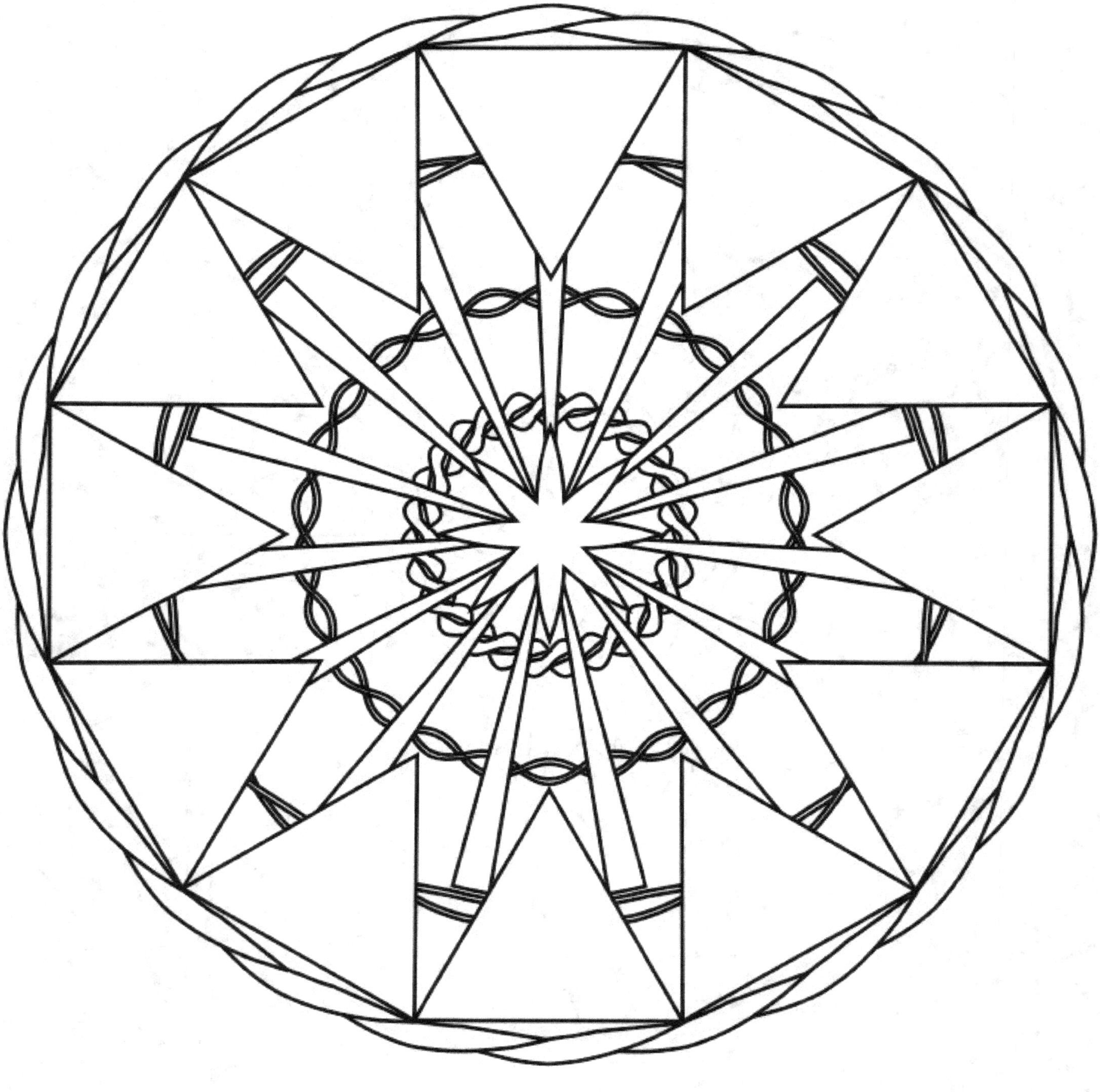

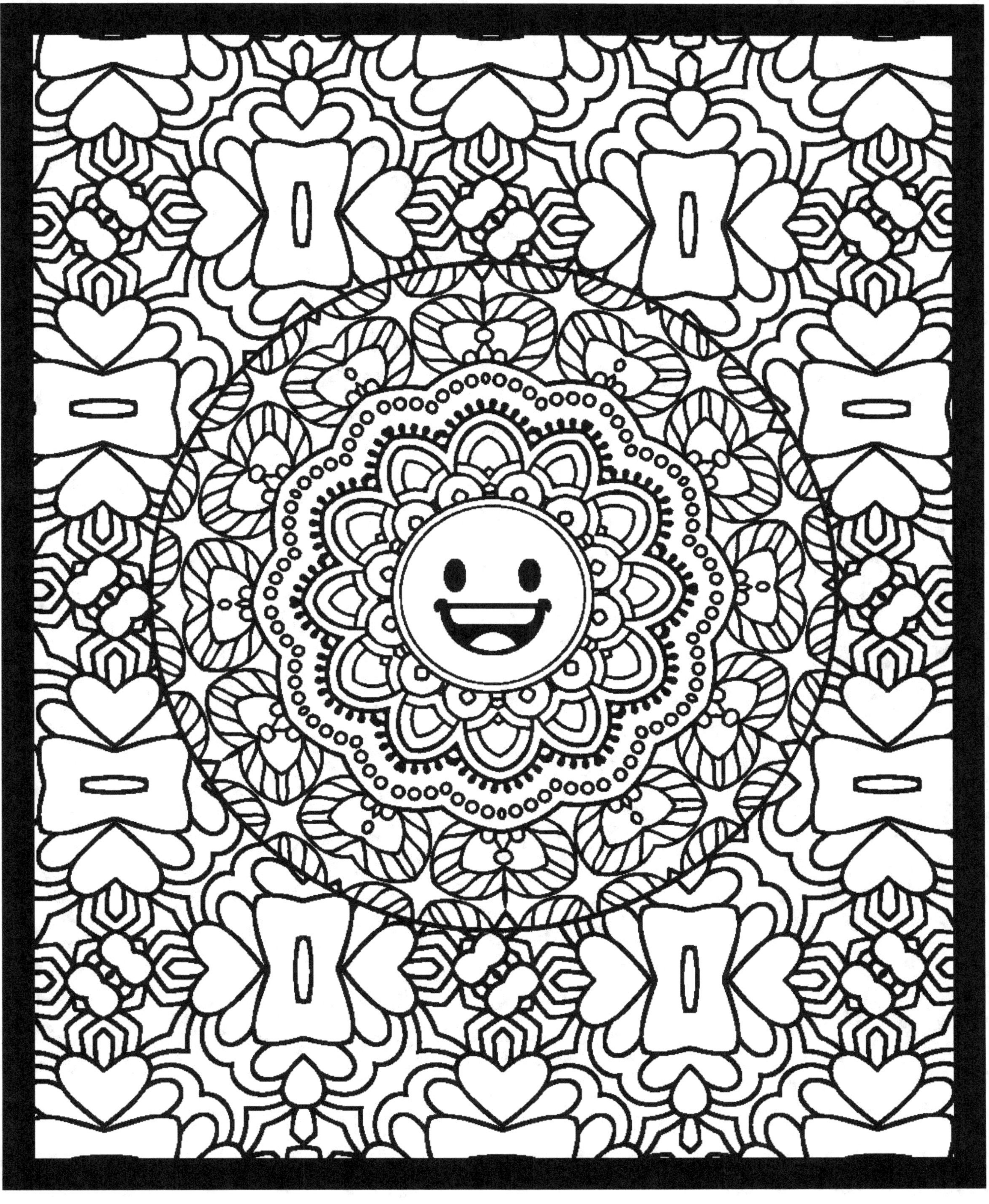

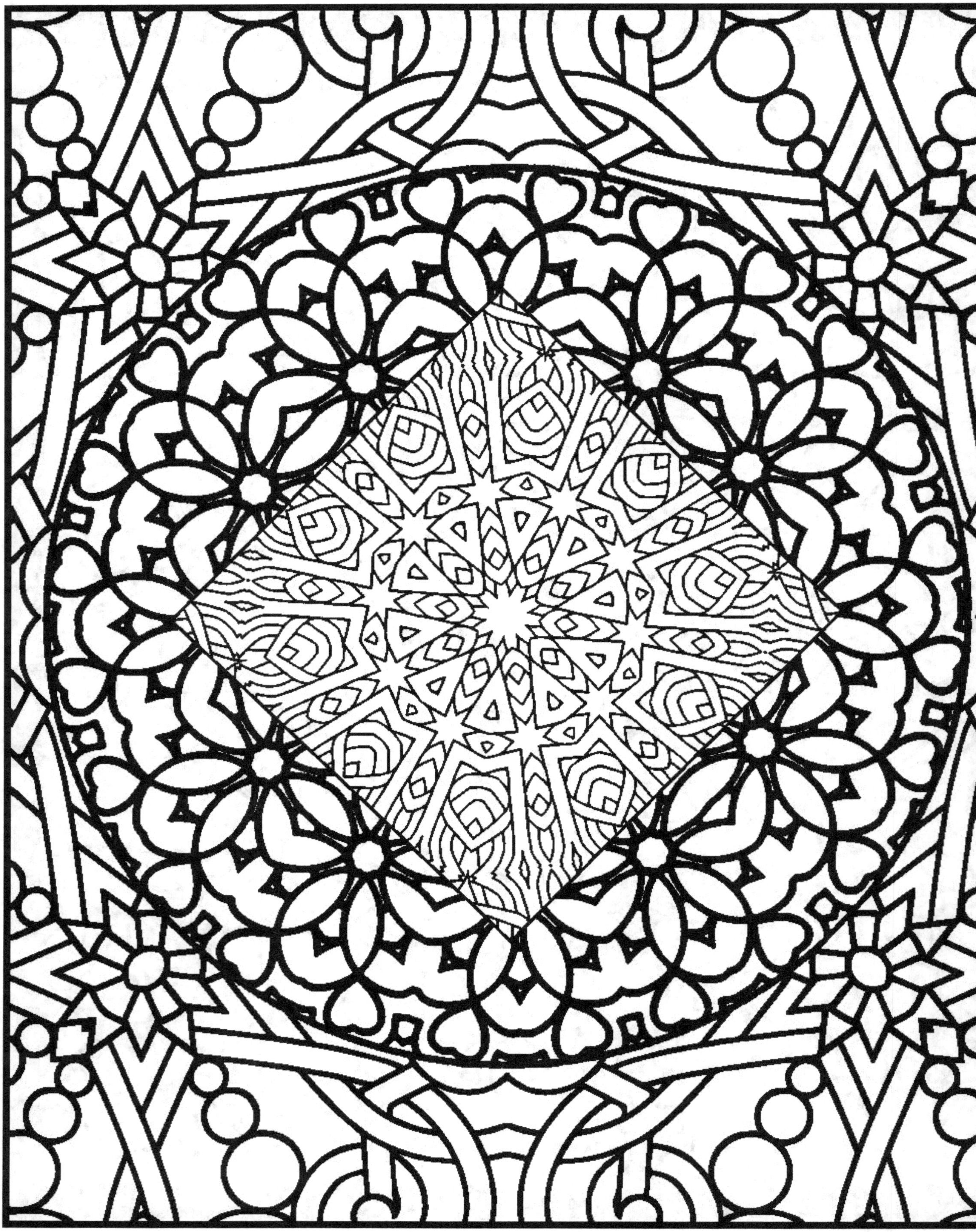

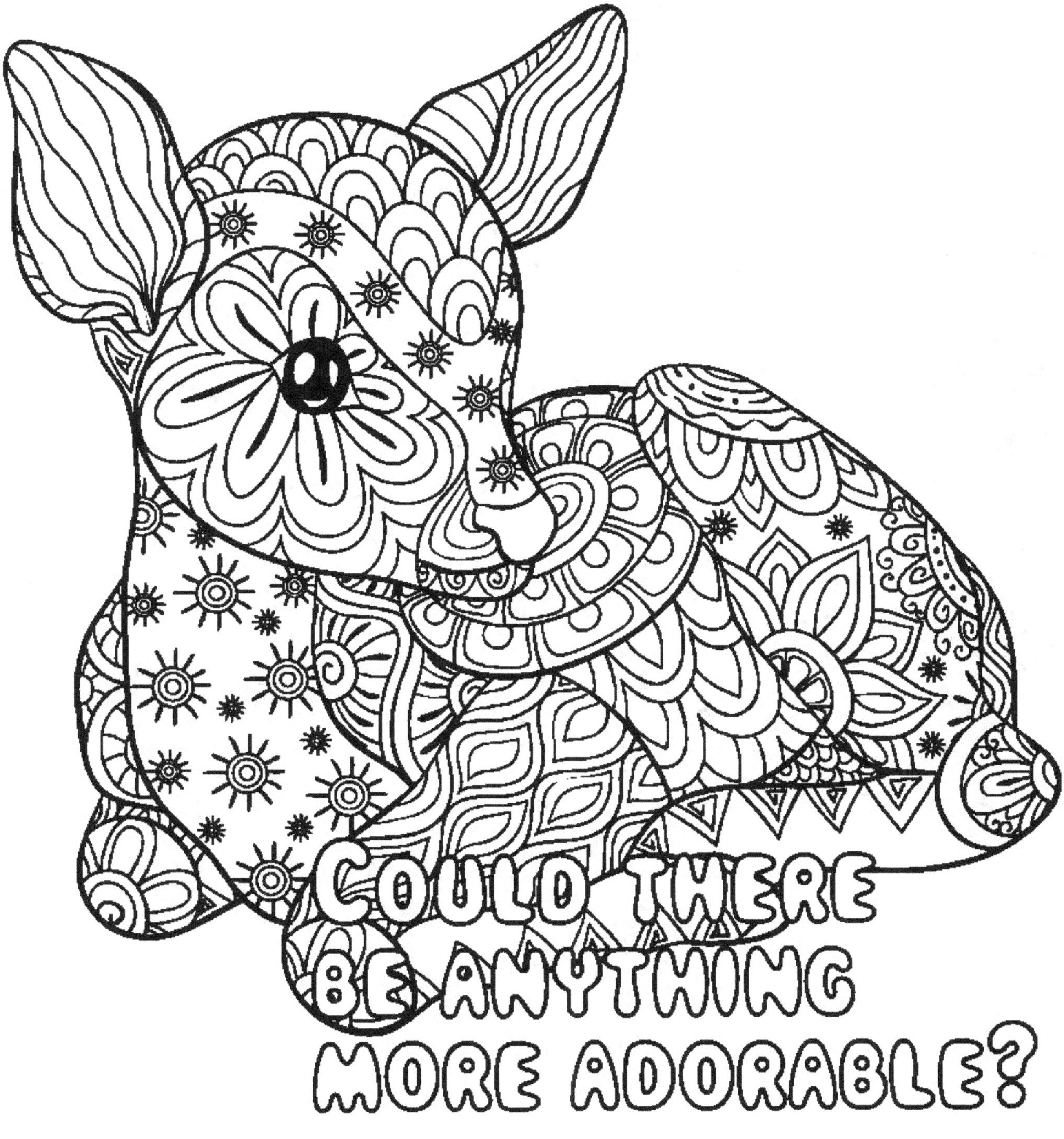
COULD THERE
BE ANYTHING
MORE ADORABLE?

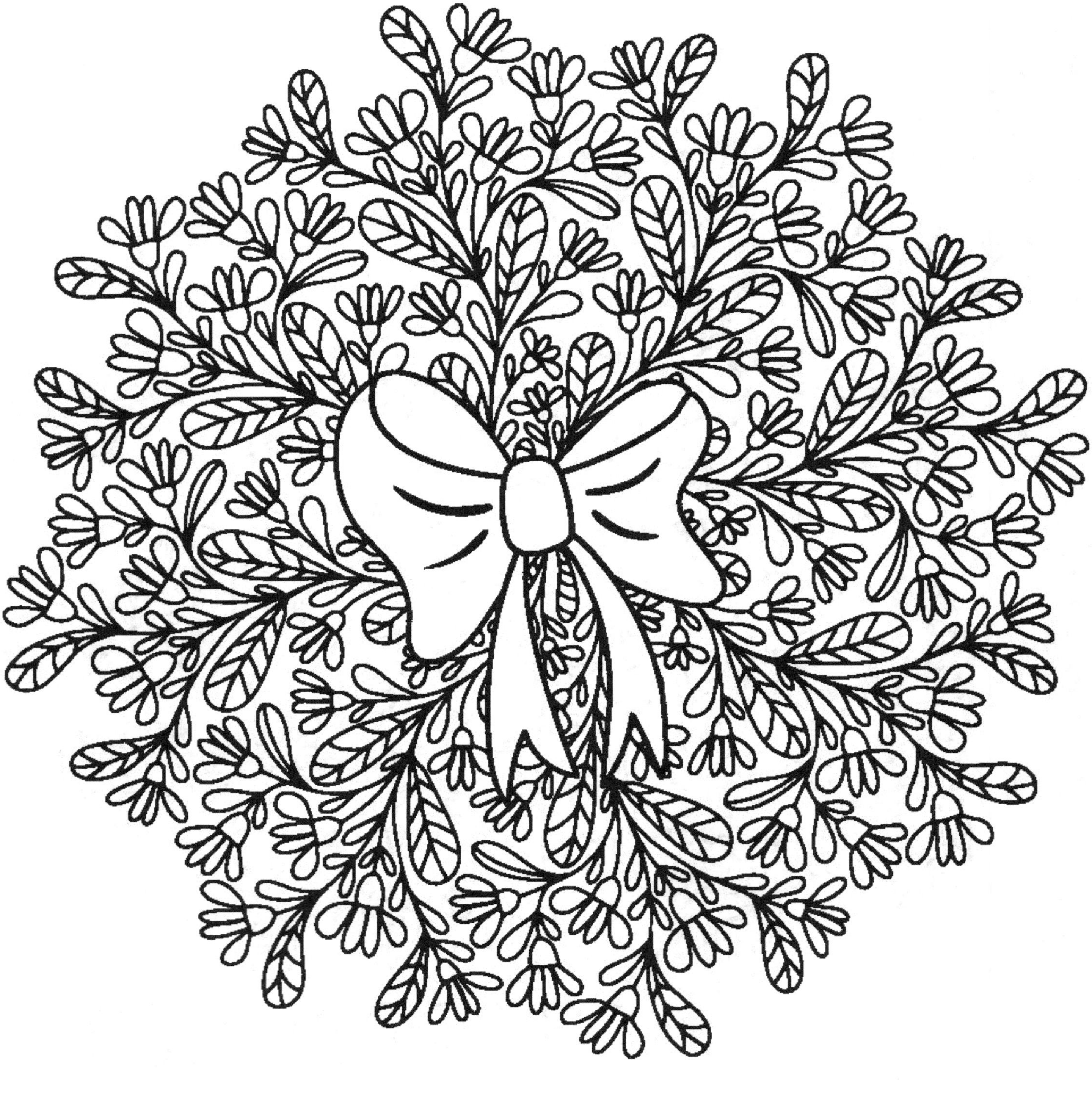

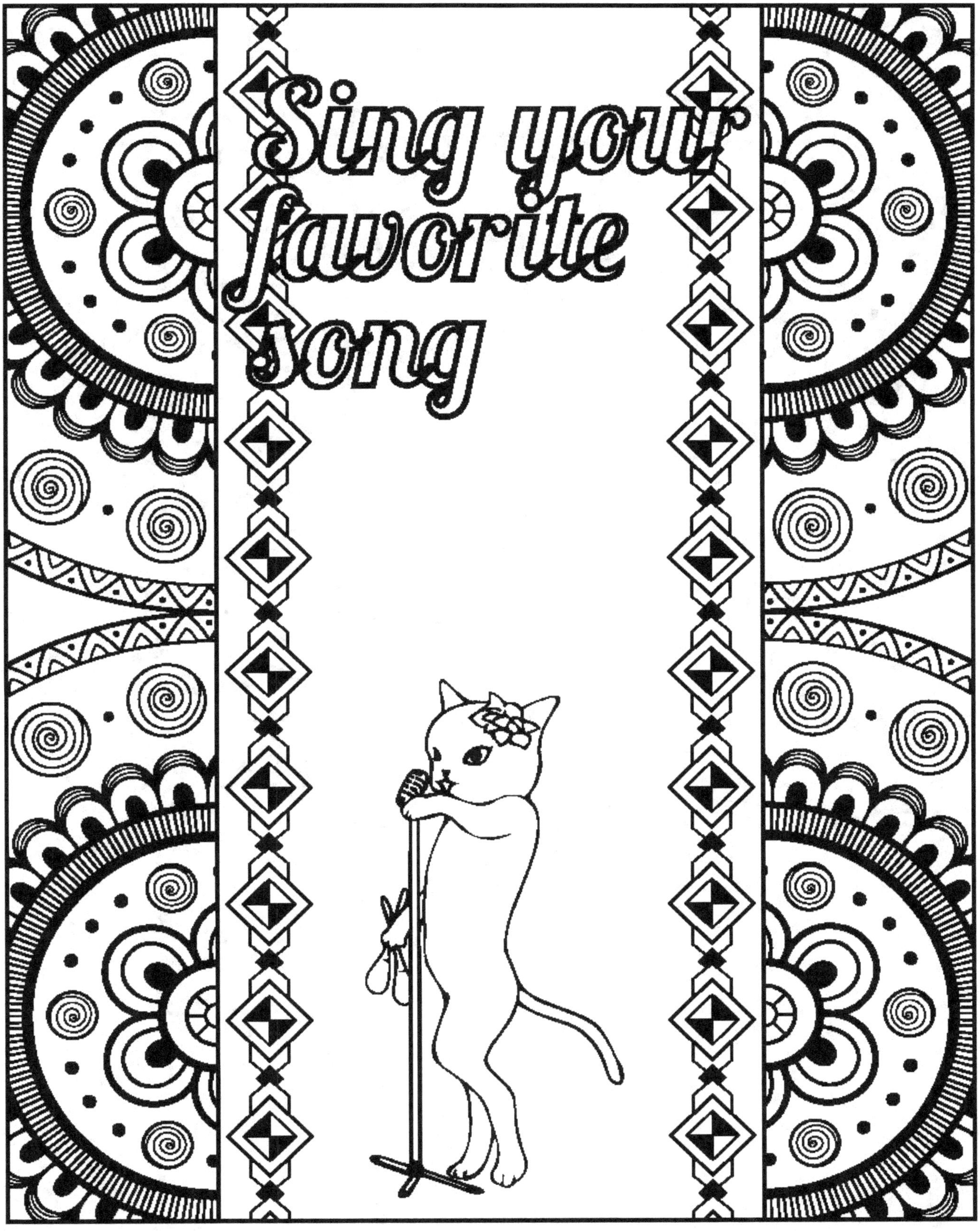
Sing your favorite song

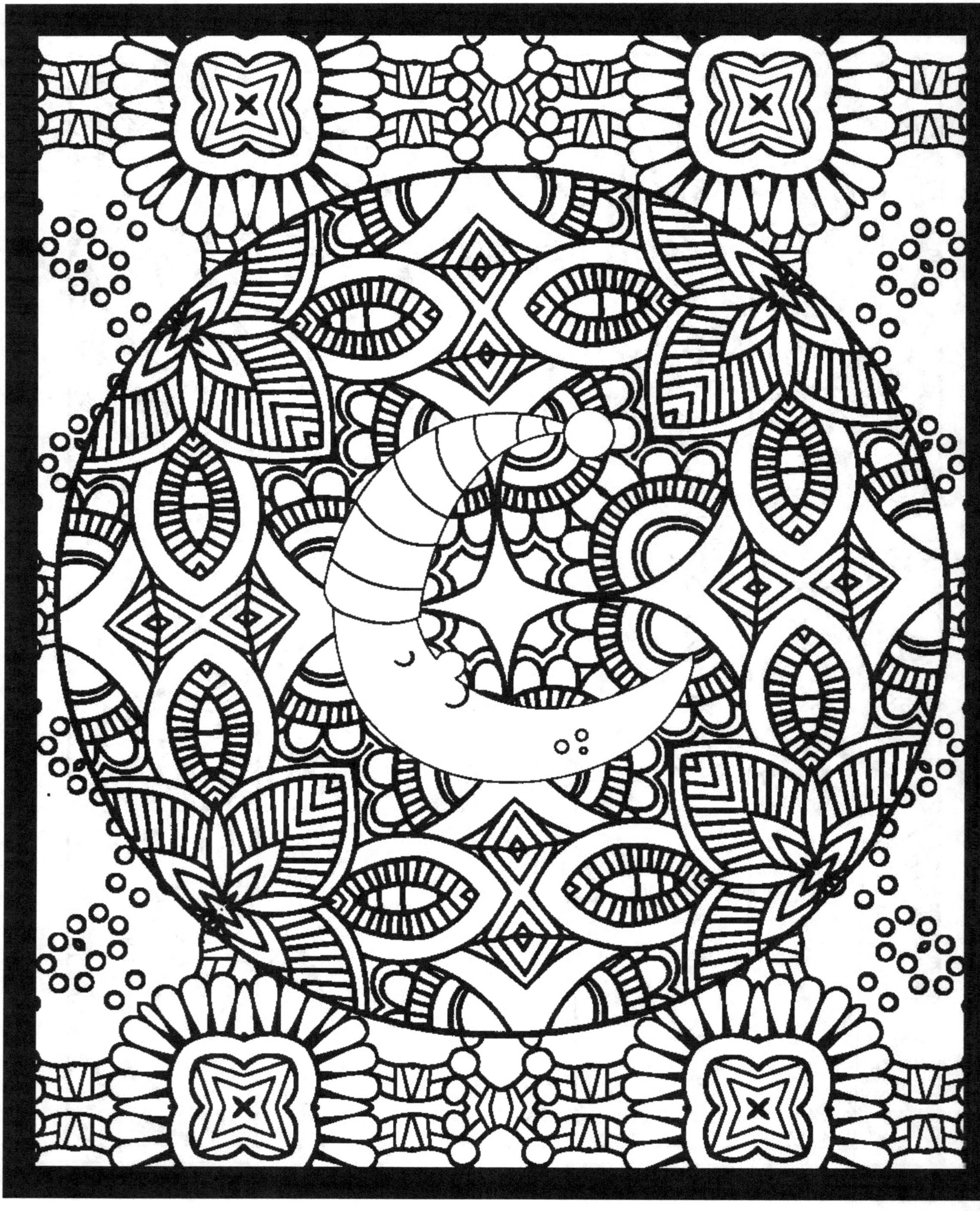

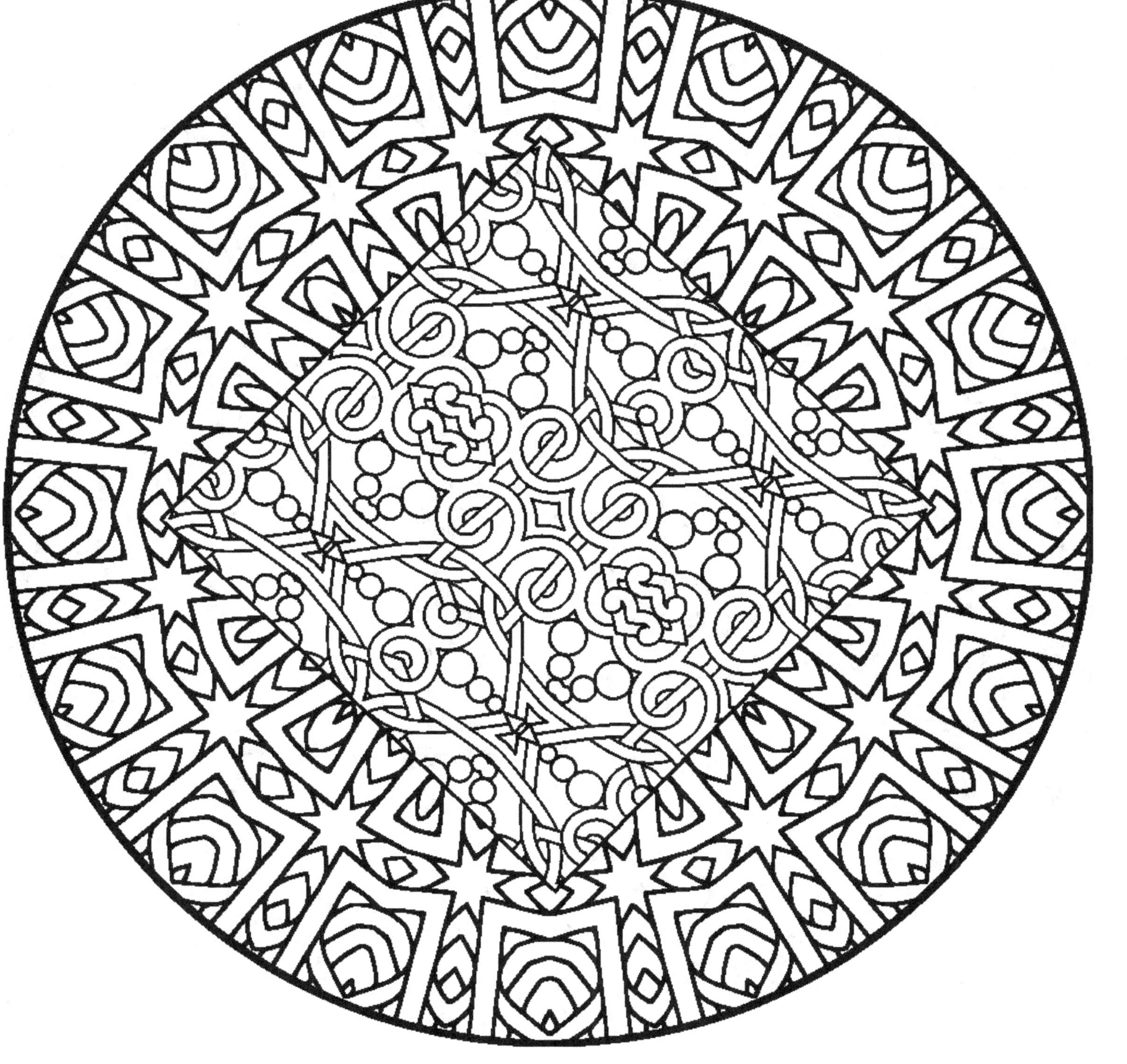

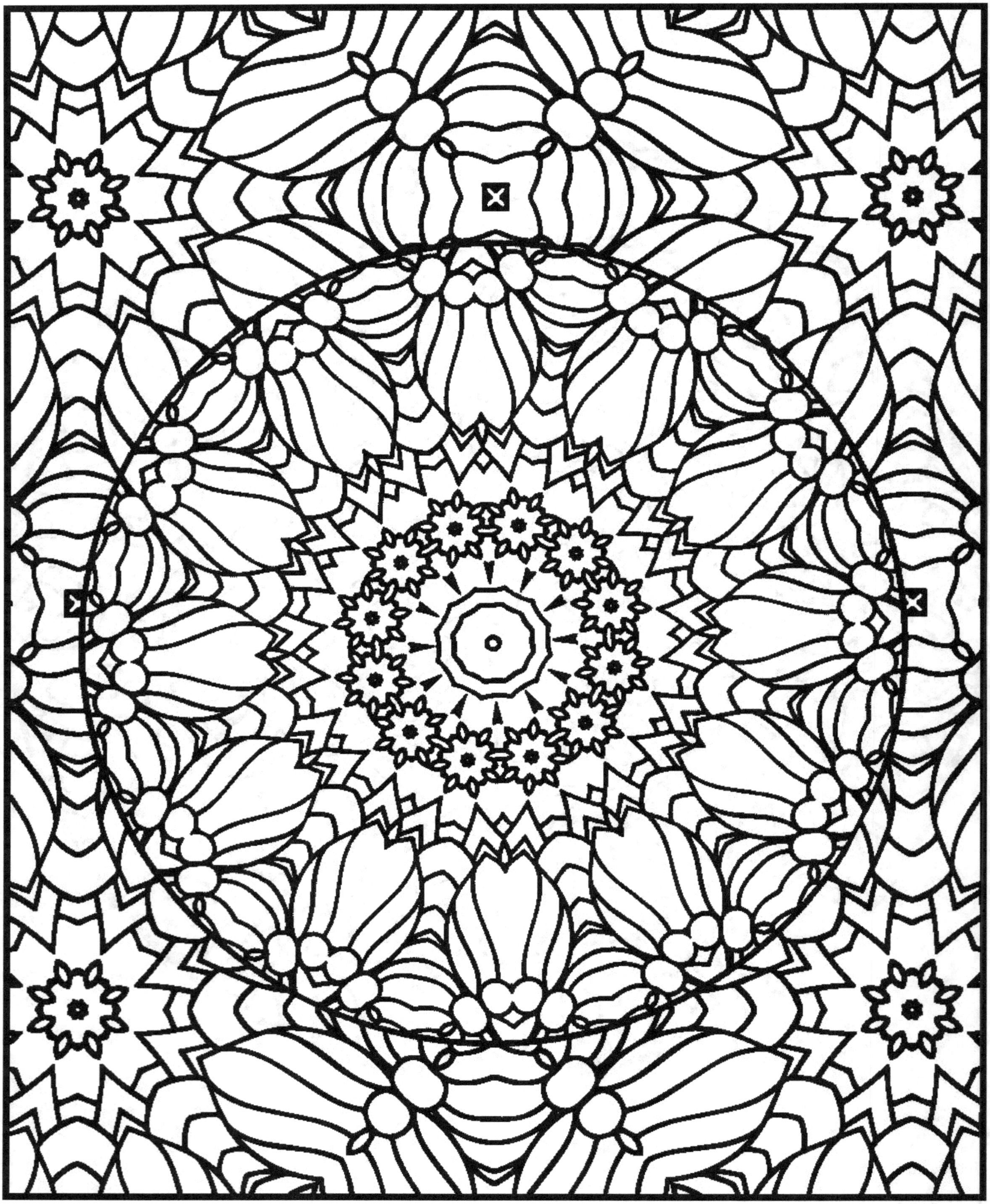

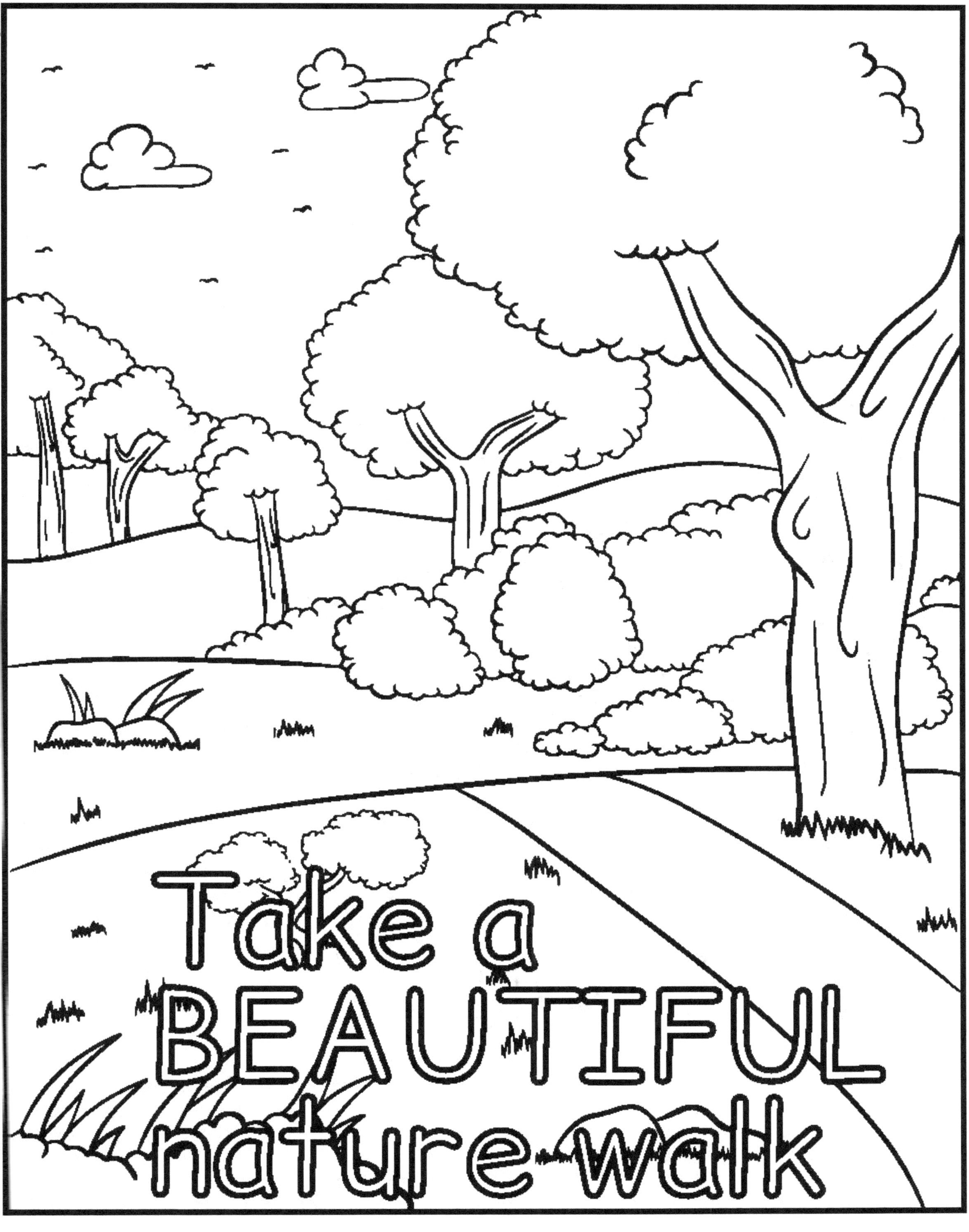
Take a
BEAUTIFUL
nature walk

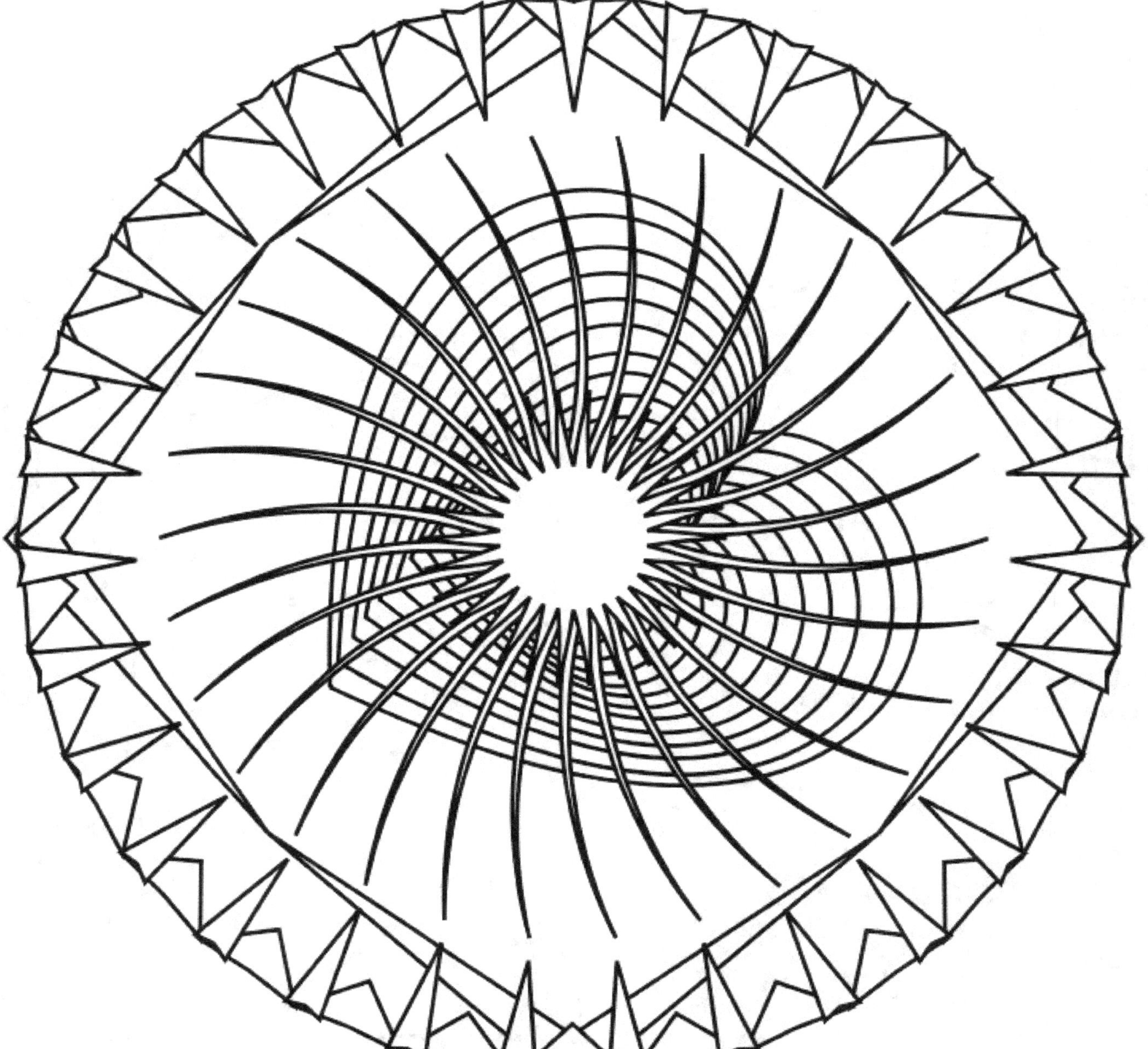

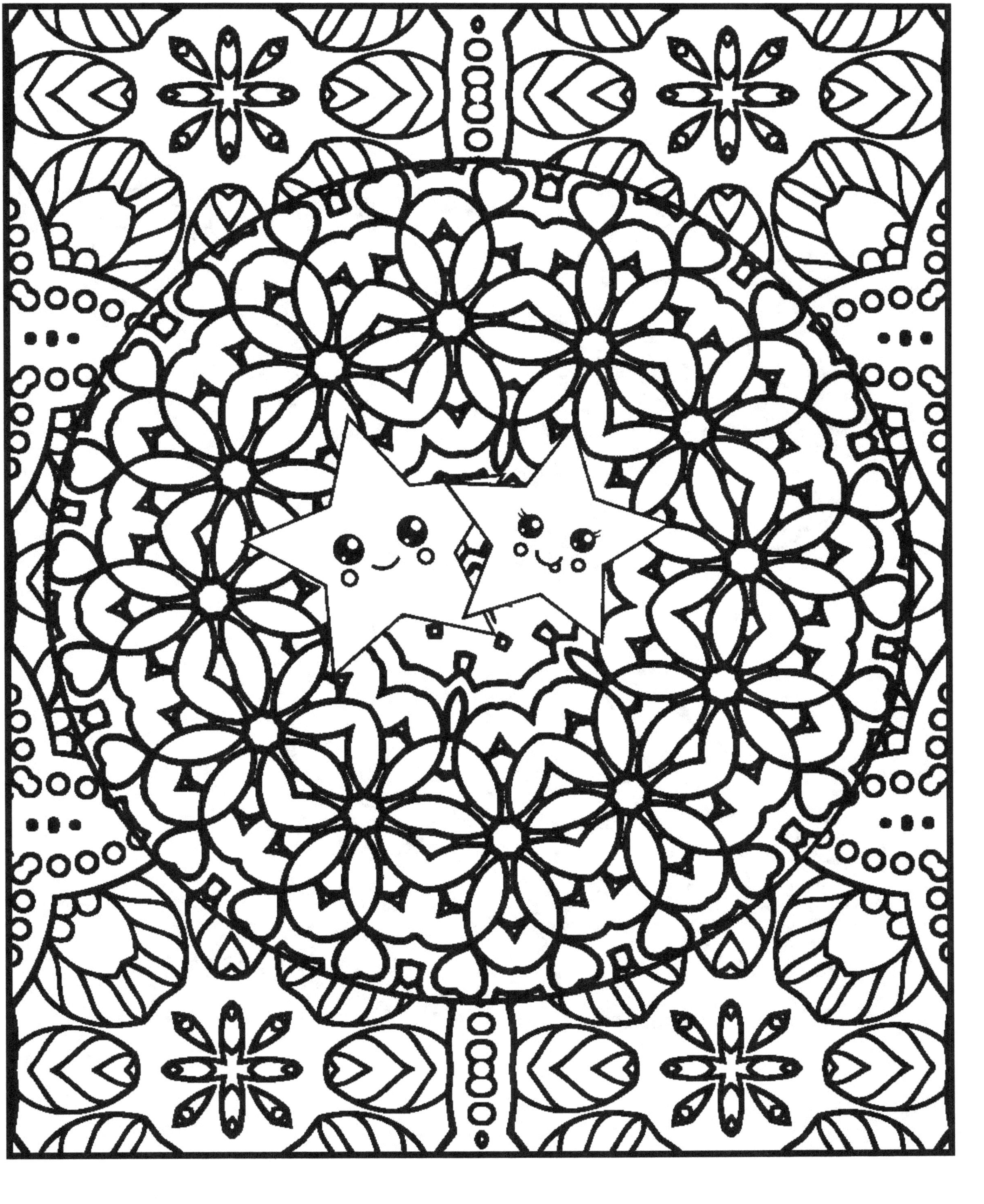

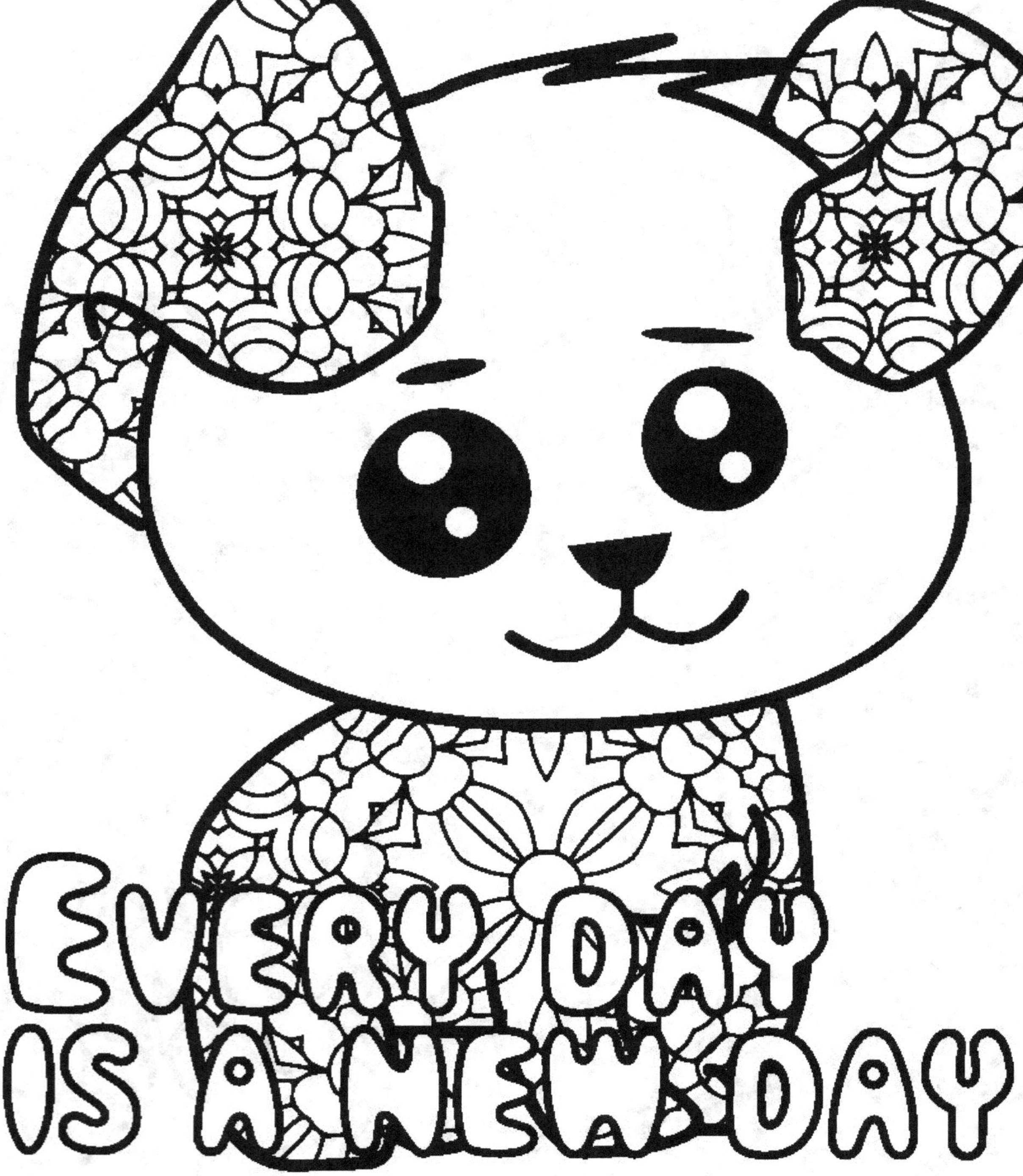
EVERY DAY
IS A NEW DAY

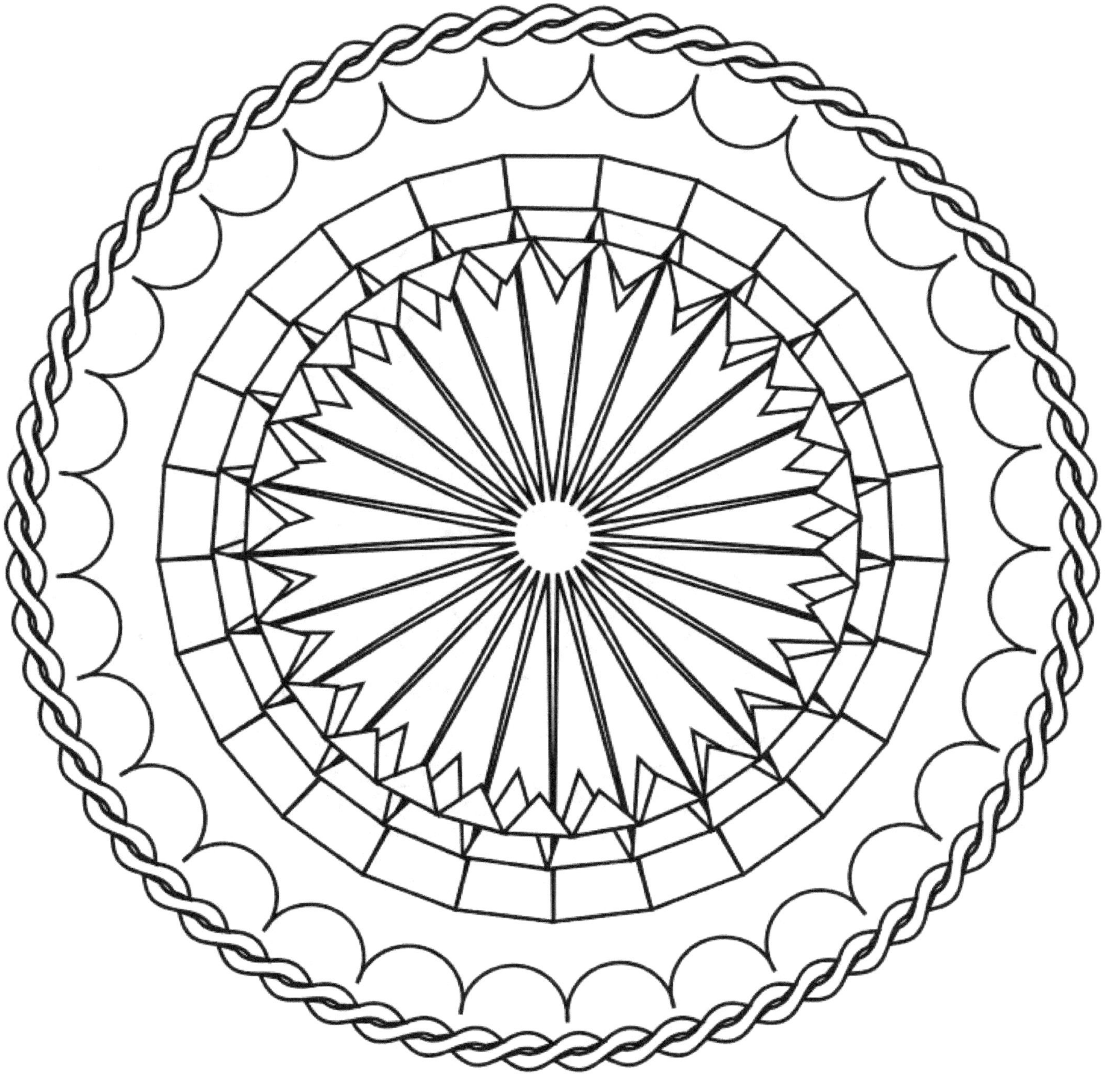

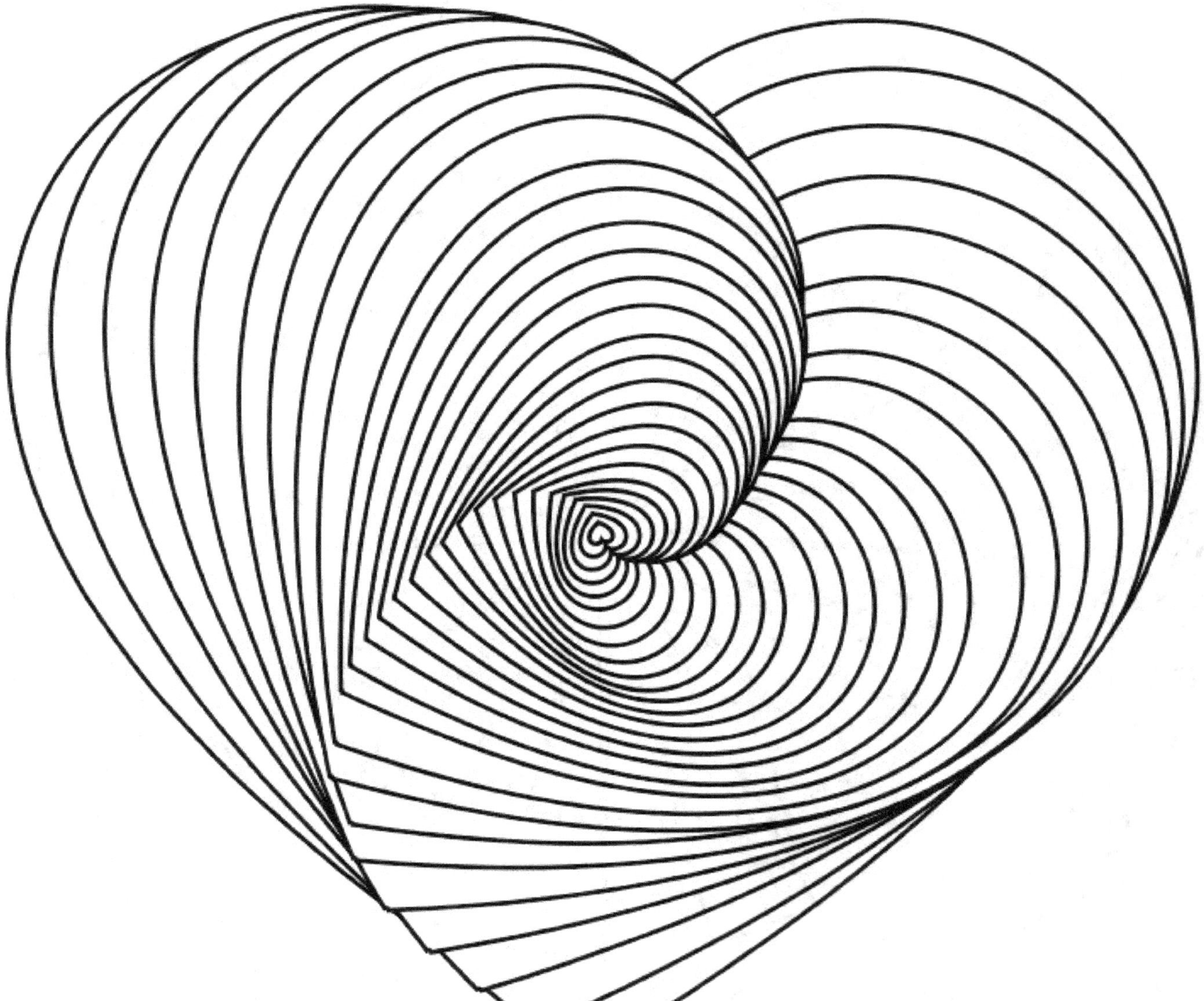

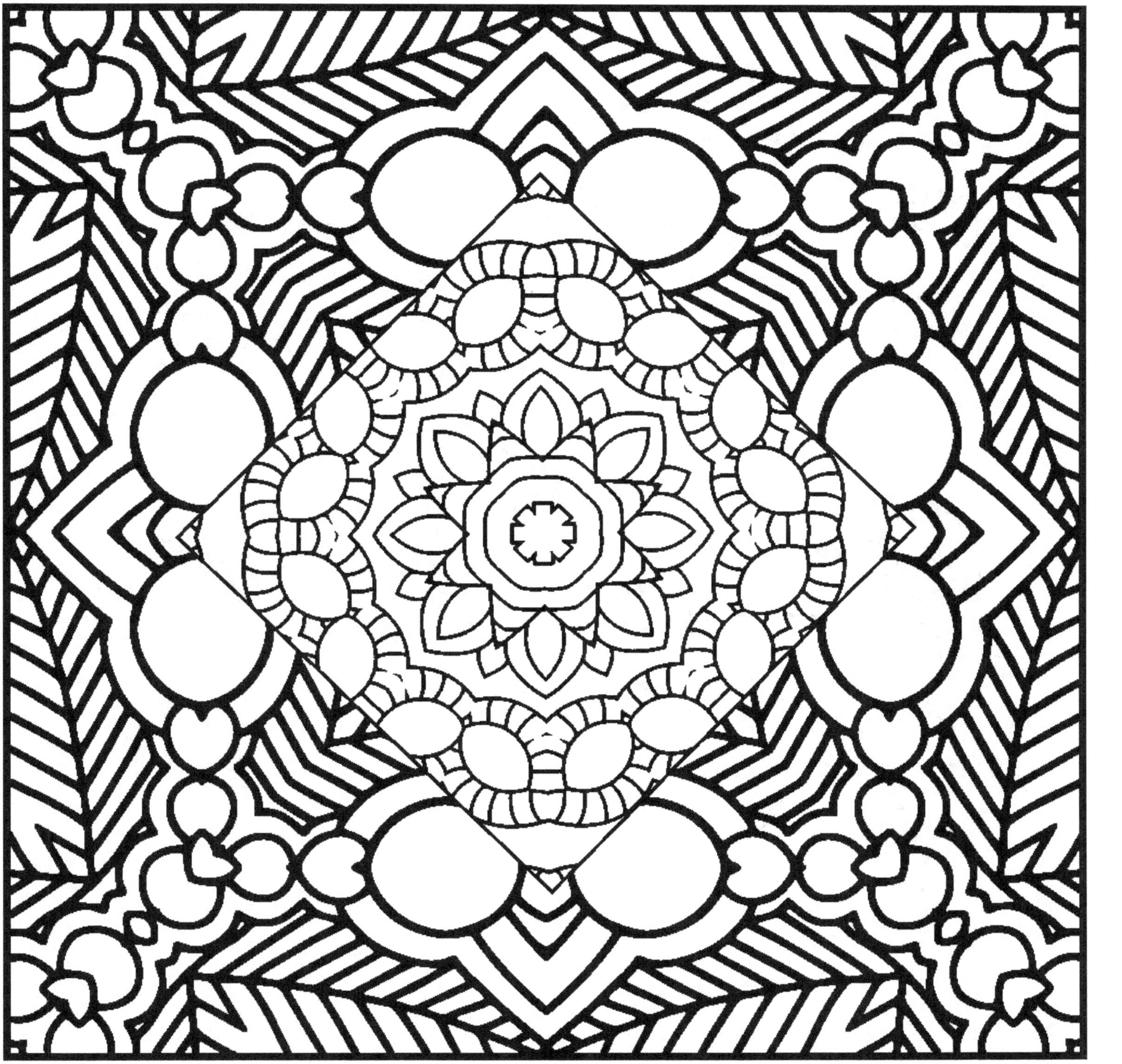

Such power
and beauty

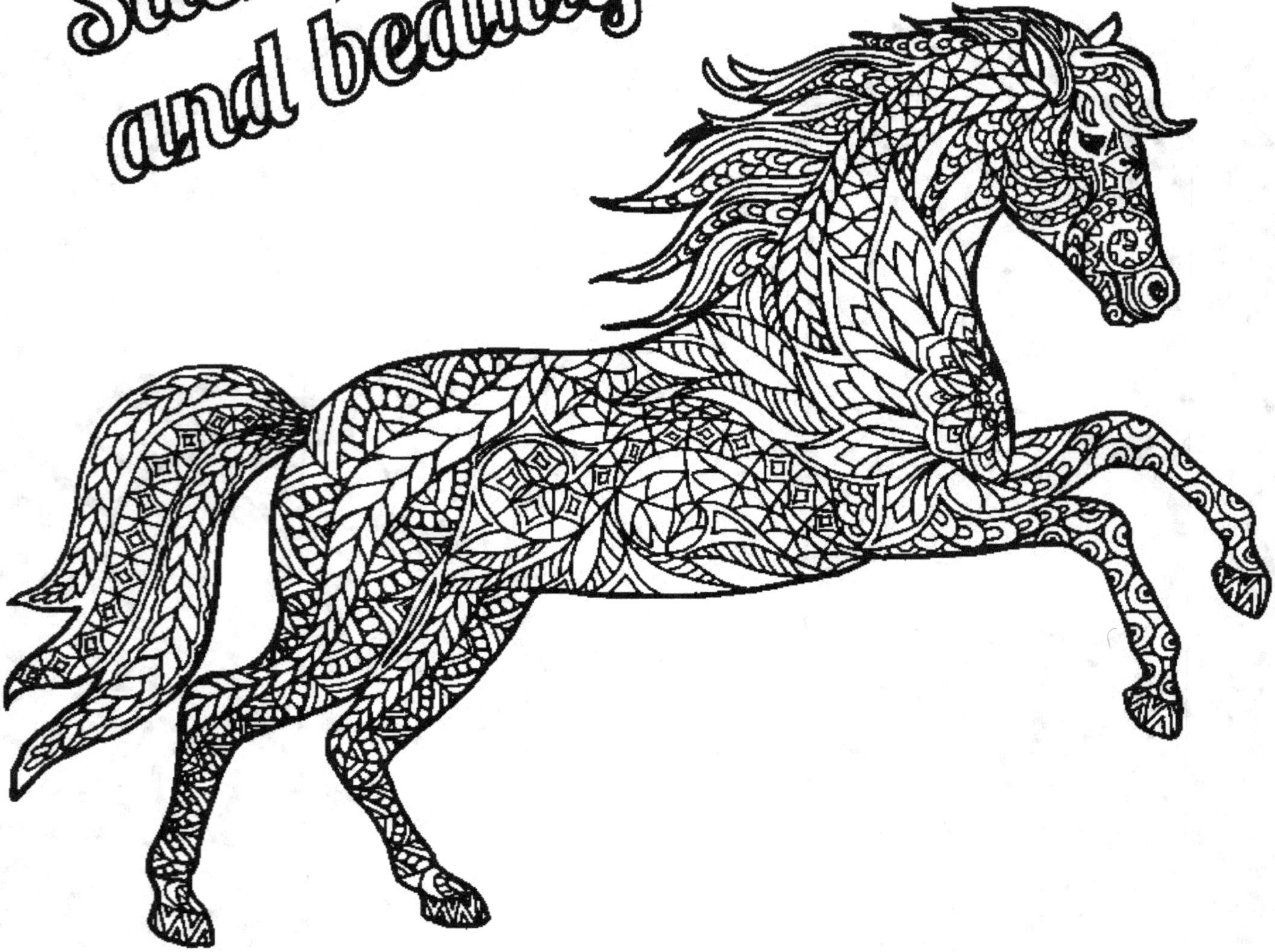

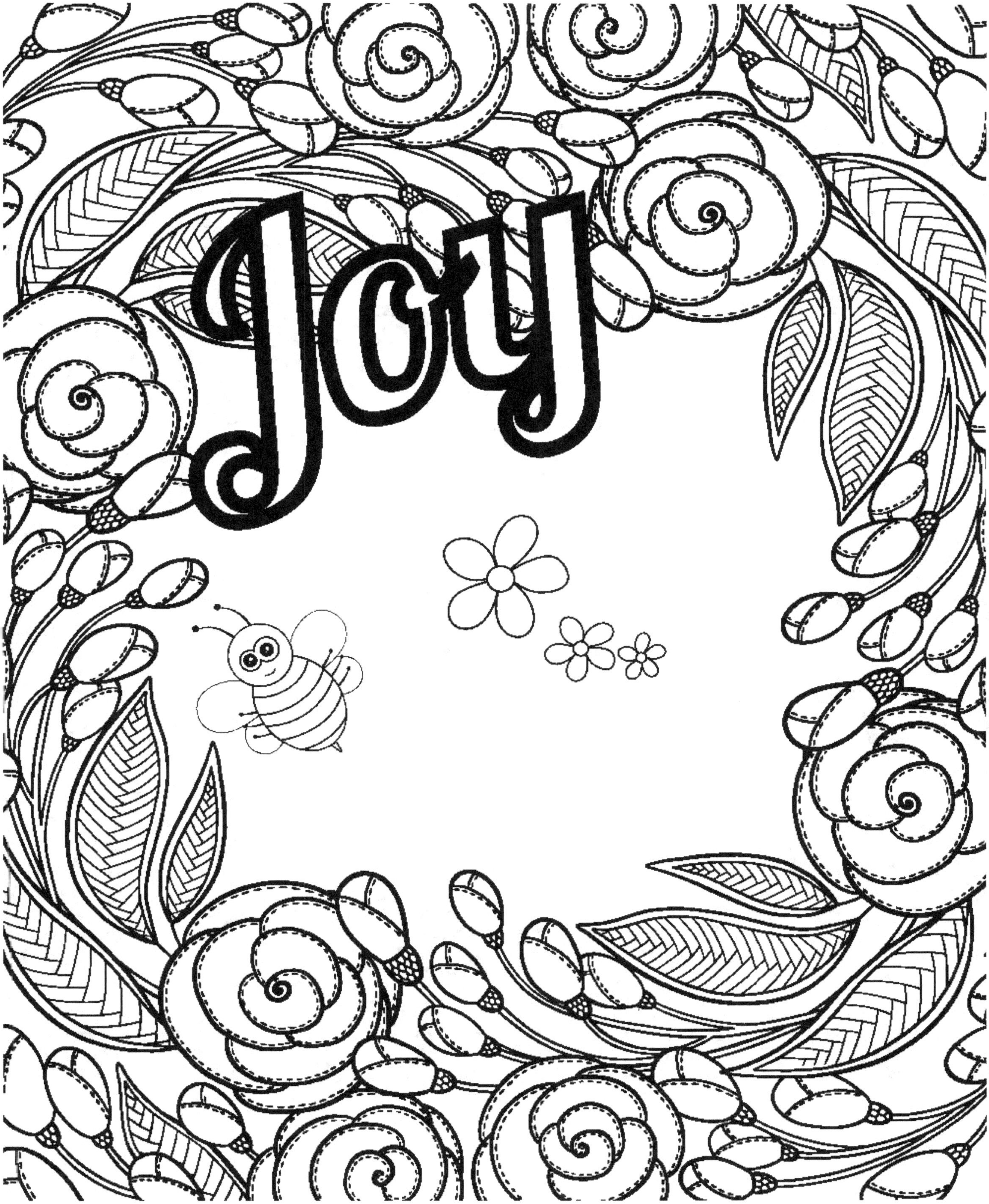
Joy

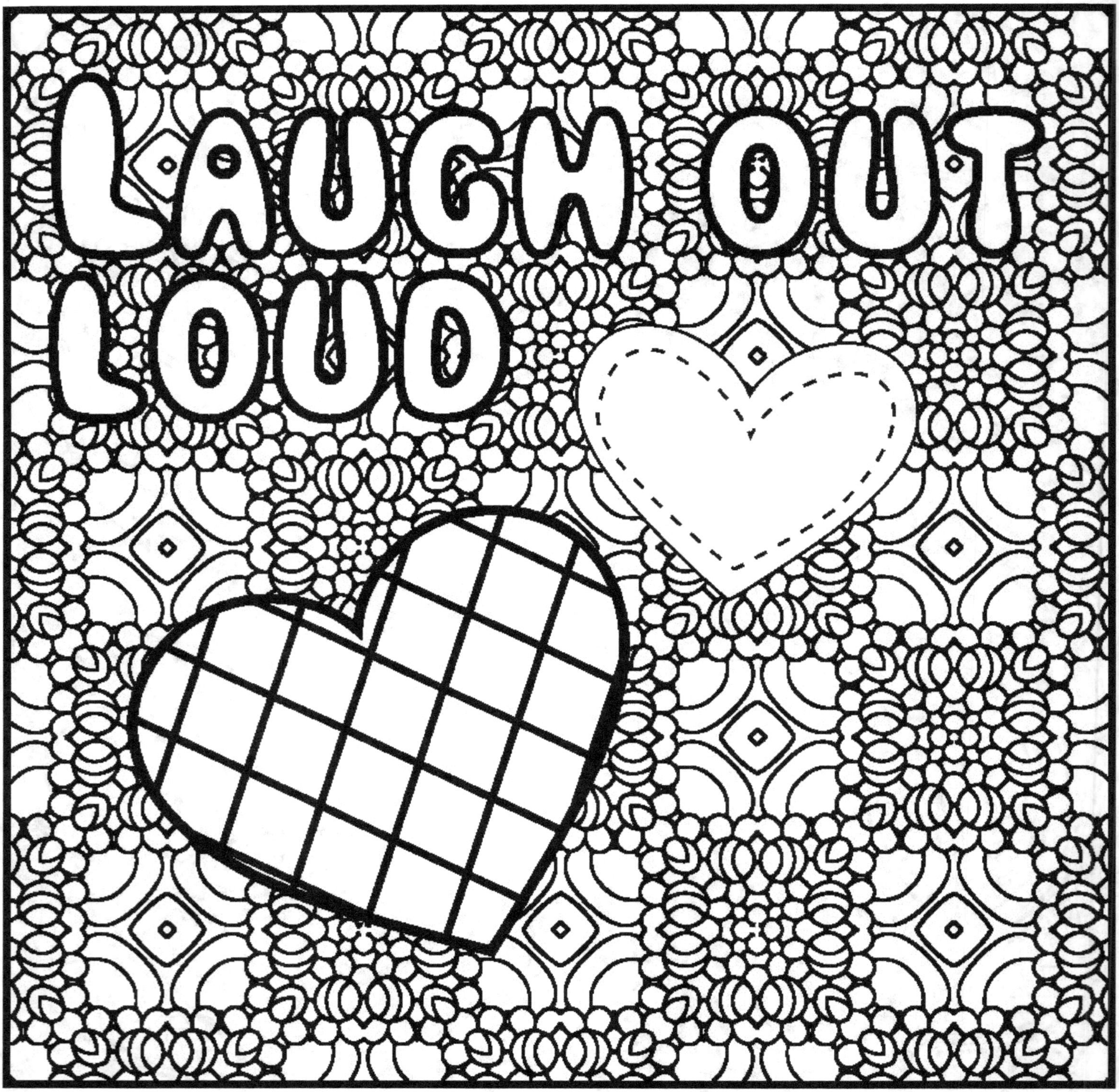
LAUGH OUT
LOUD

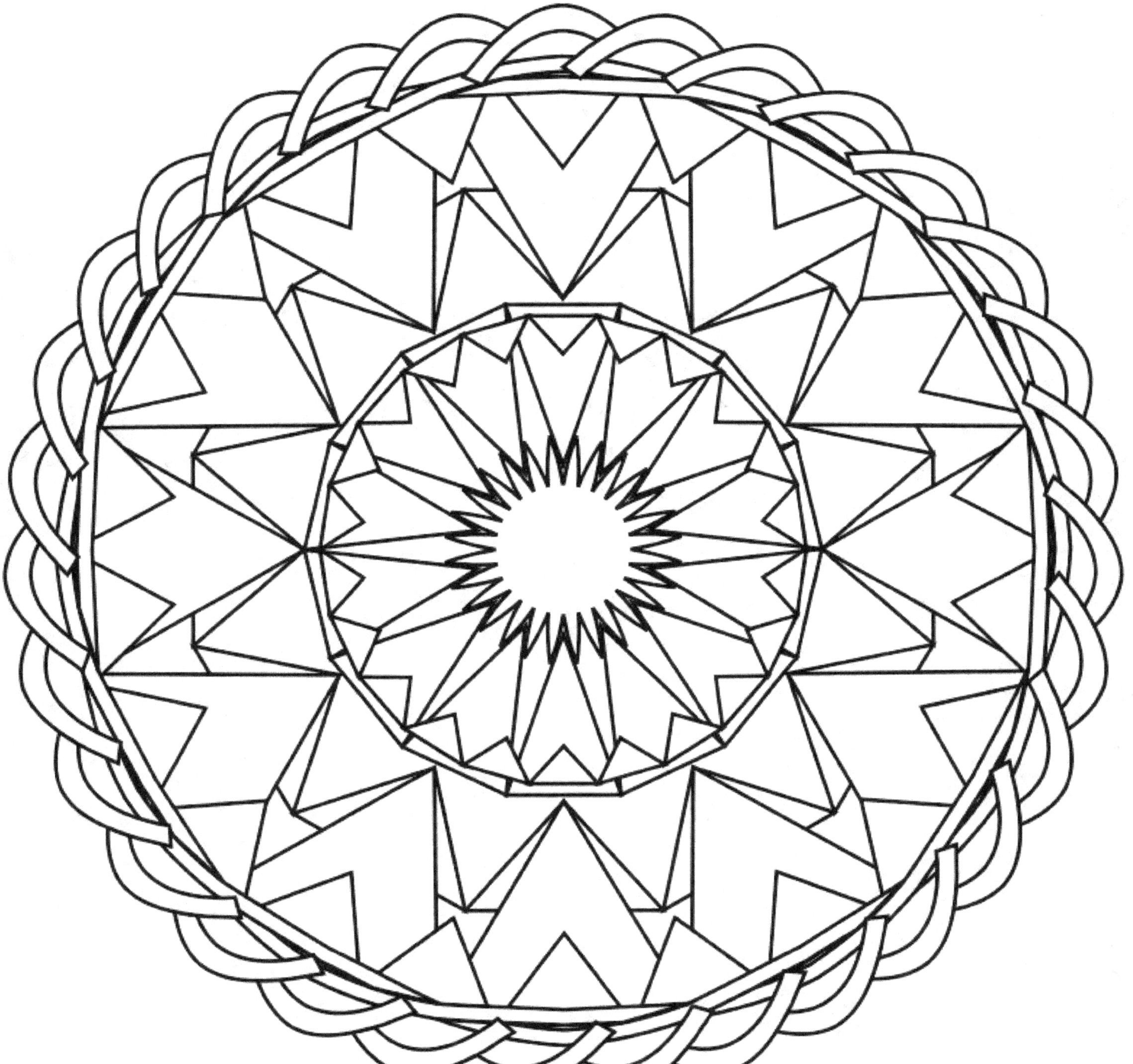

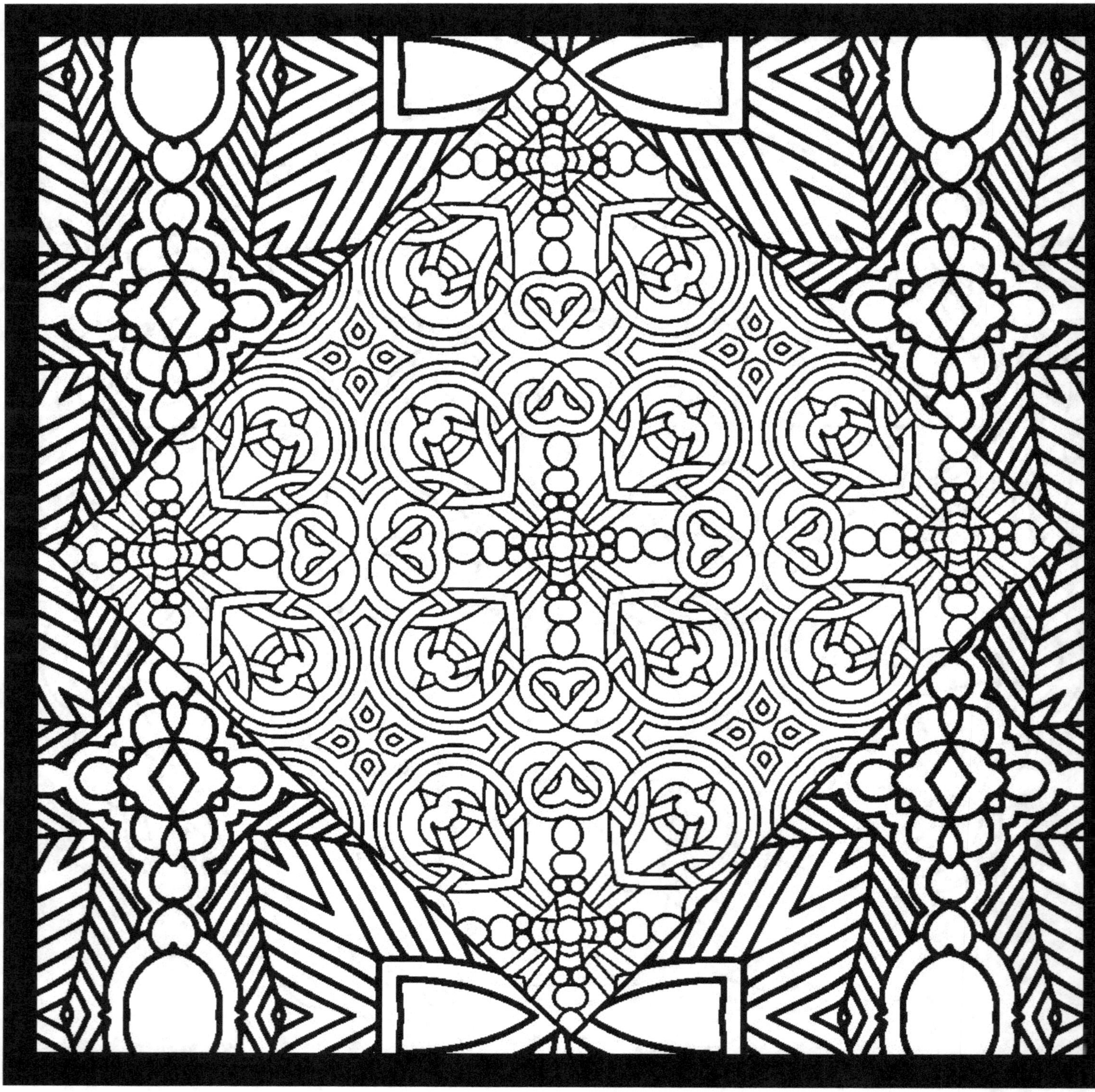

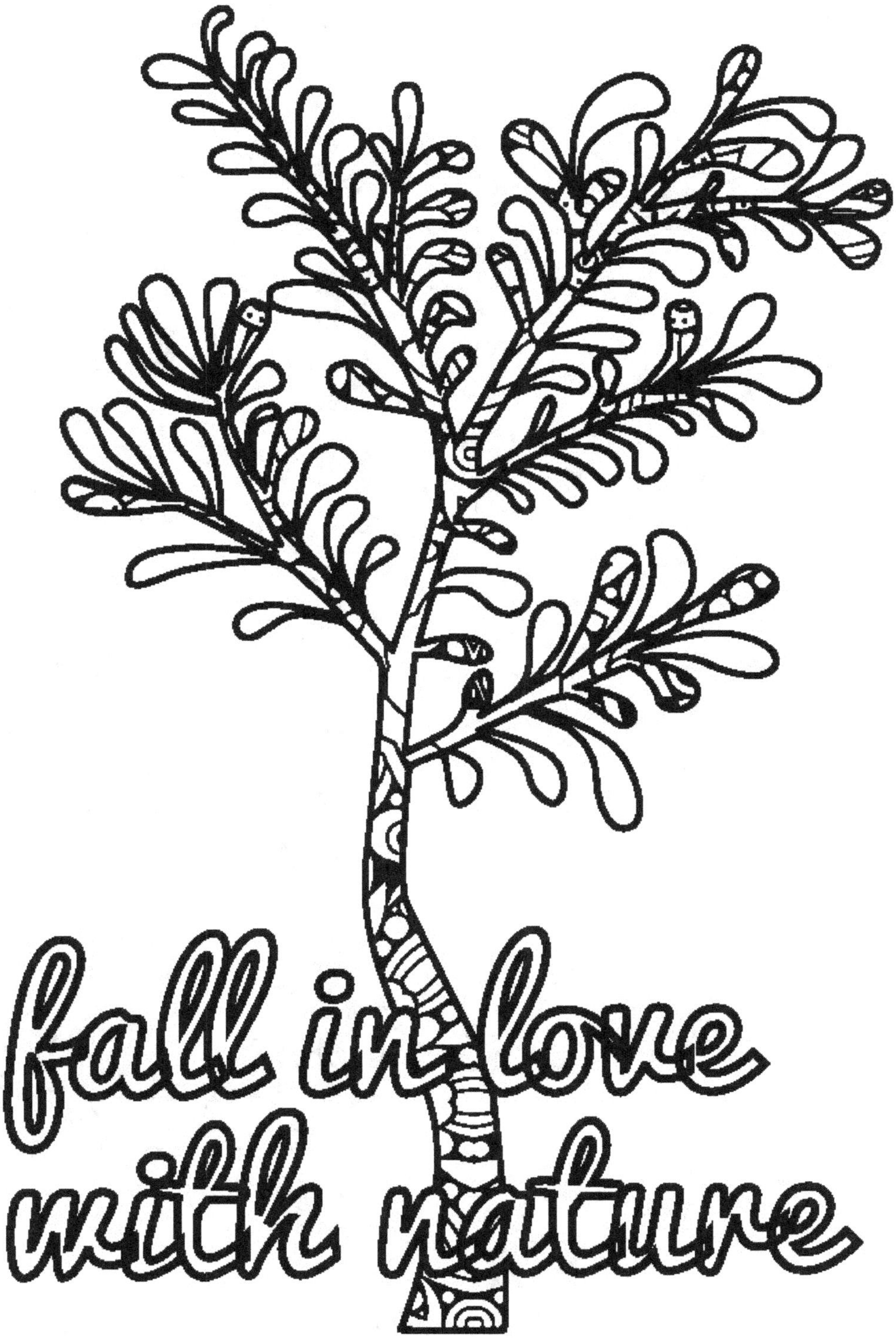
fall in love
with nature

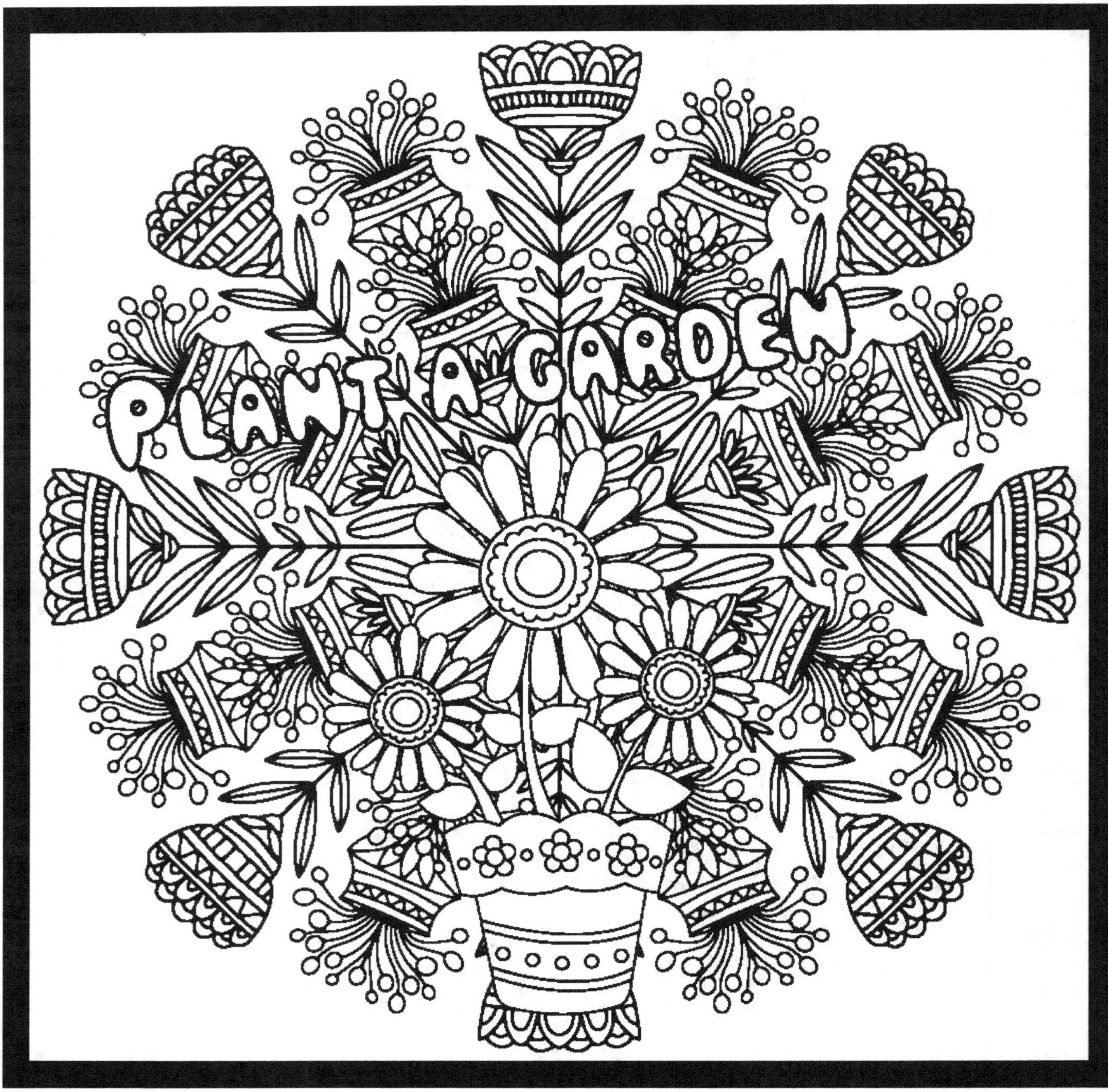
PLANT A GARDEN

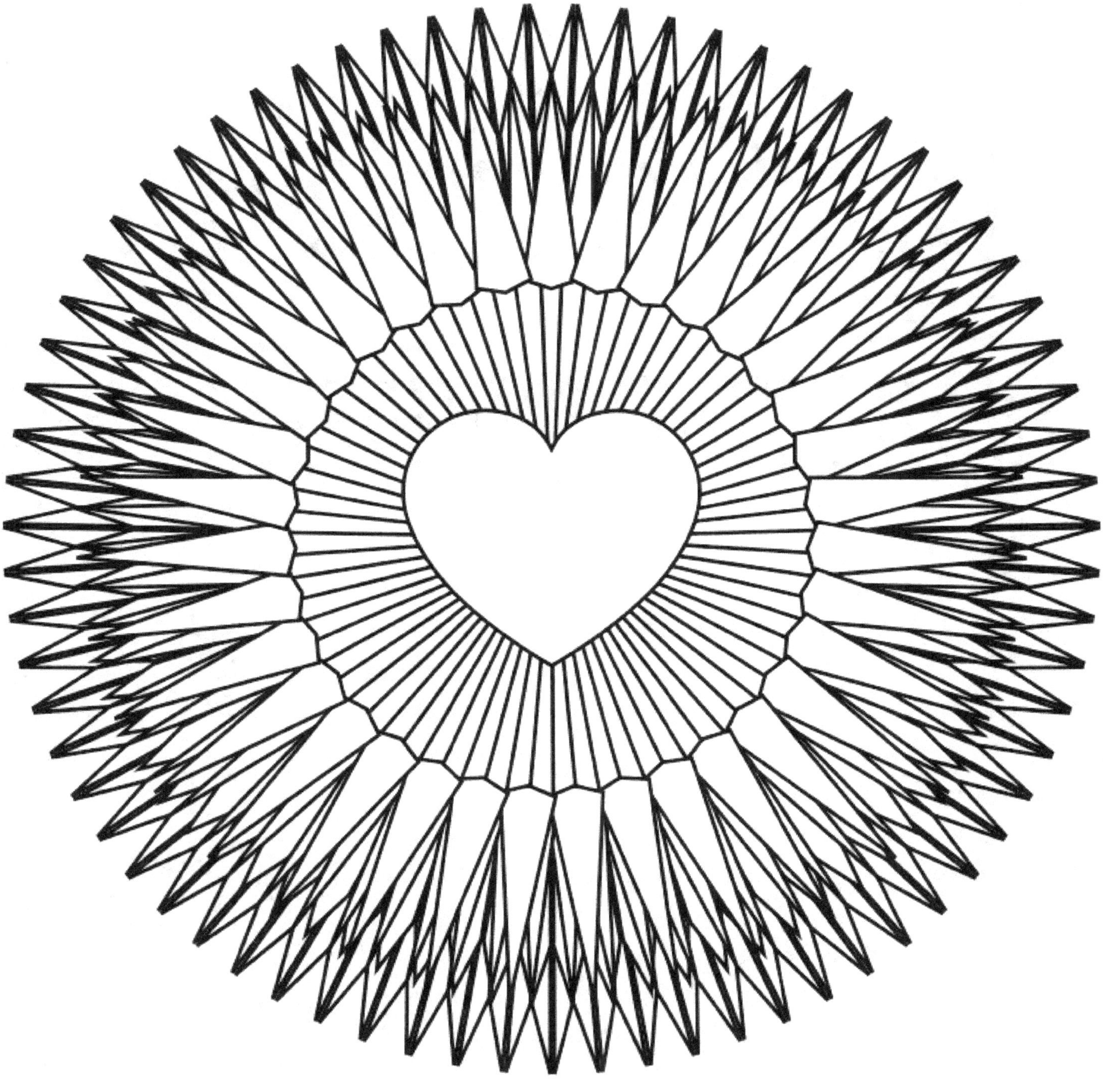

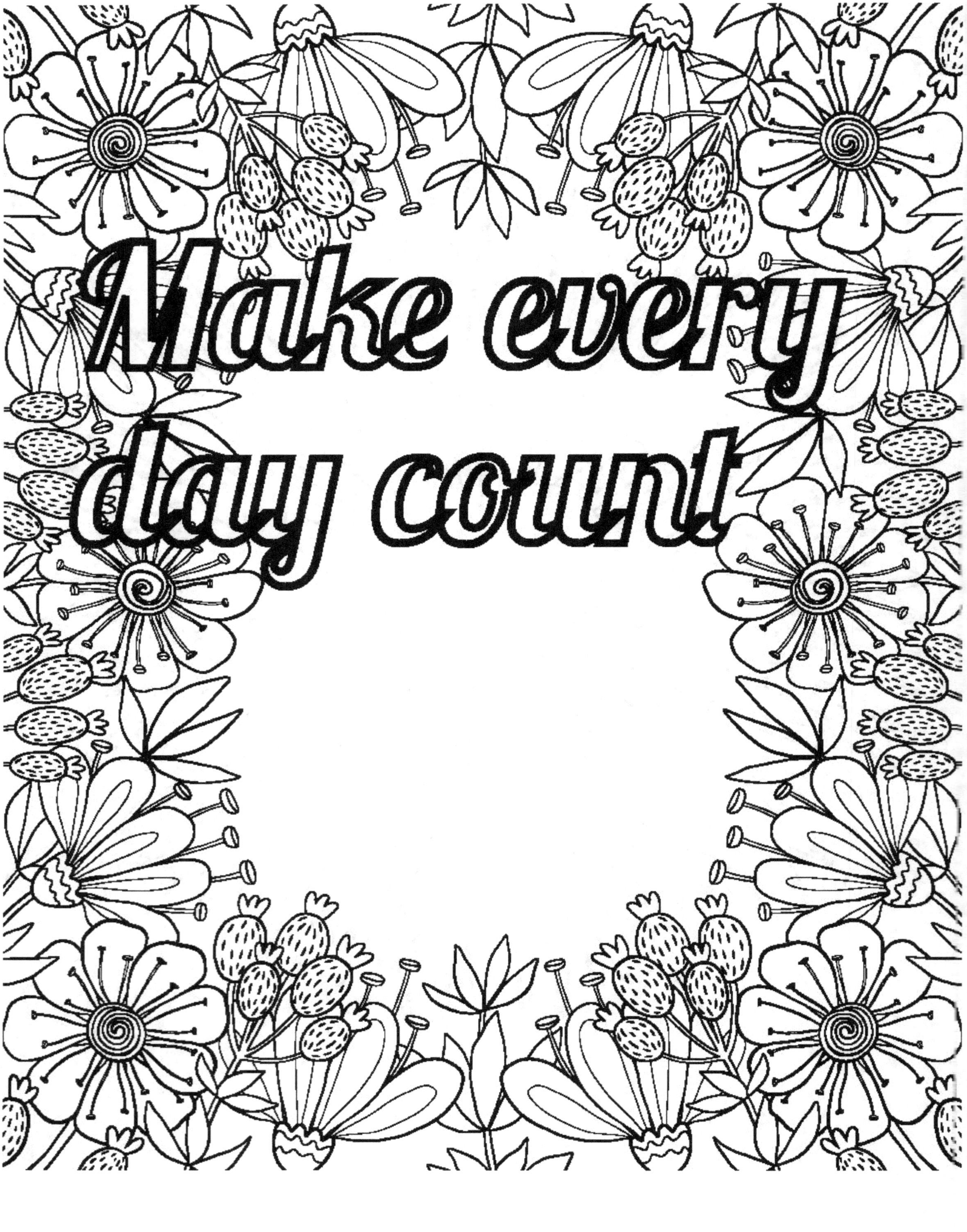
Make every
day count

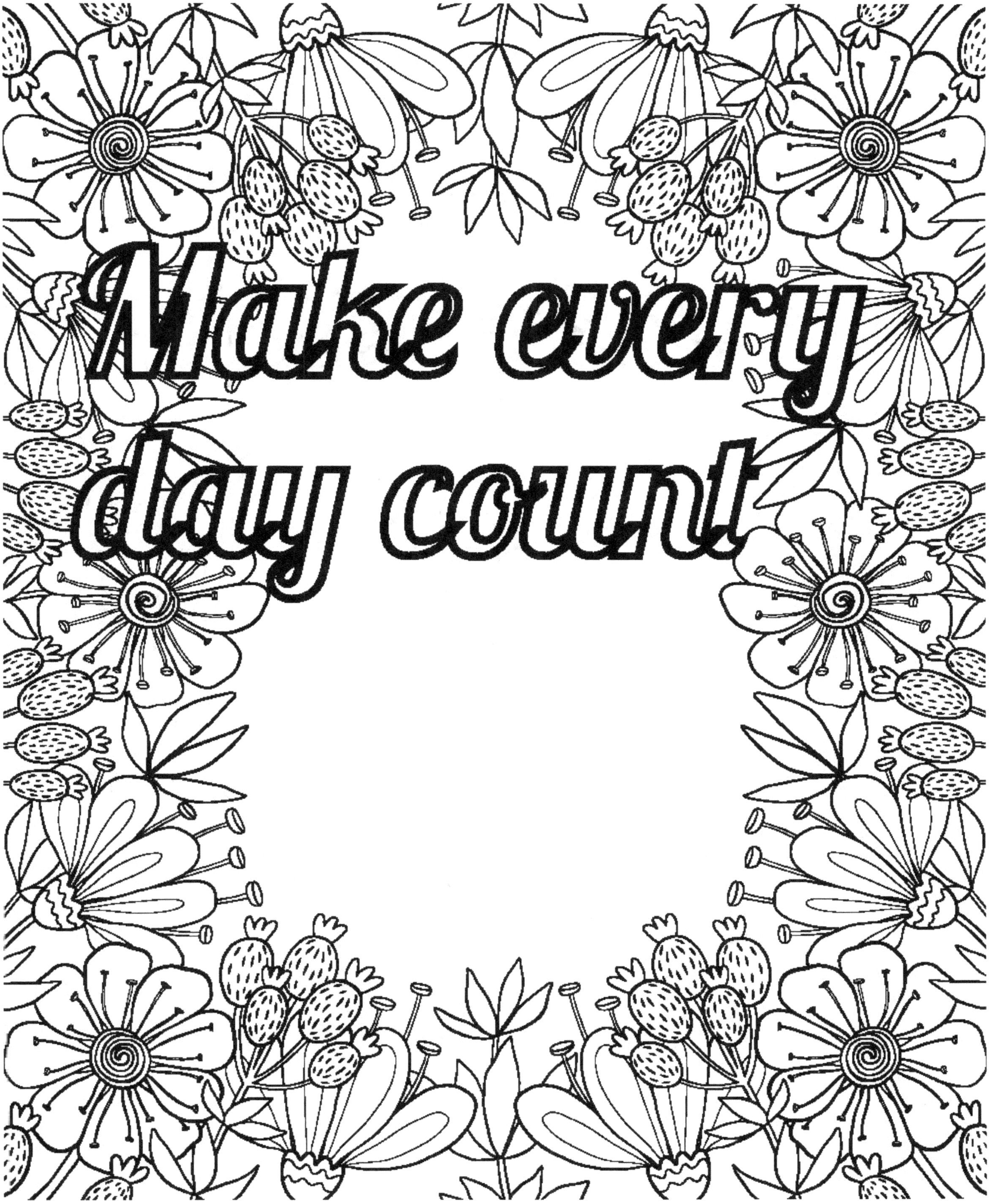
Make every
day count

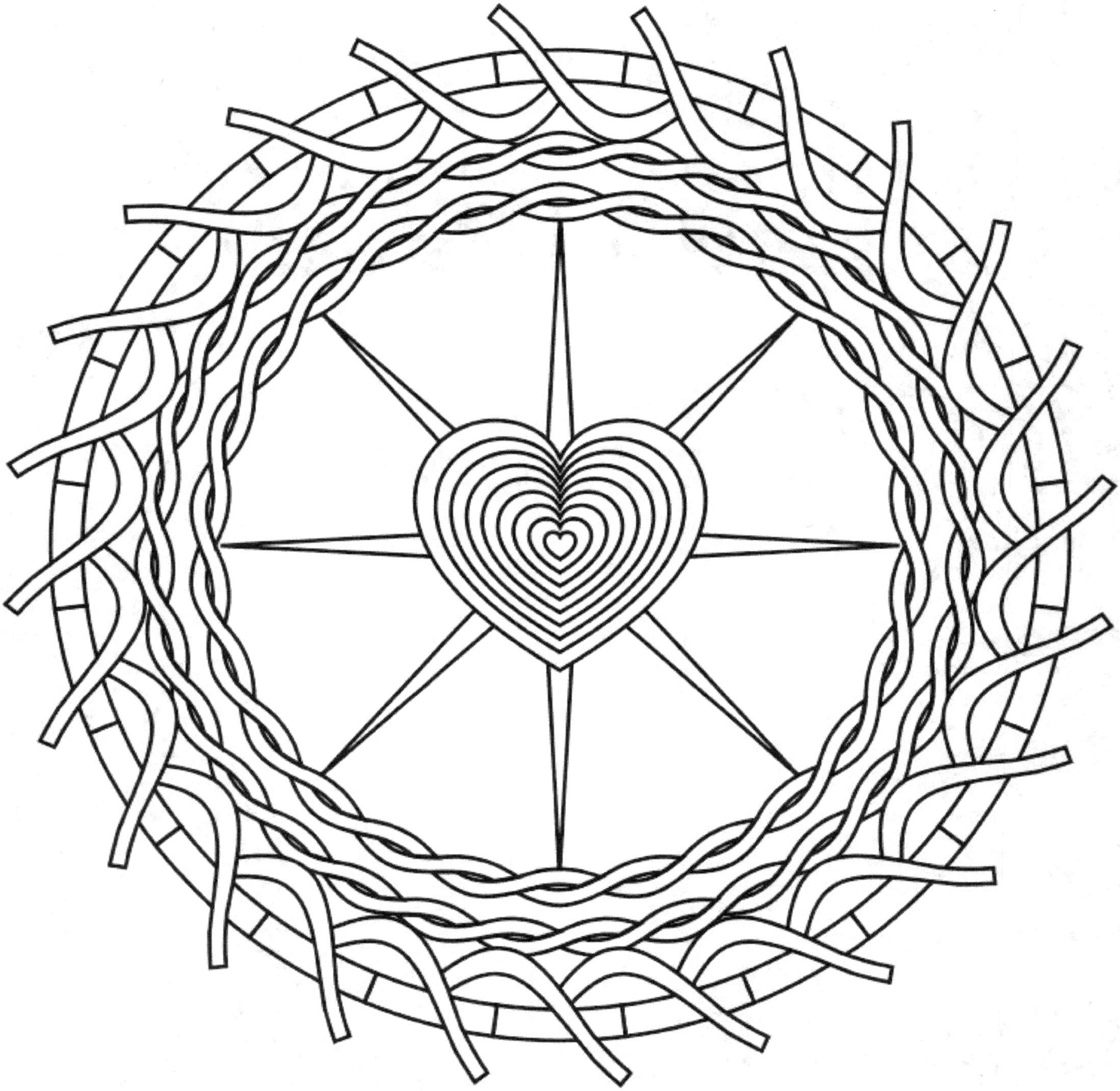

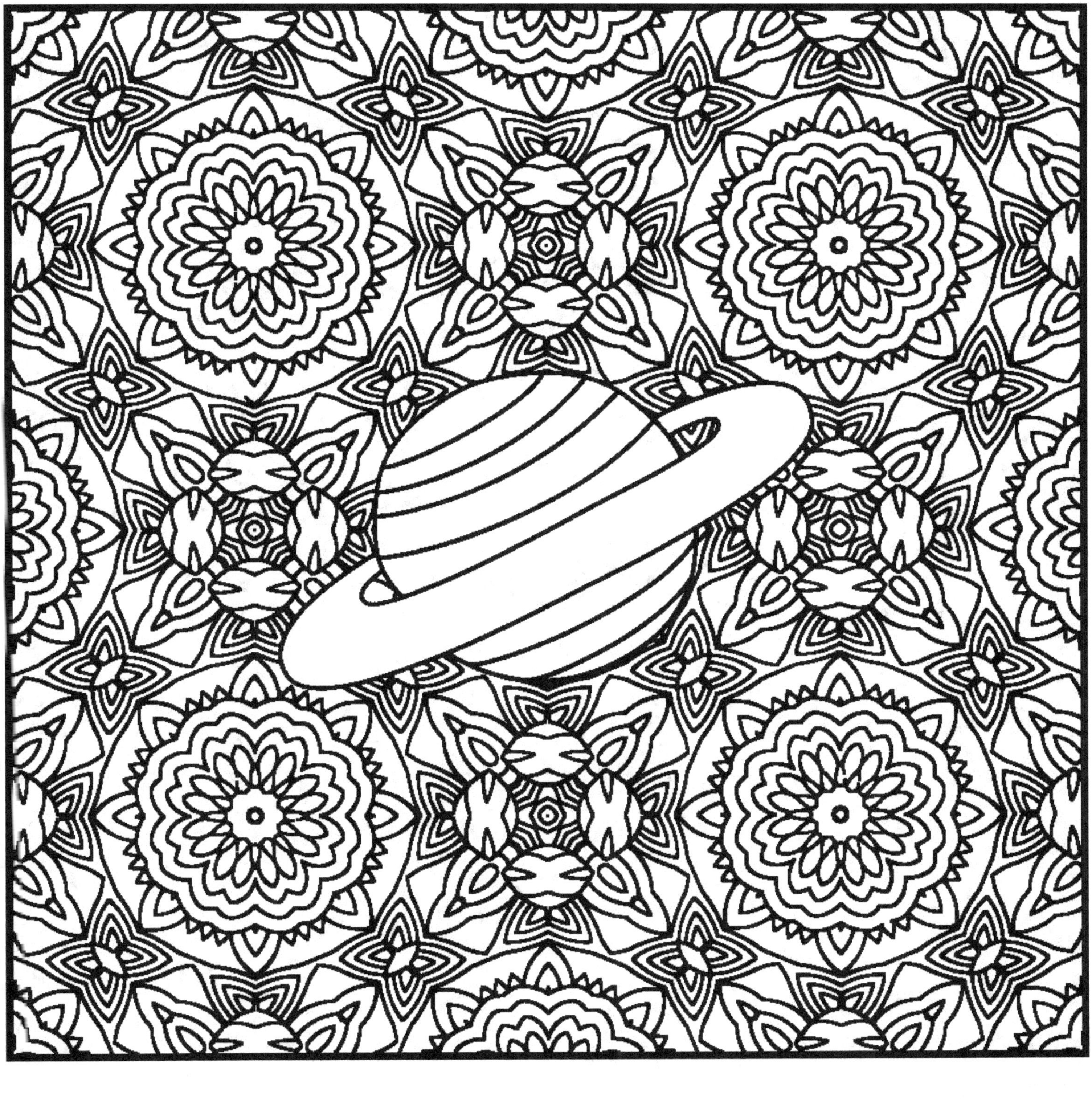

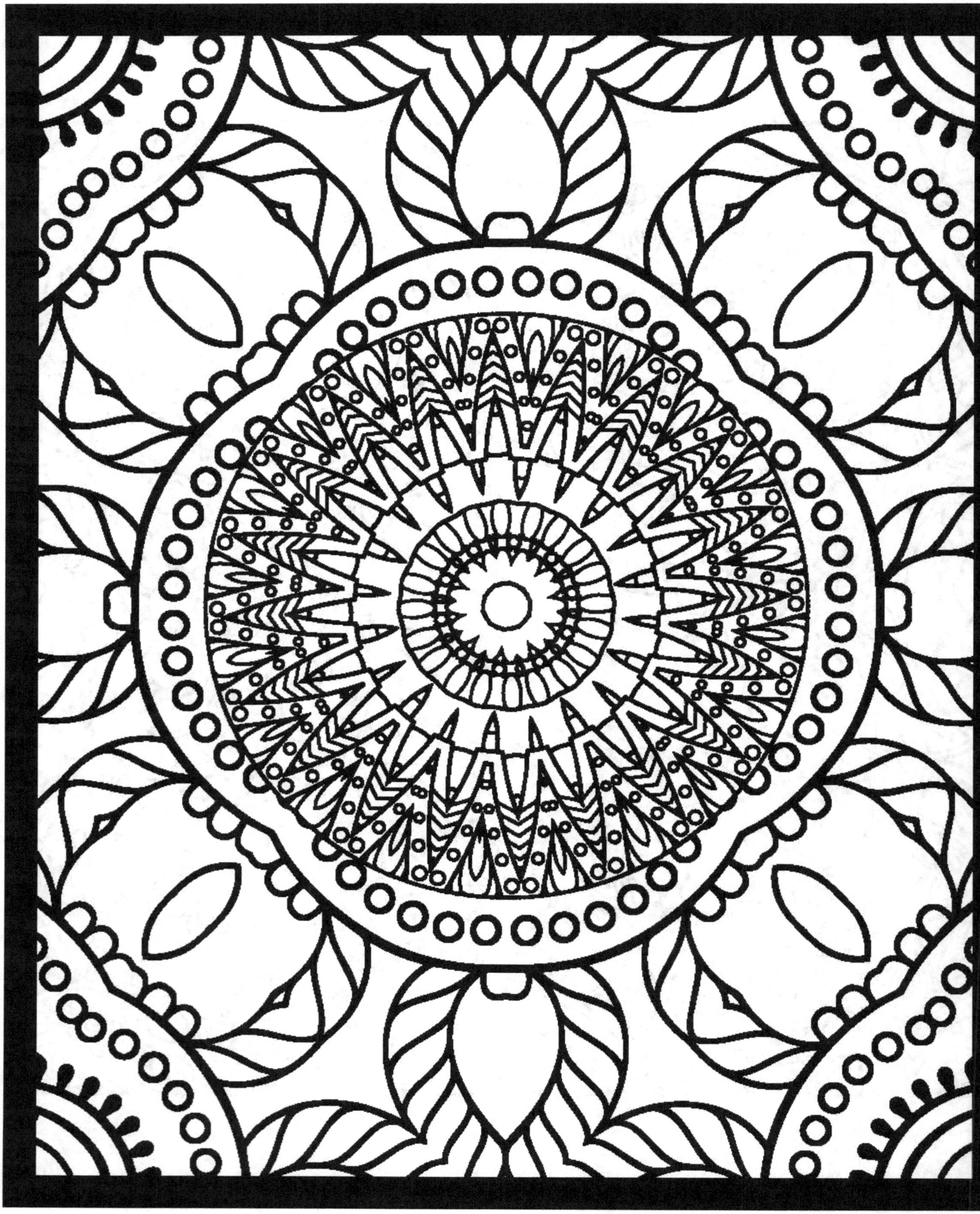

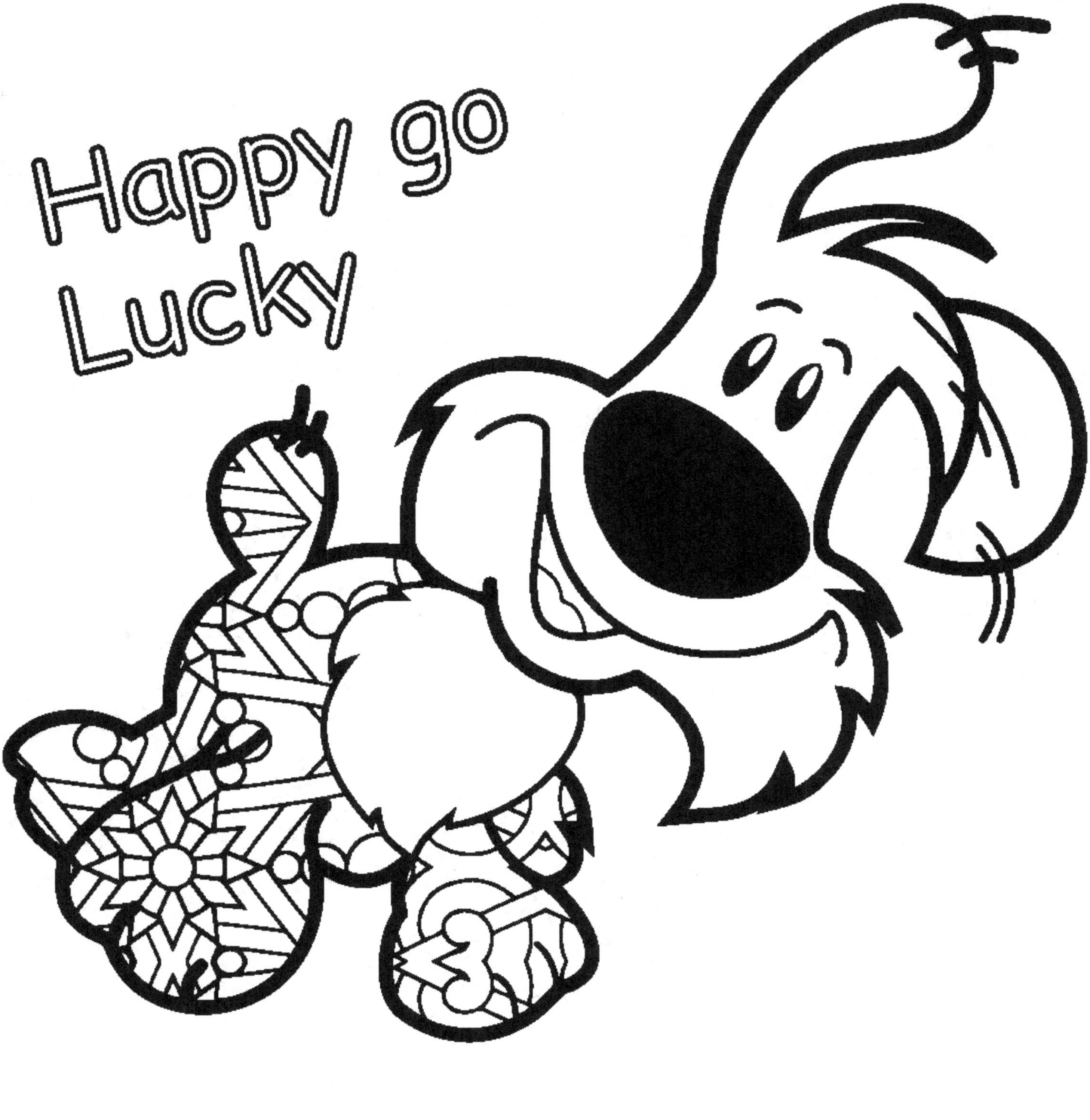
Happy go
Lucky

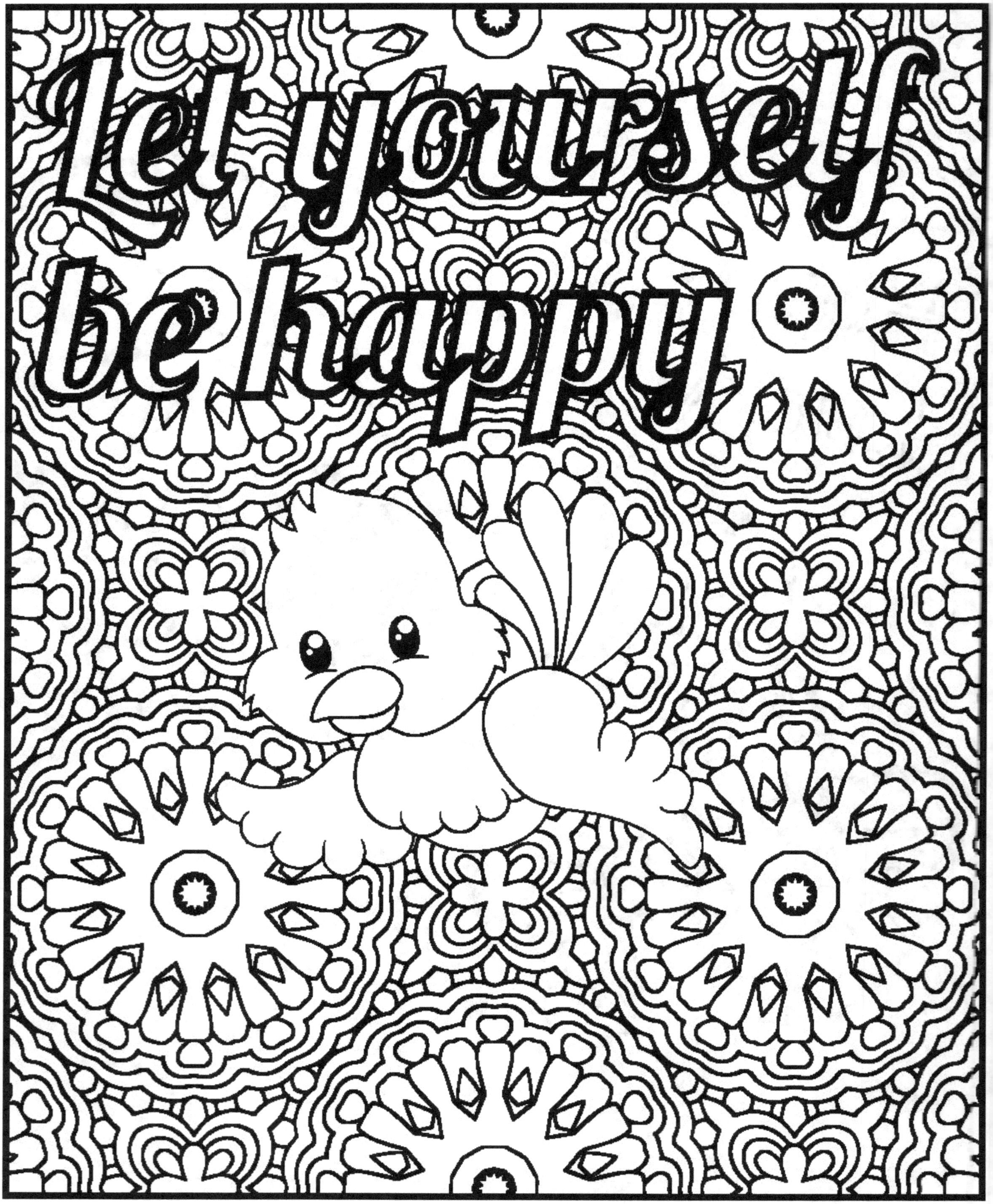
Let yourself
be happy

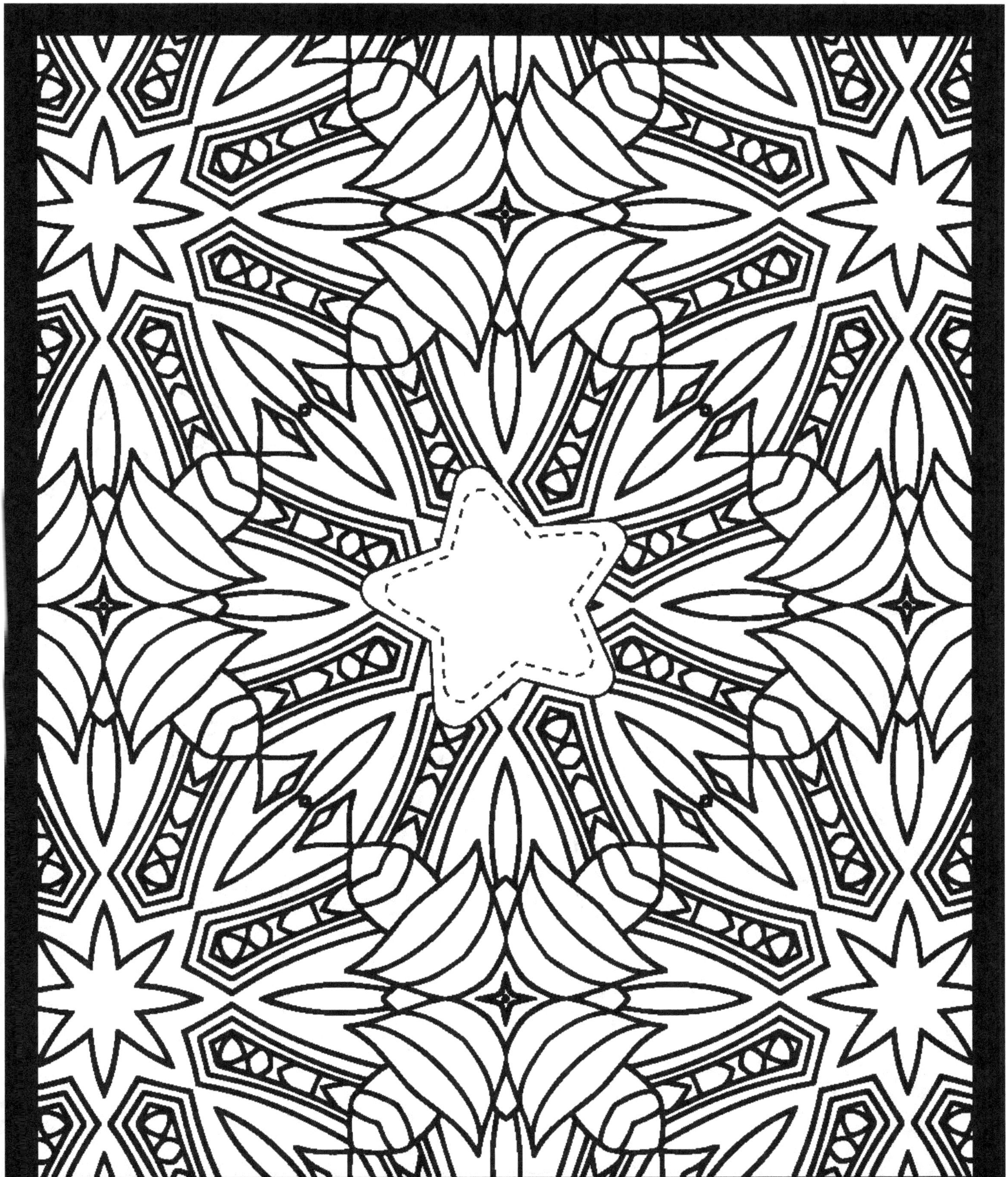

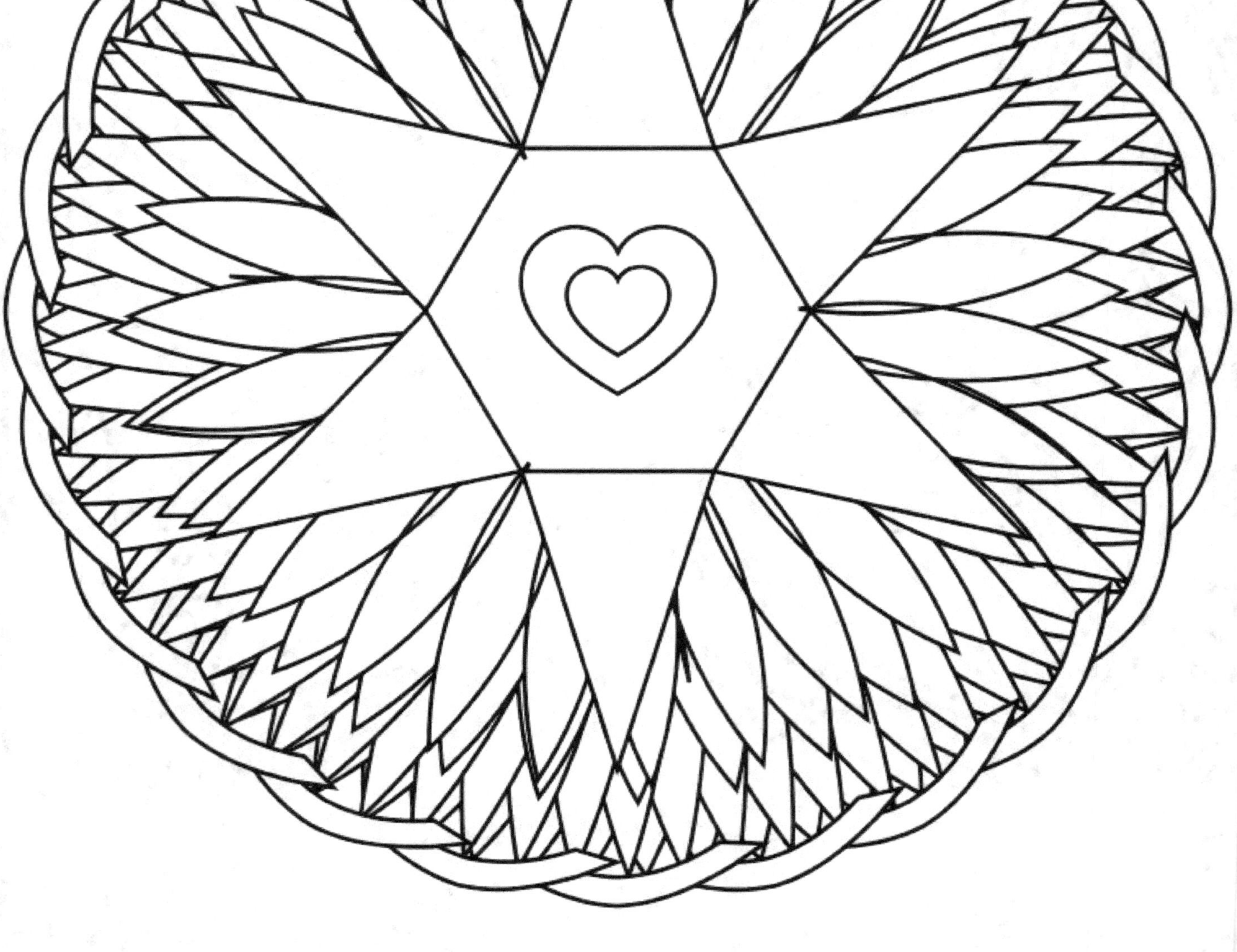

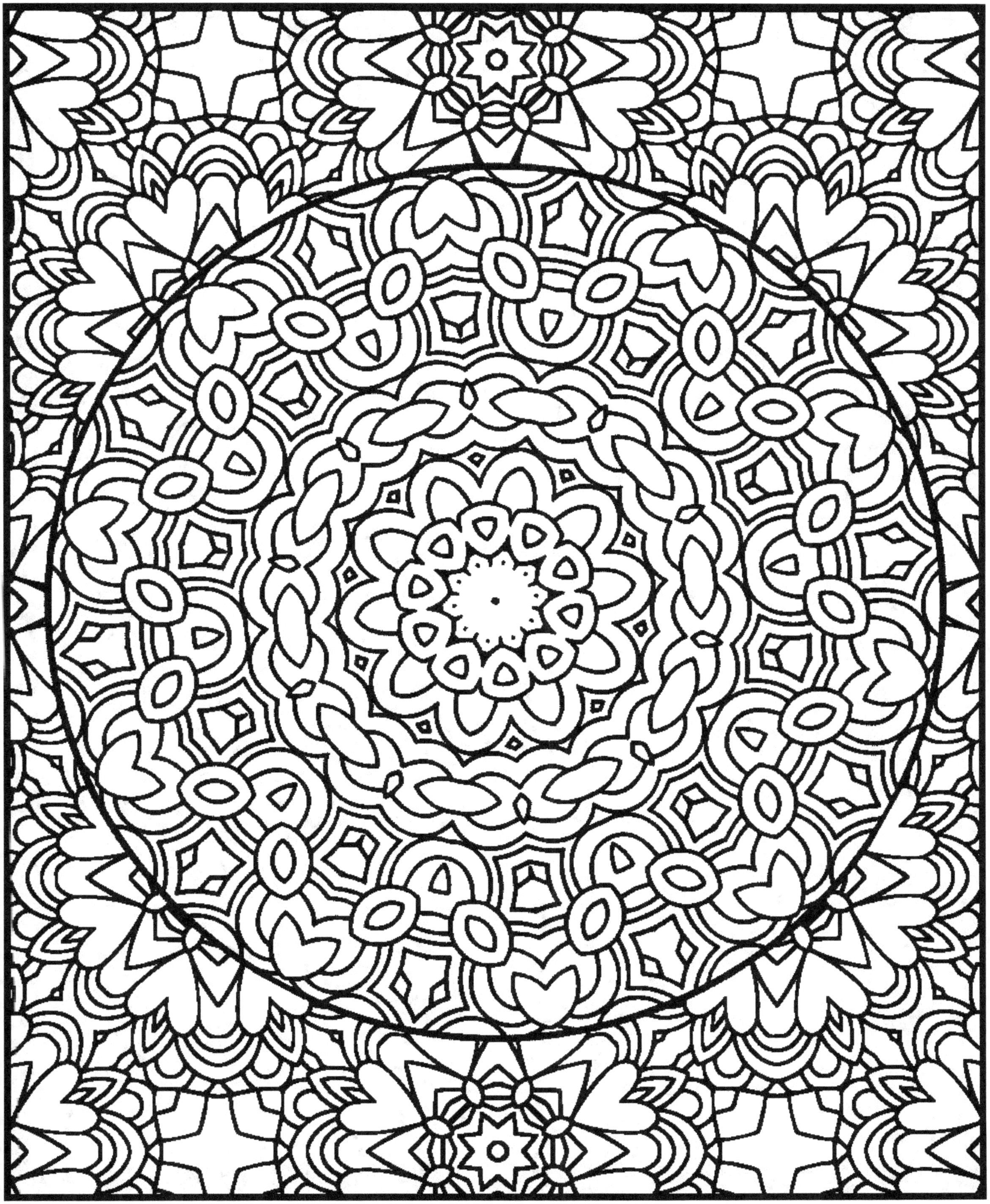

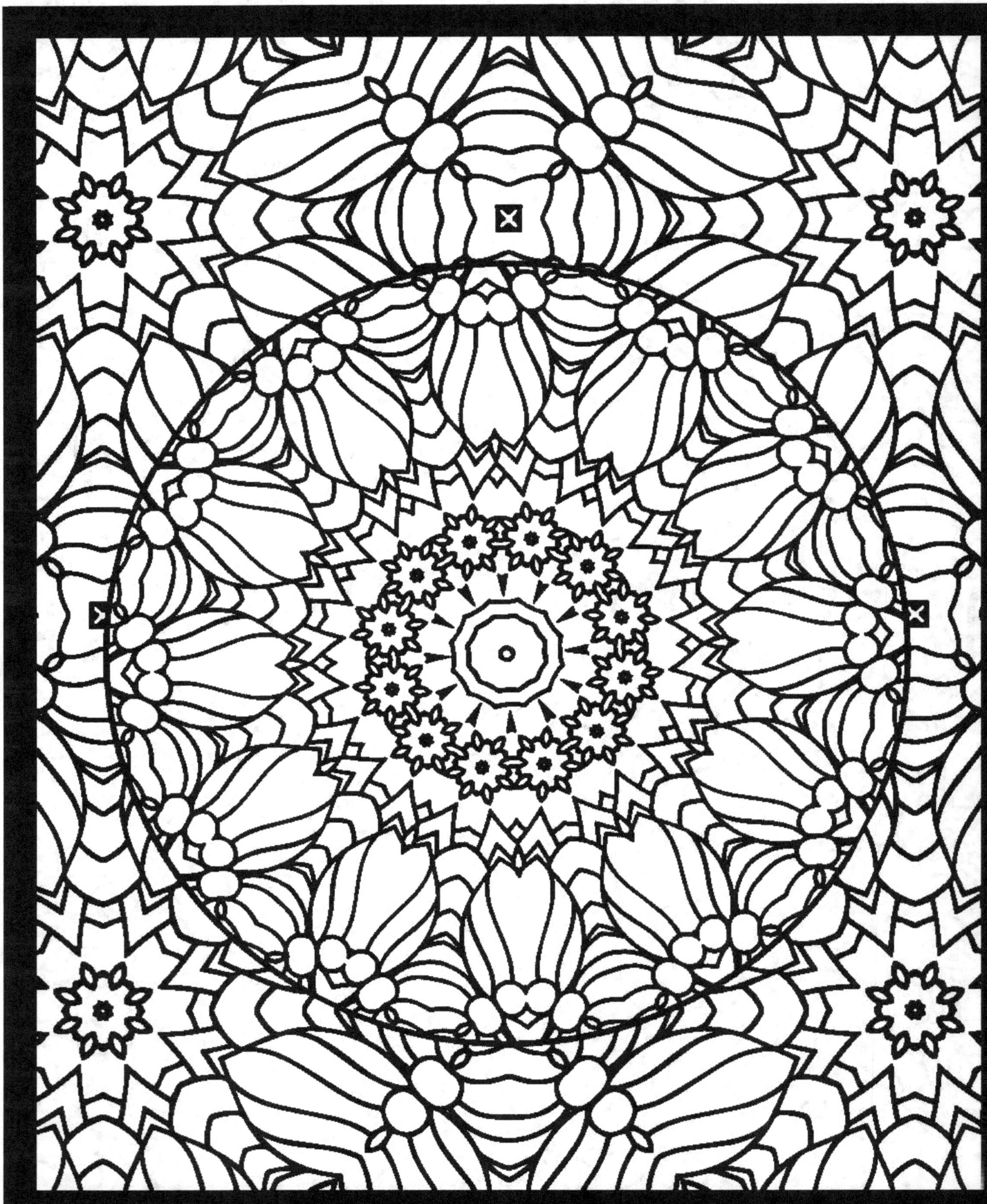

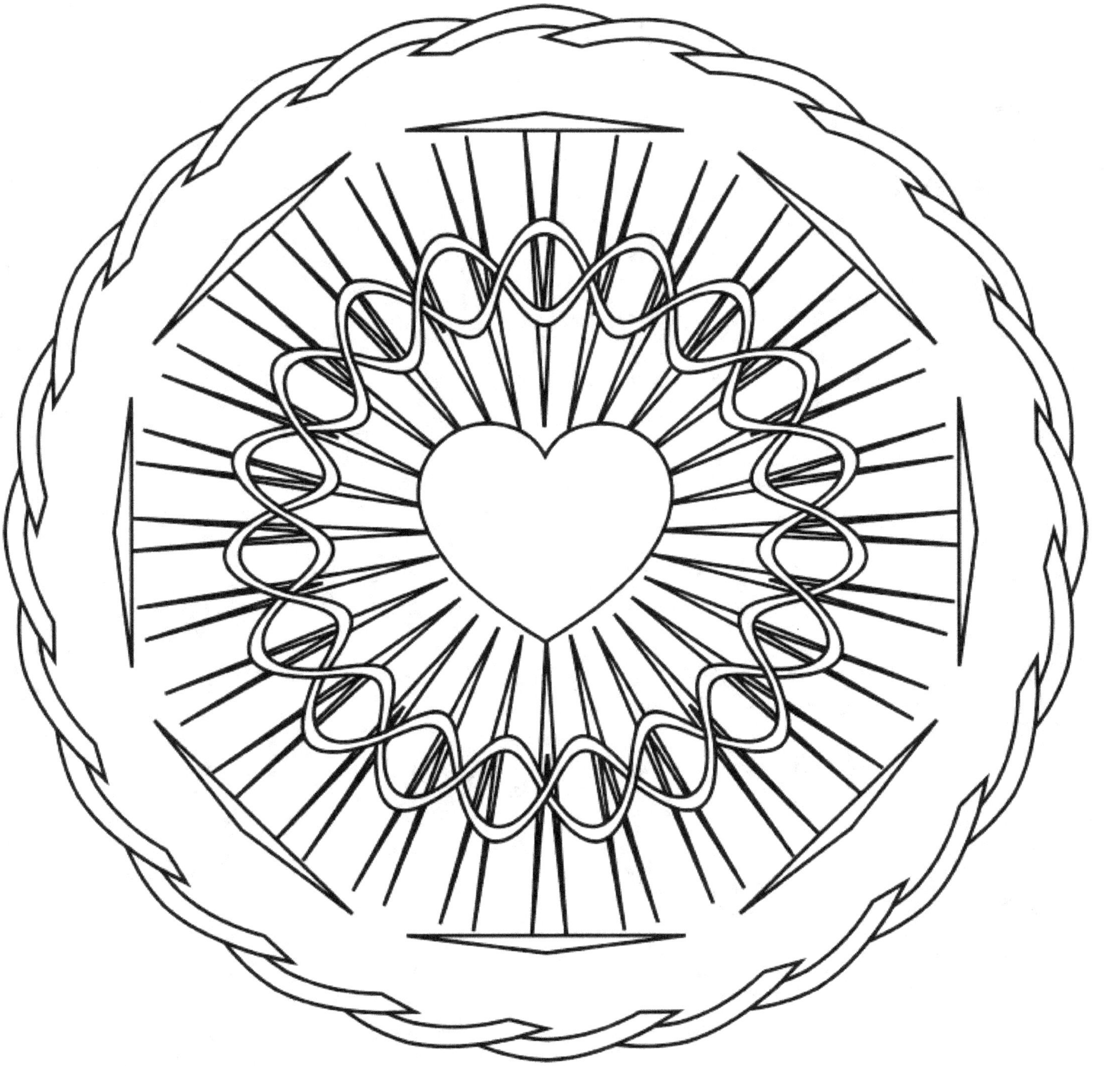

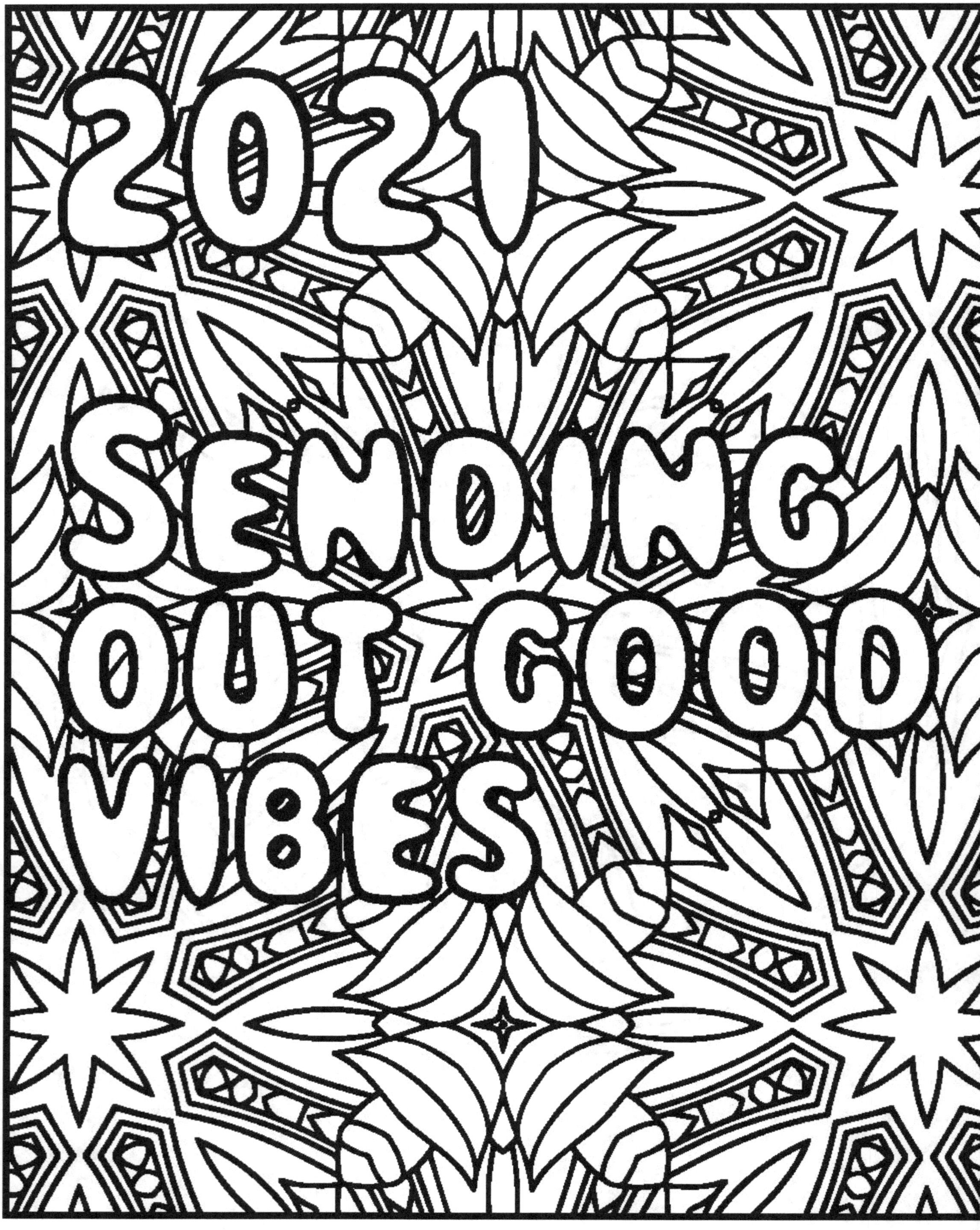
2021
SENDING
OUT GOOD
VIBES

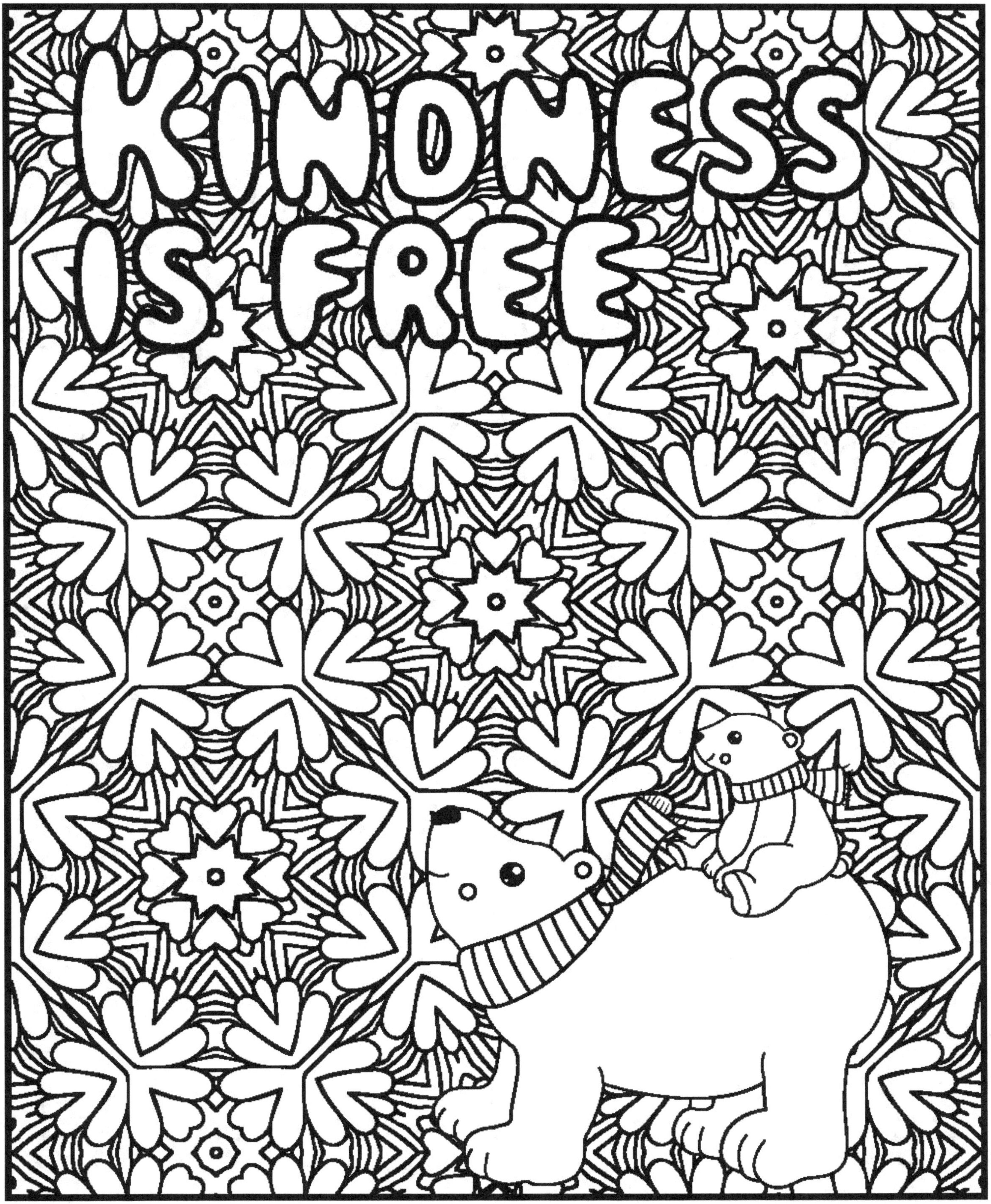
KINDNESS
IS FREE

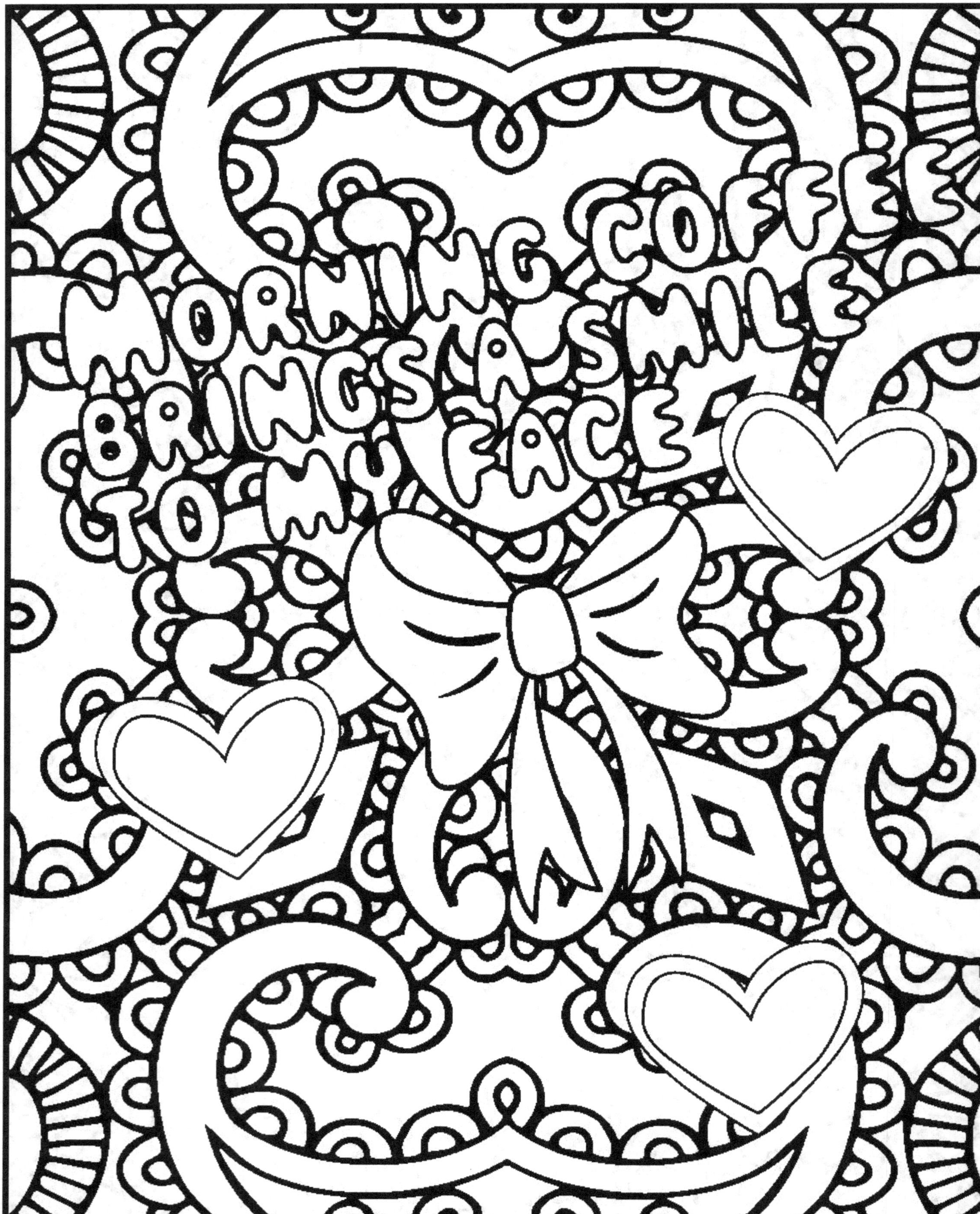
MORNING COFFEE
BRINGS A SMILE
TO MY FACE

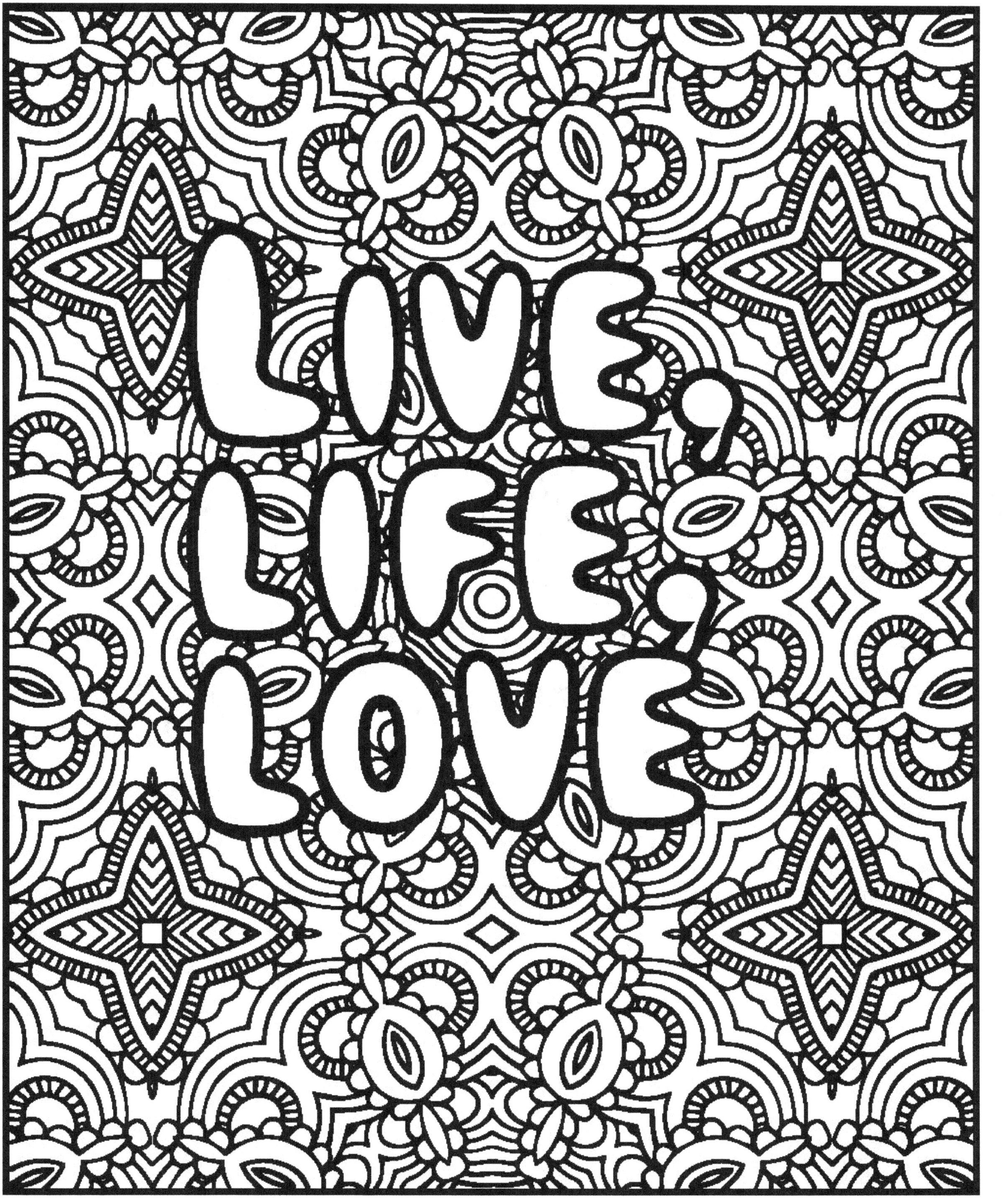
LIVE, LIFE, LOVE

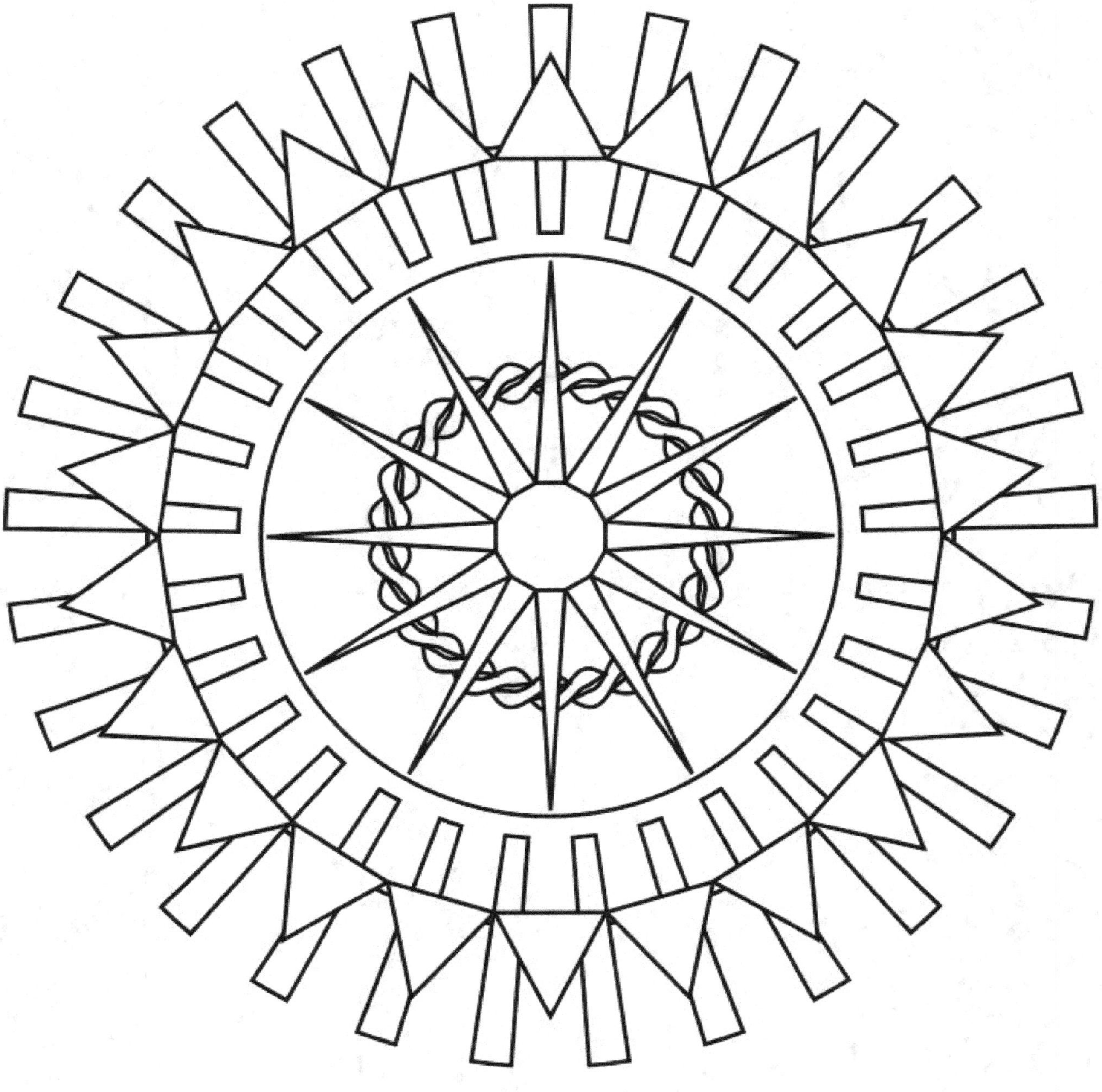

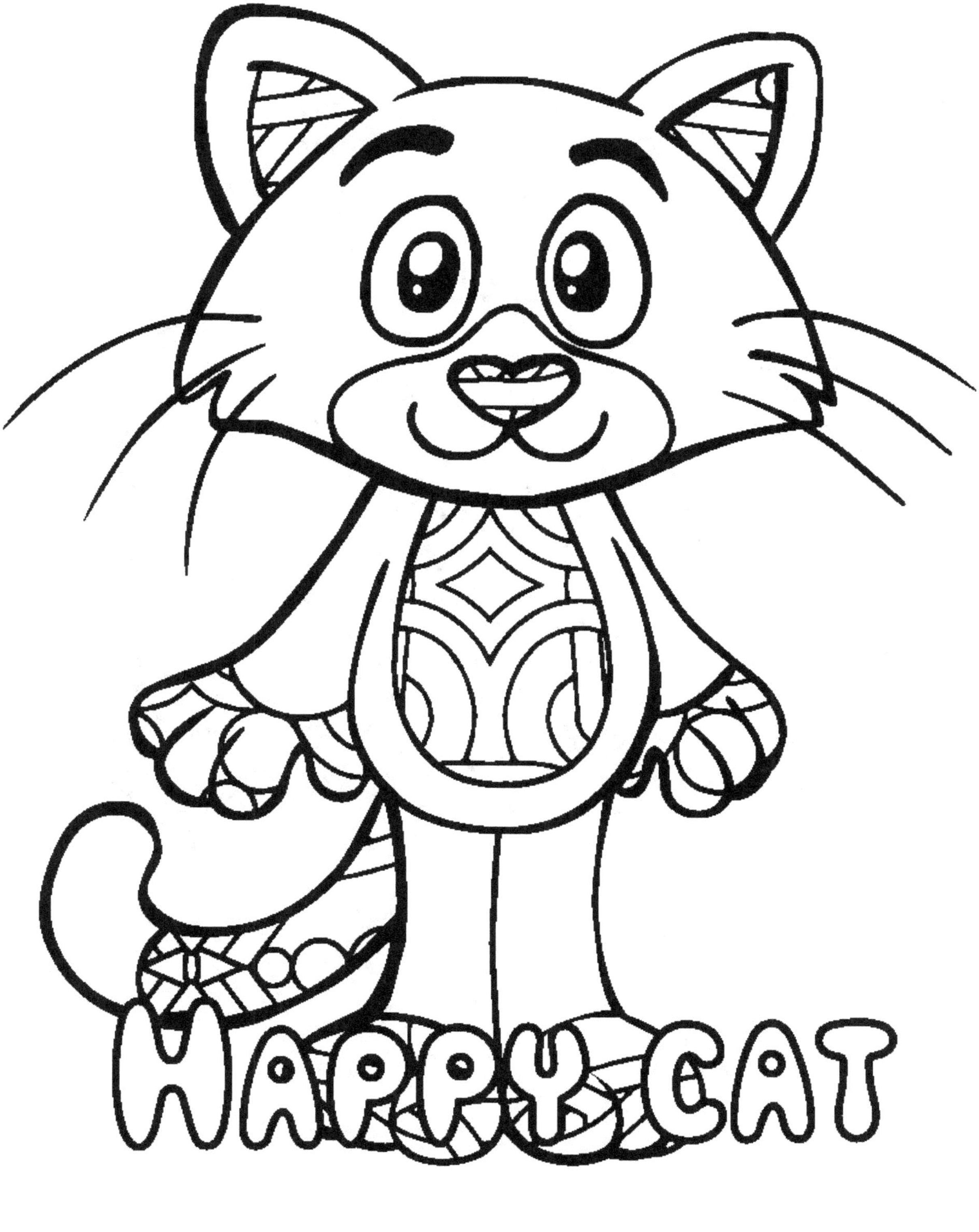
HAPPY CAT

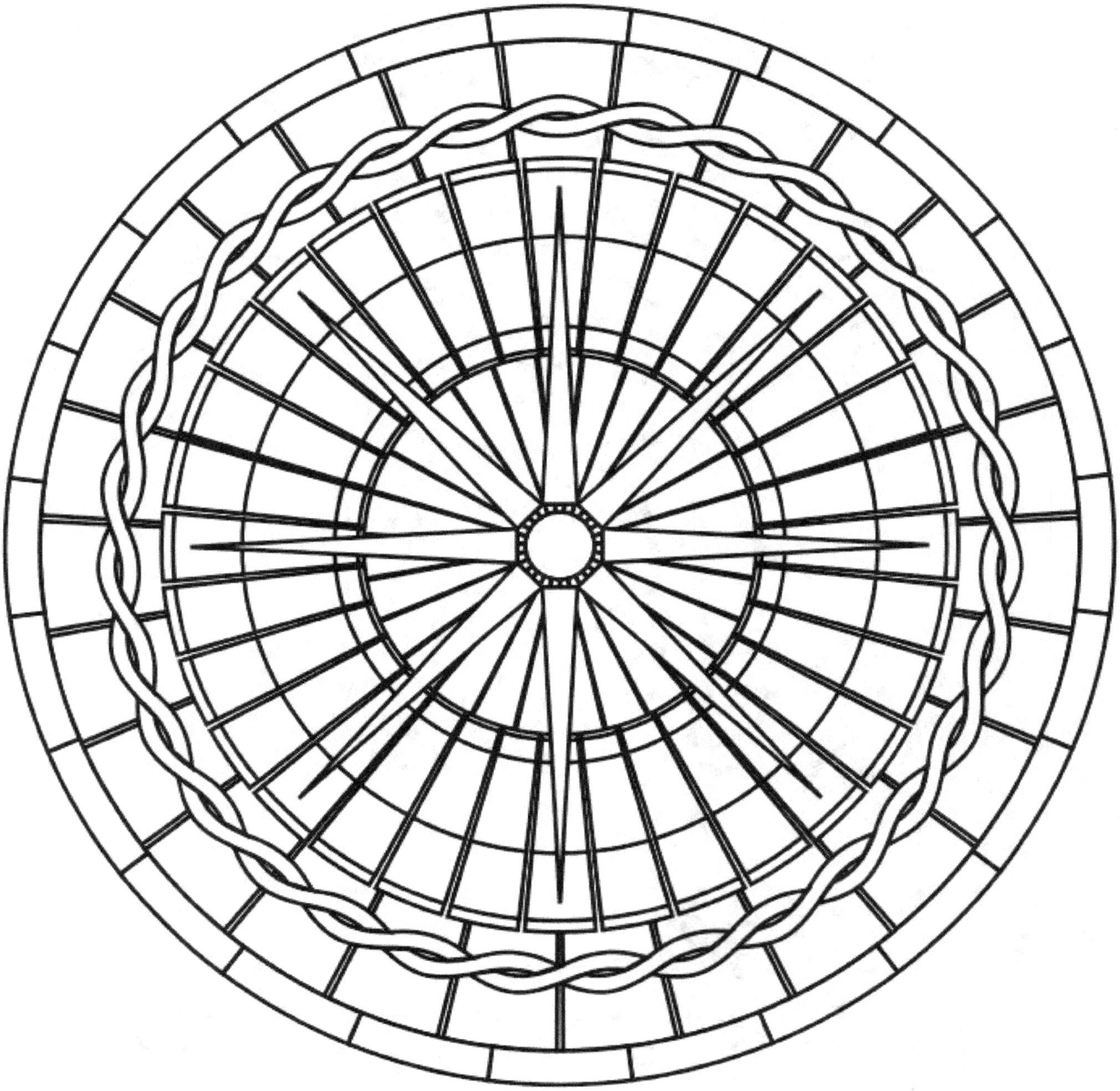

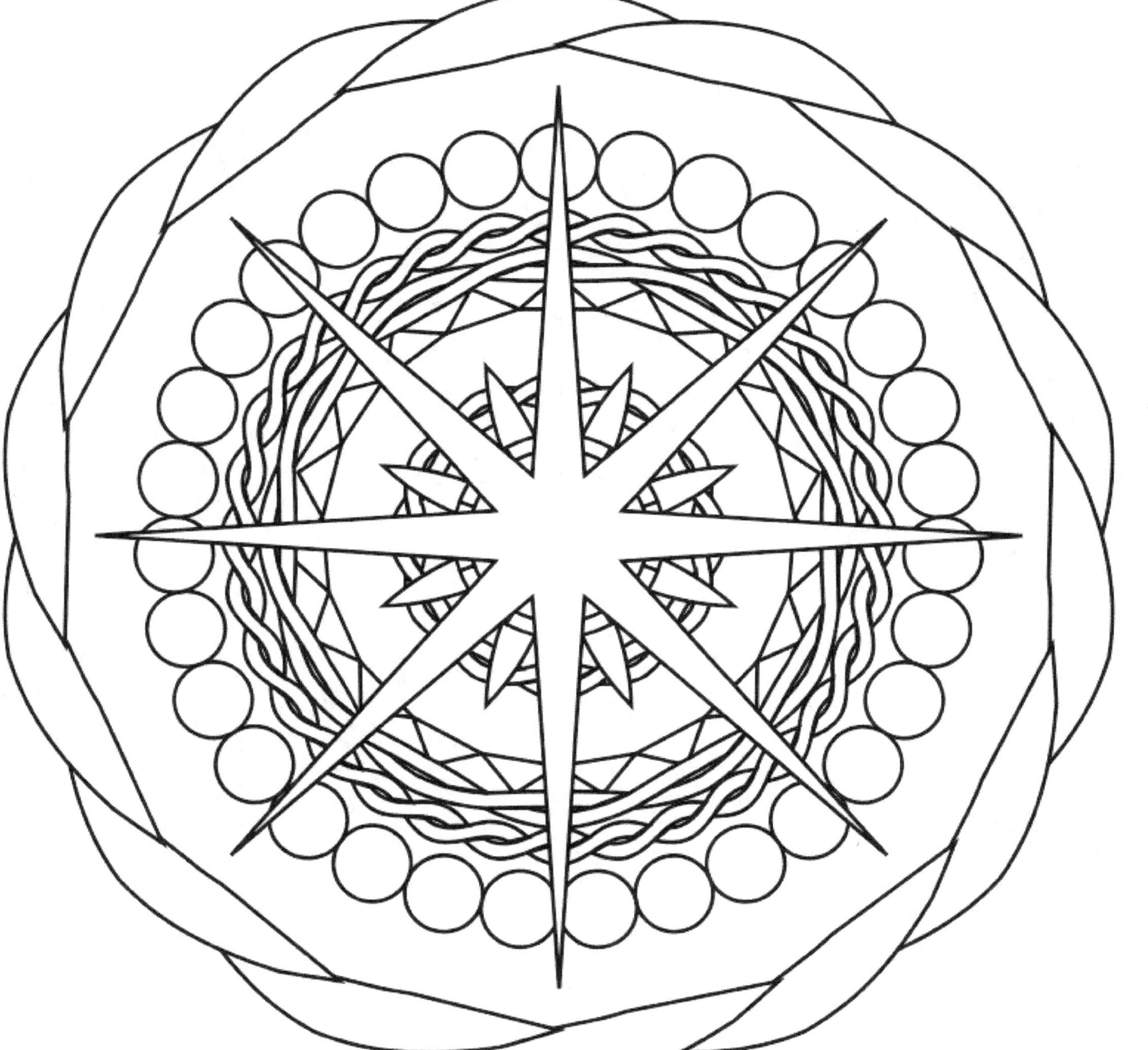

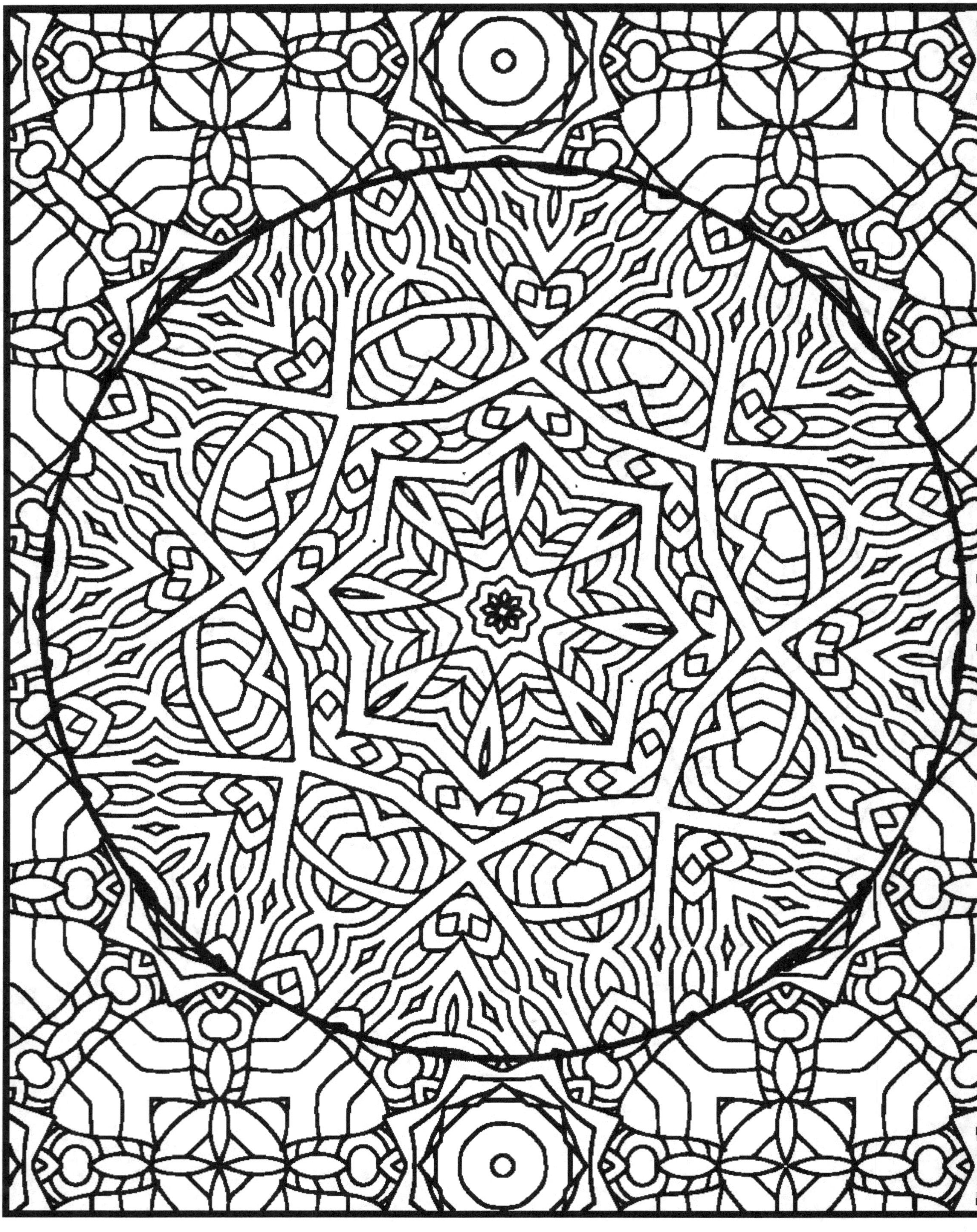

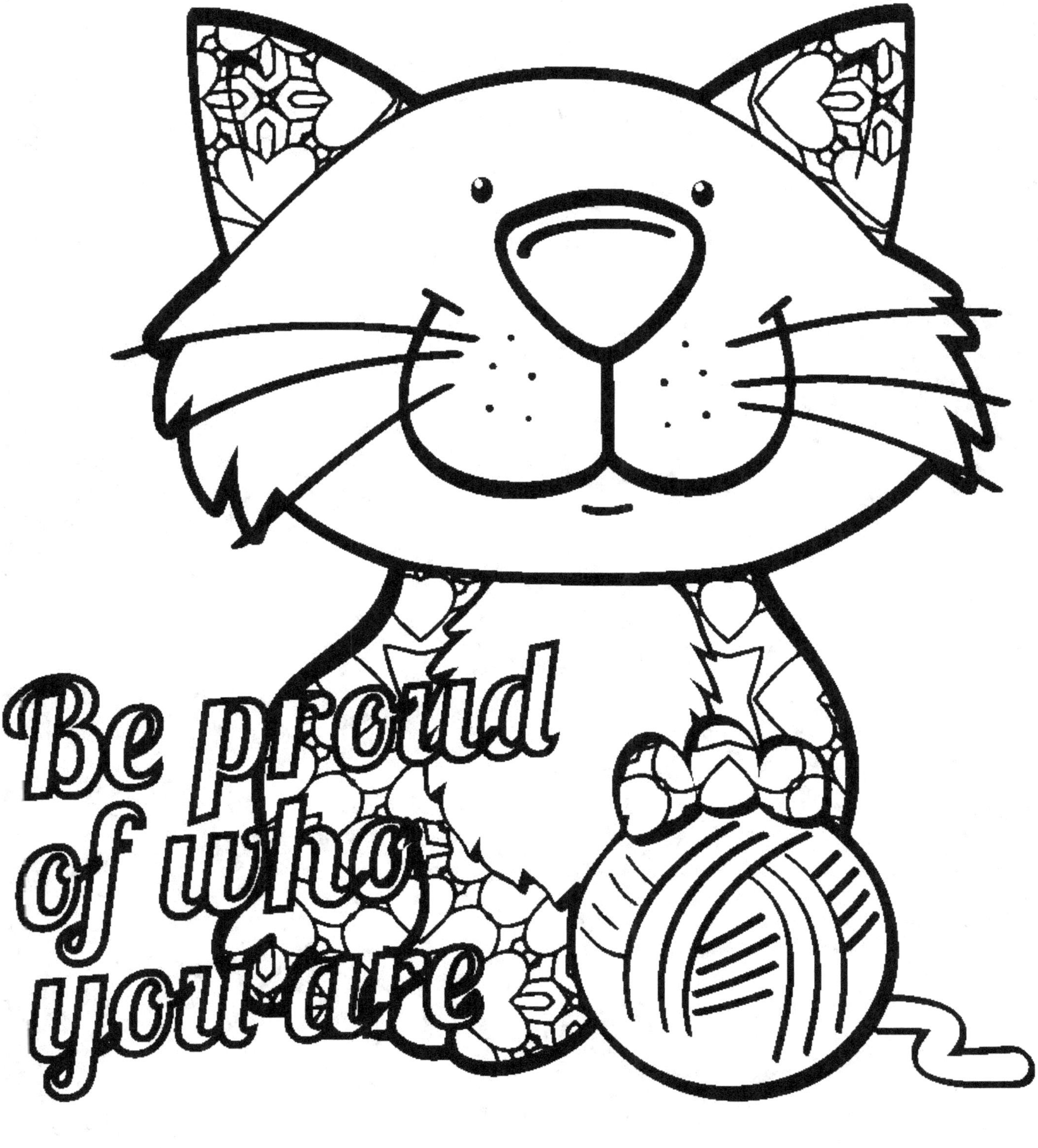
Be proud
of who
you are

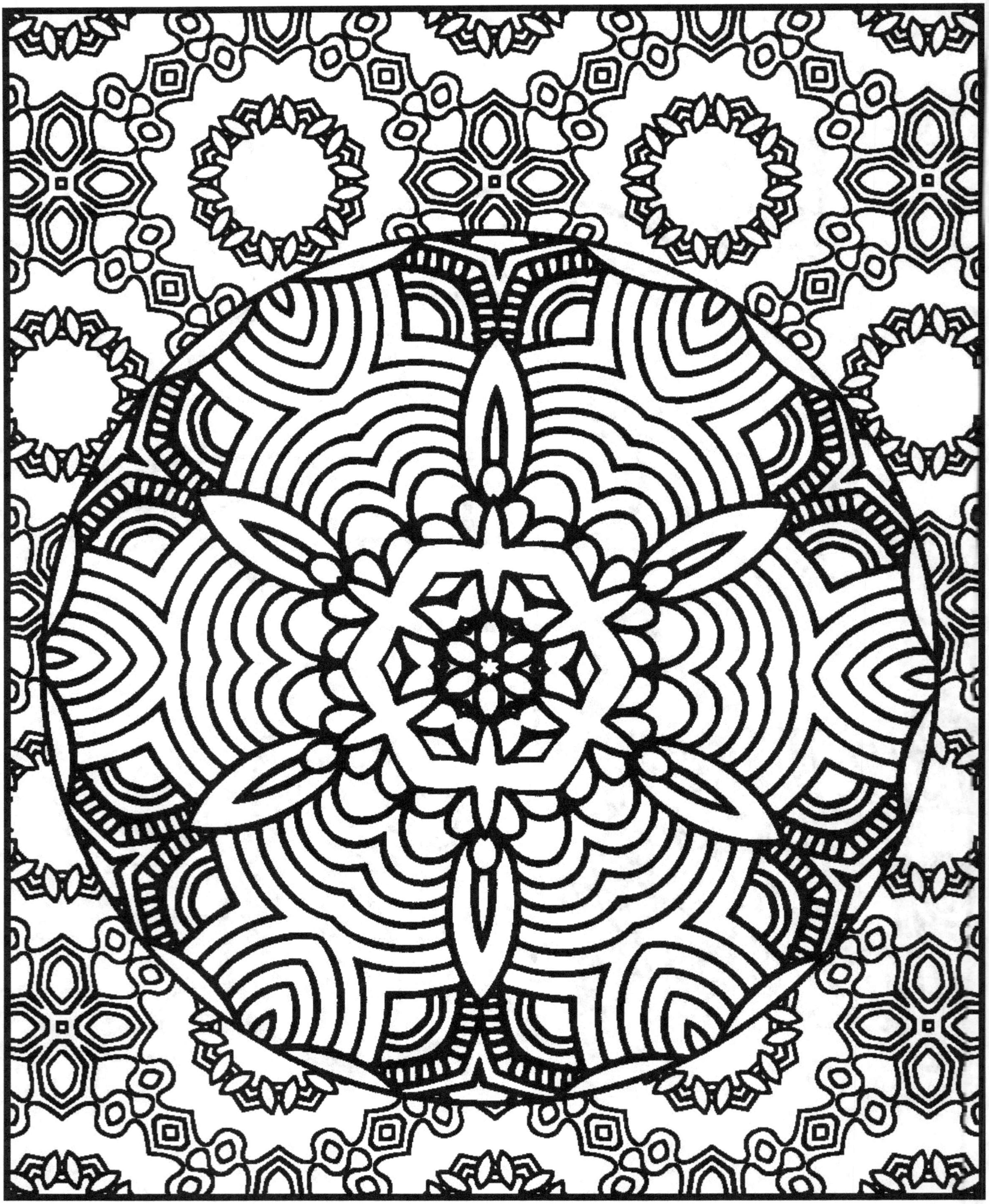

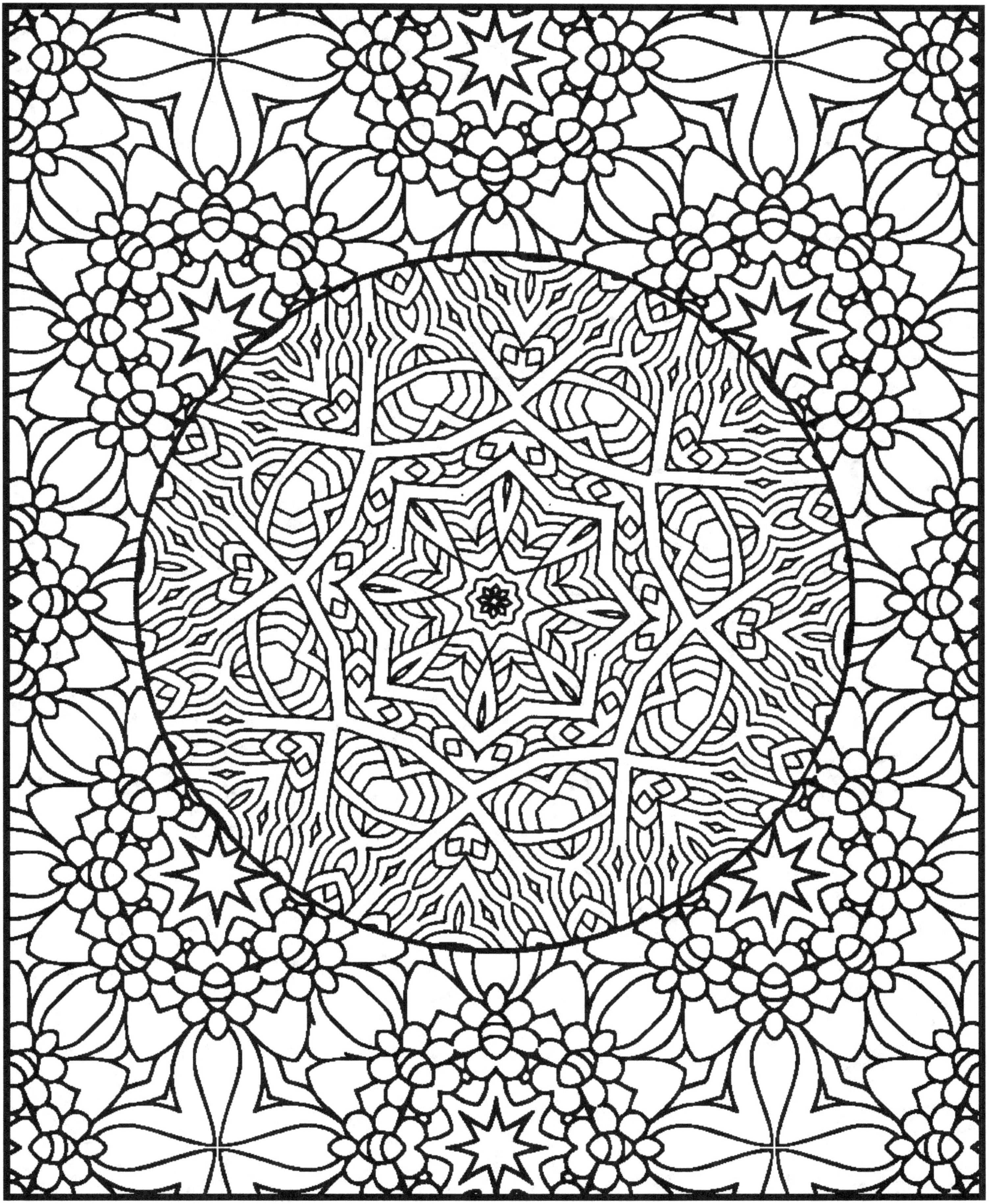

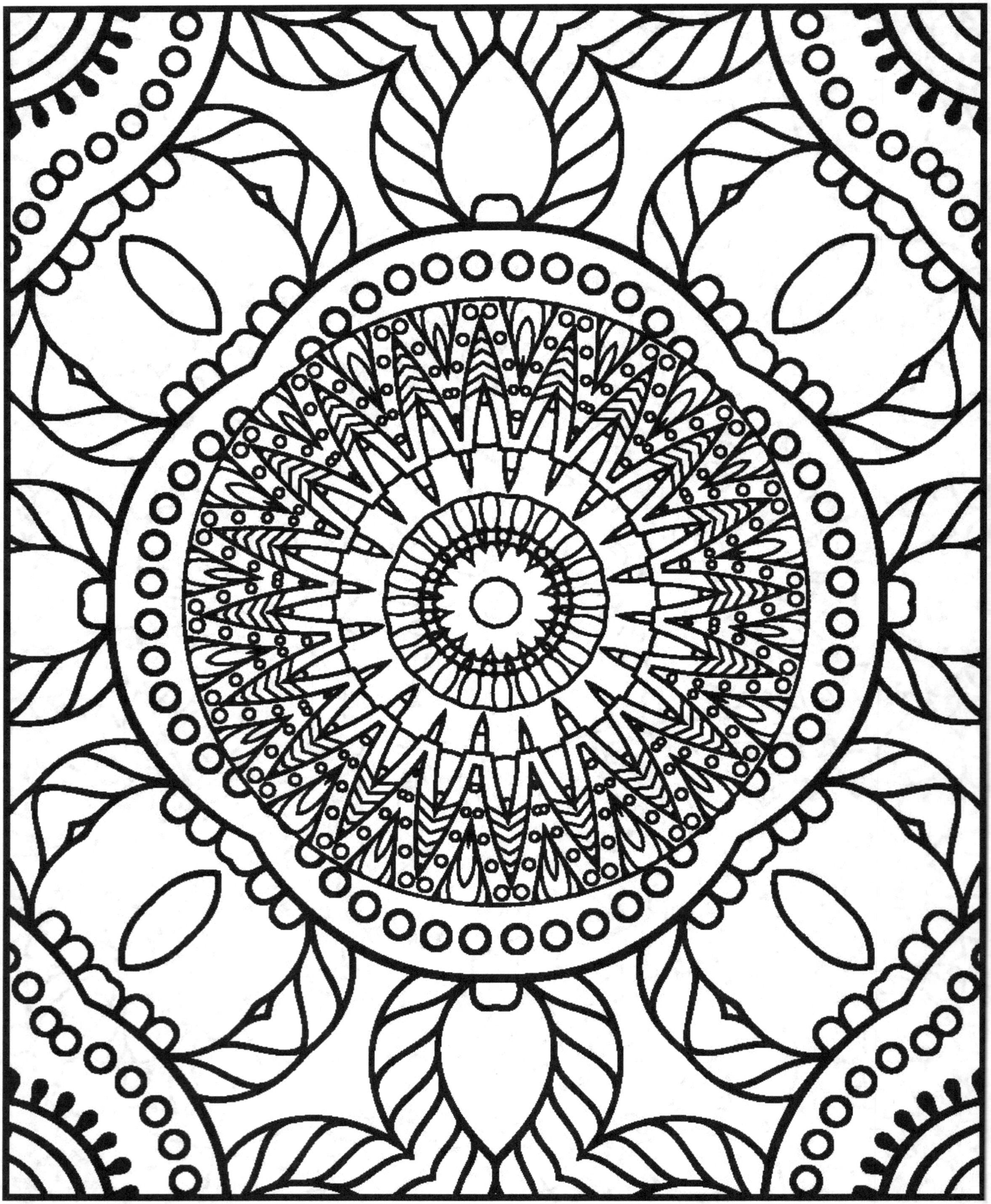

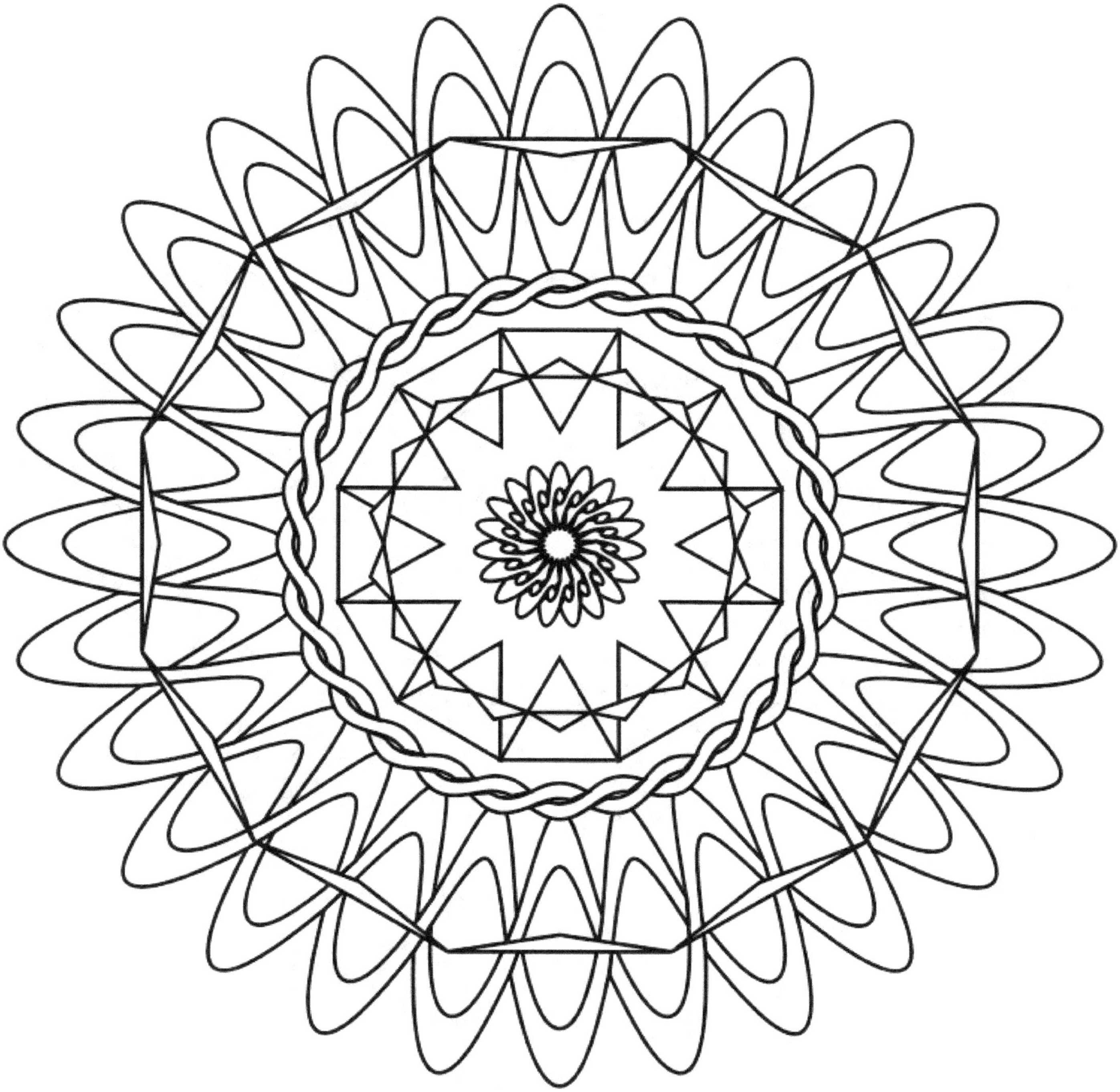

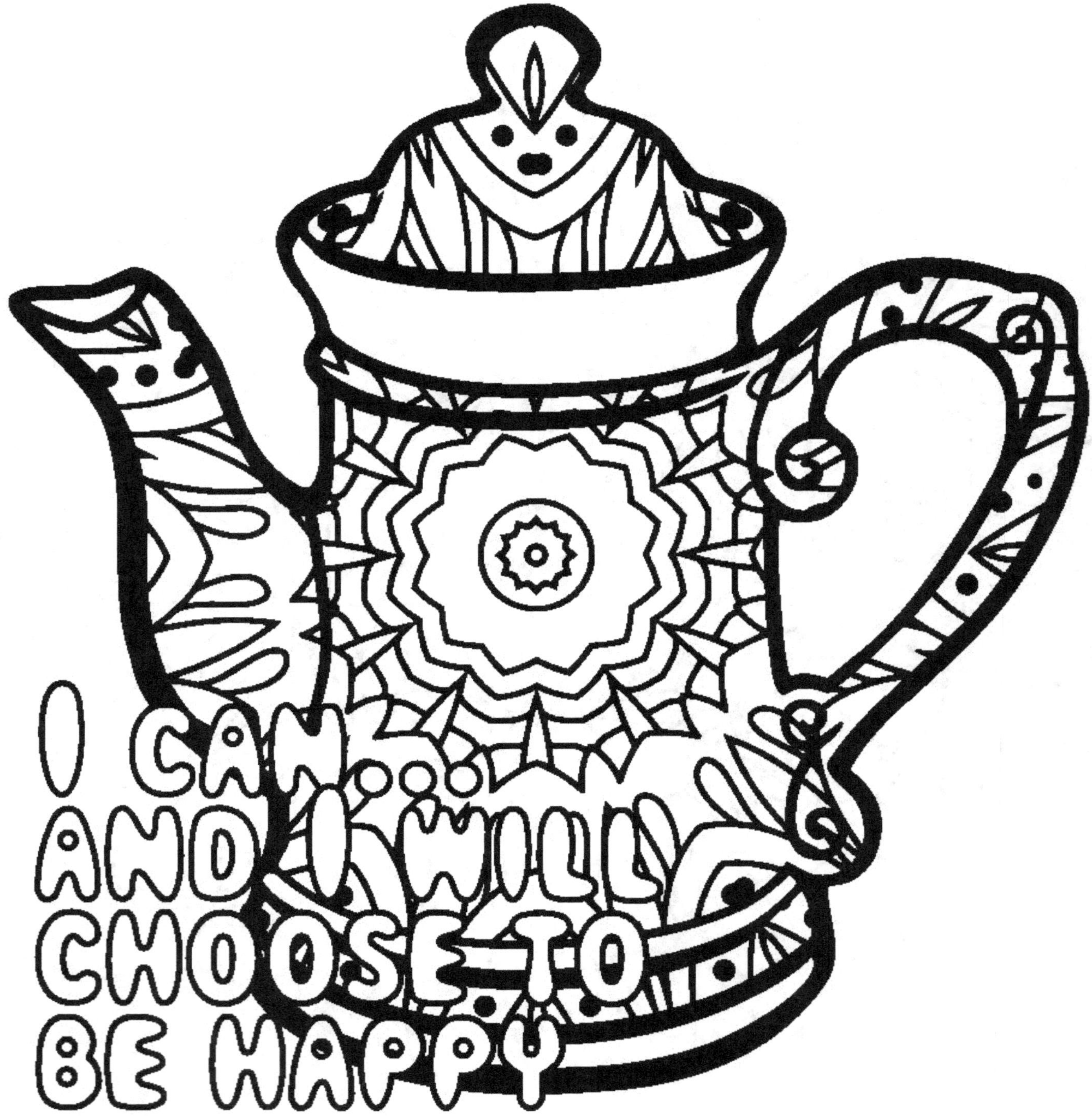
I CAN...
AND I WILL
CHOOSE TO
BE HAPPY

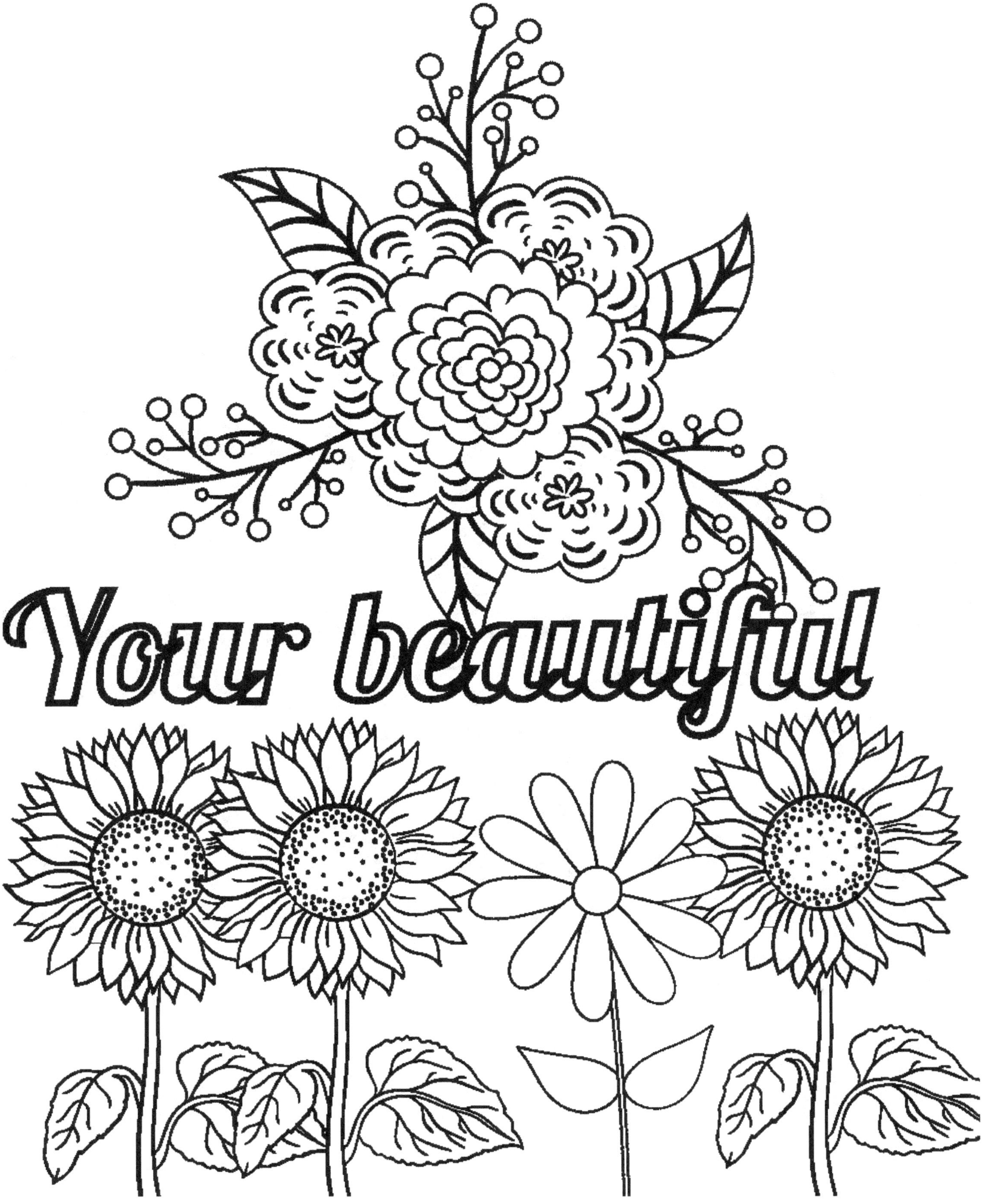
Your beautiful

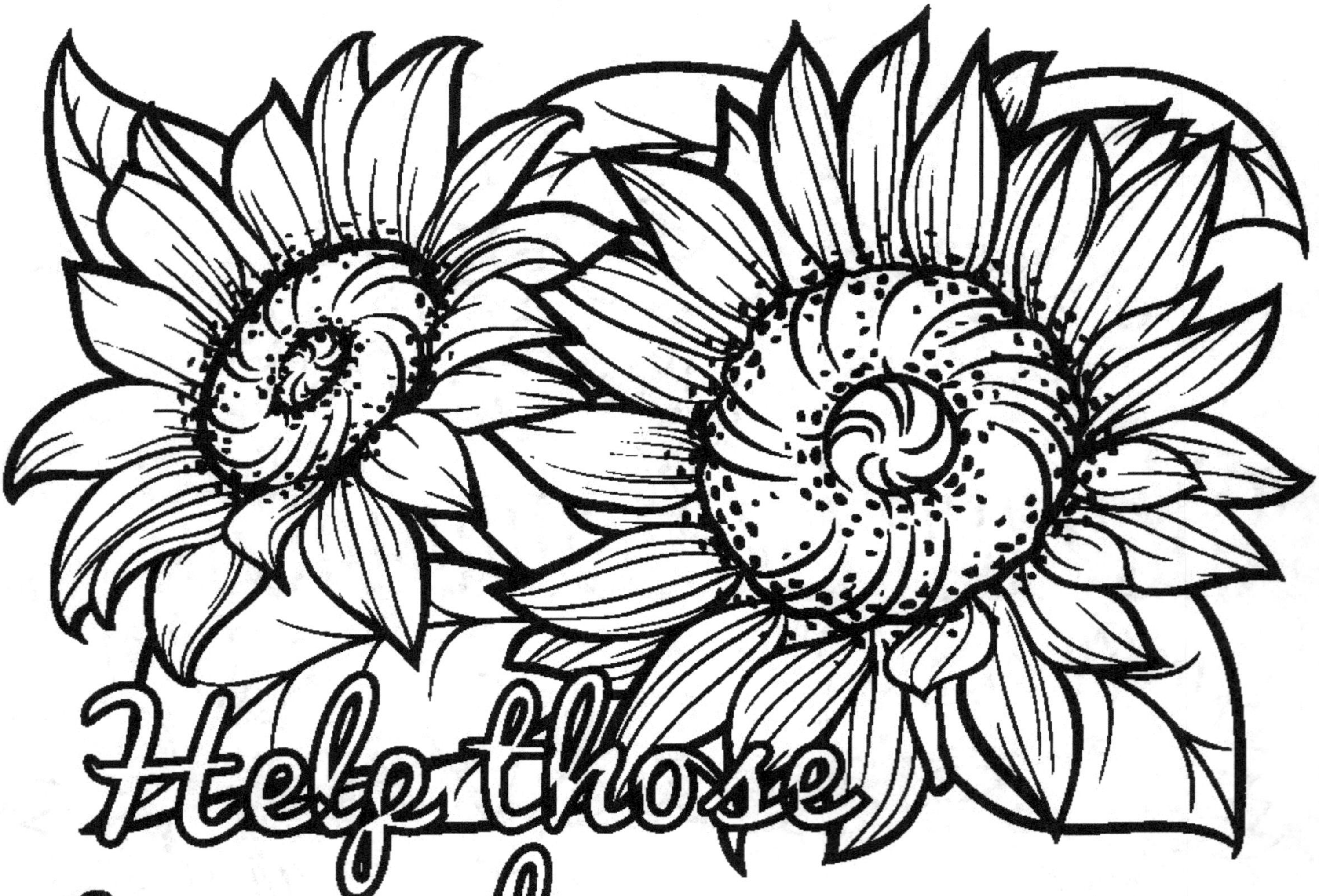
Help those
in need

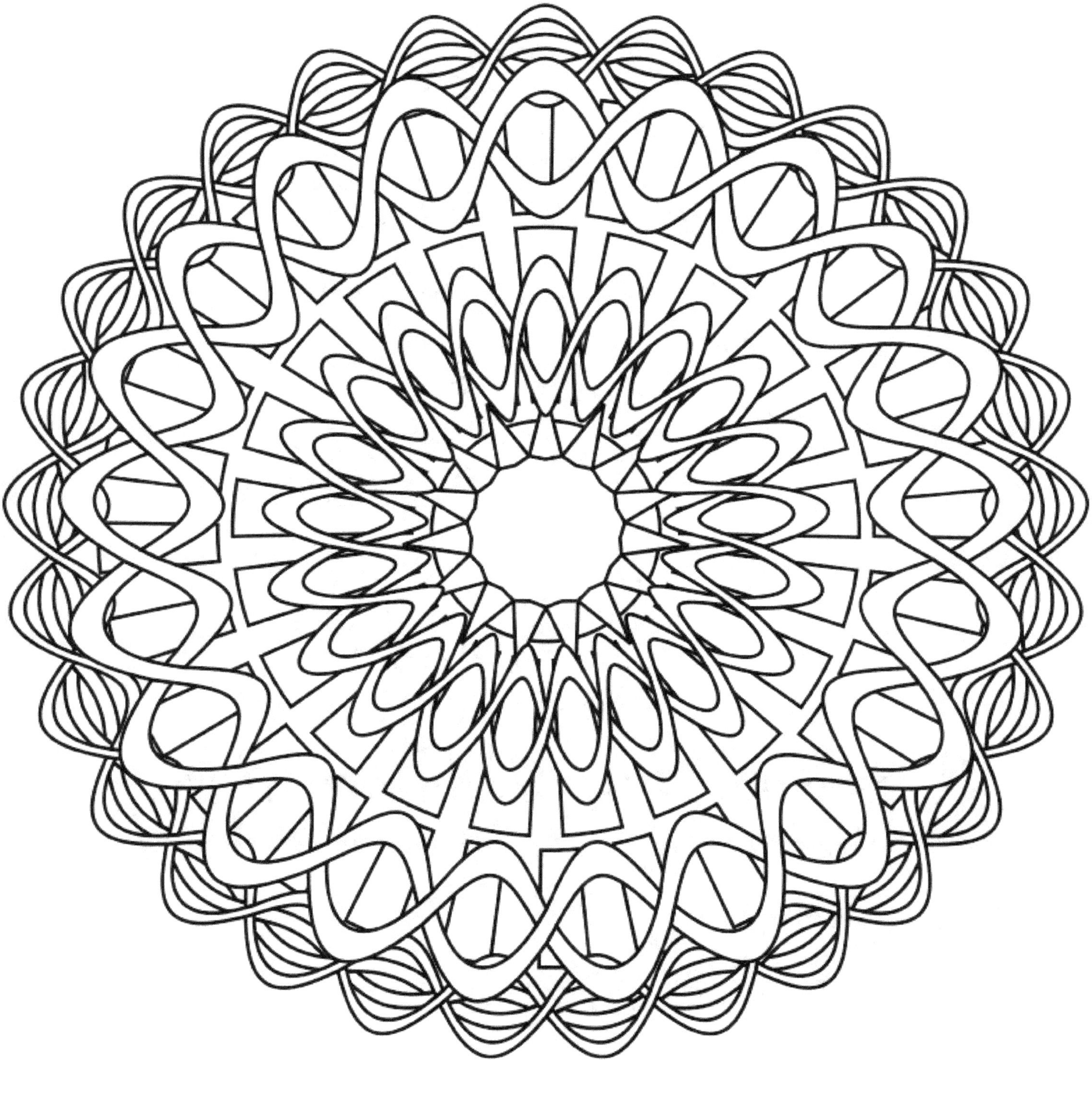

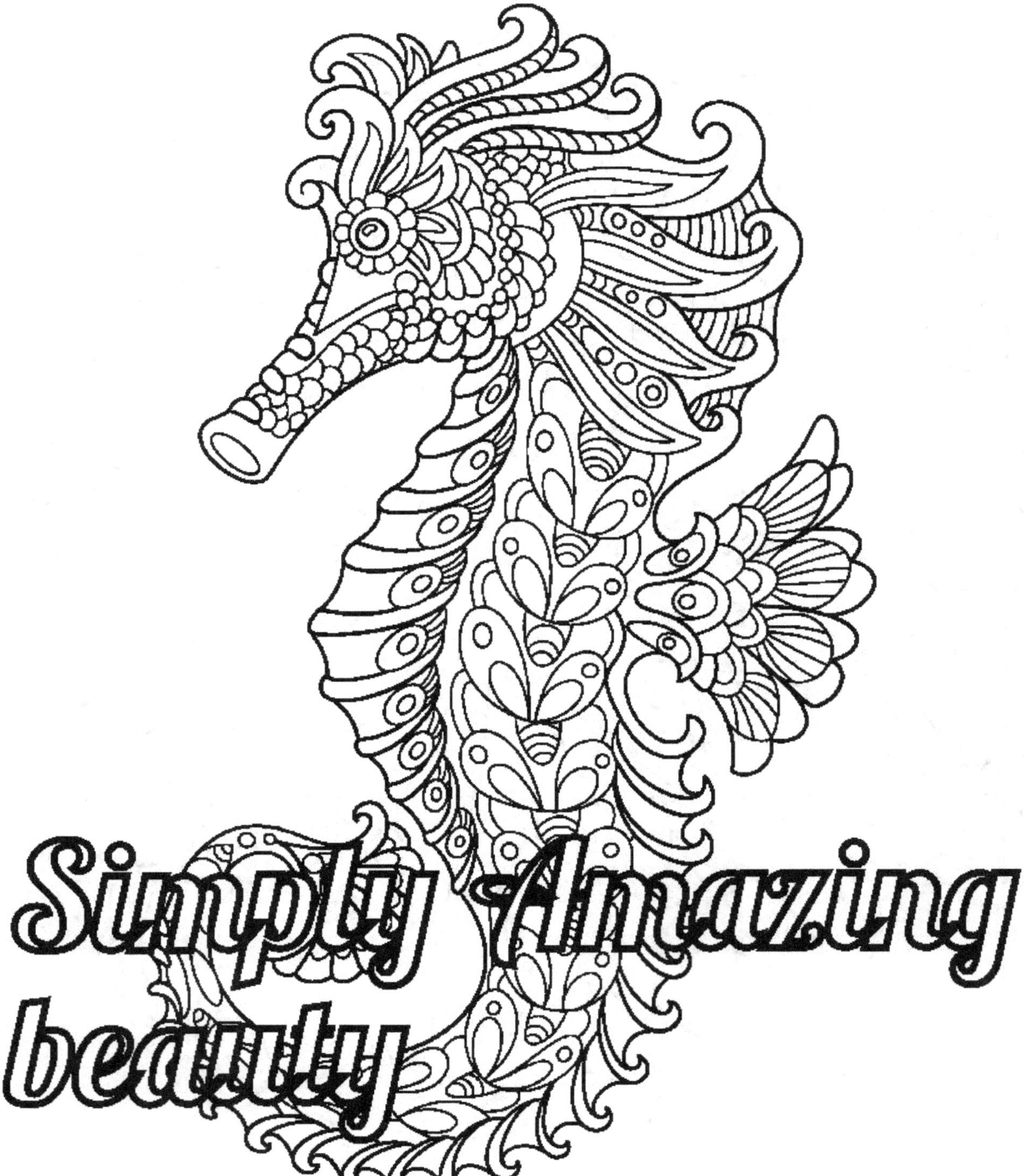
Simply Amazing
beauty

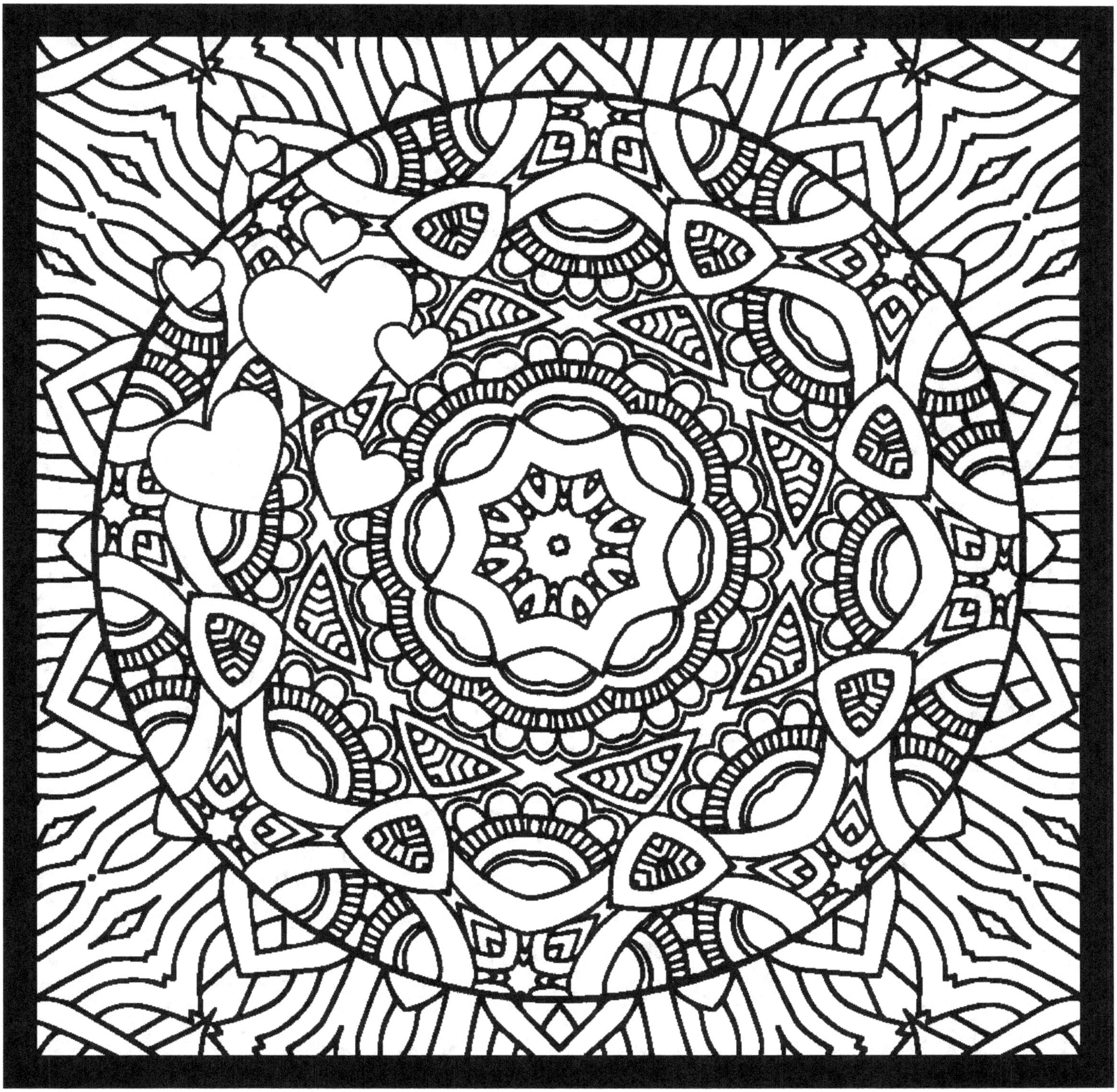

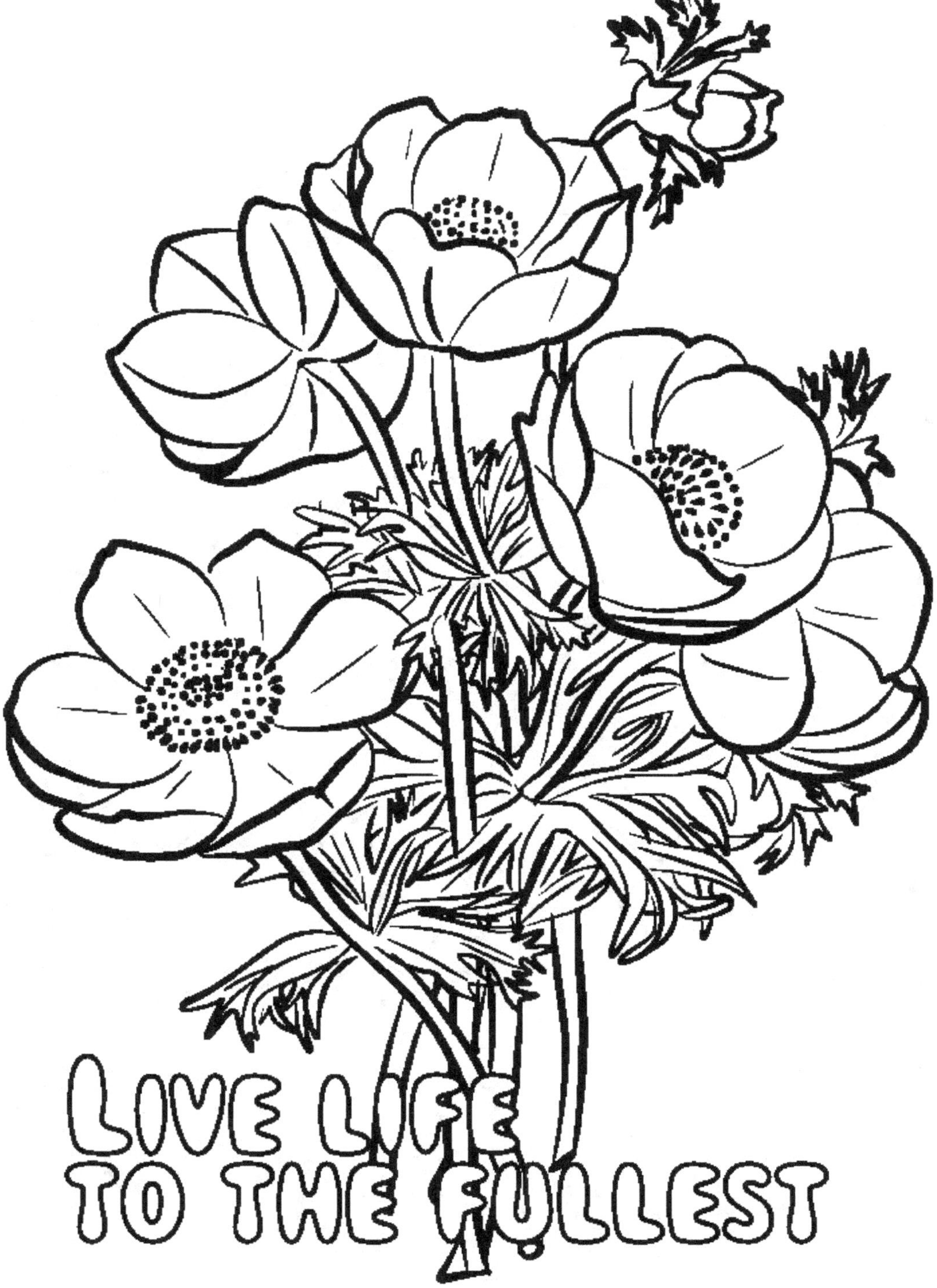
LIVE LIFE
TO THE FULLEST

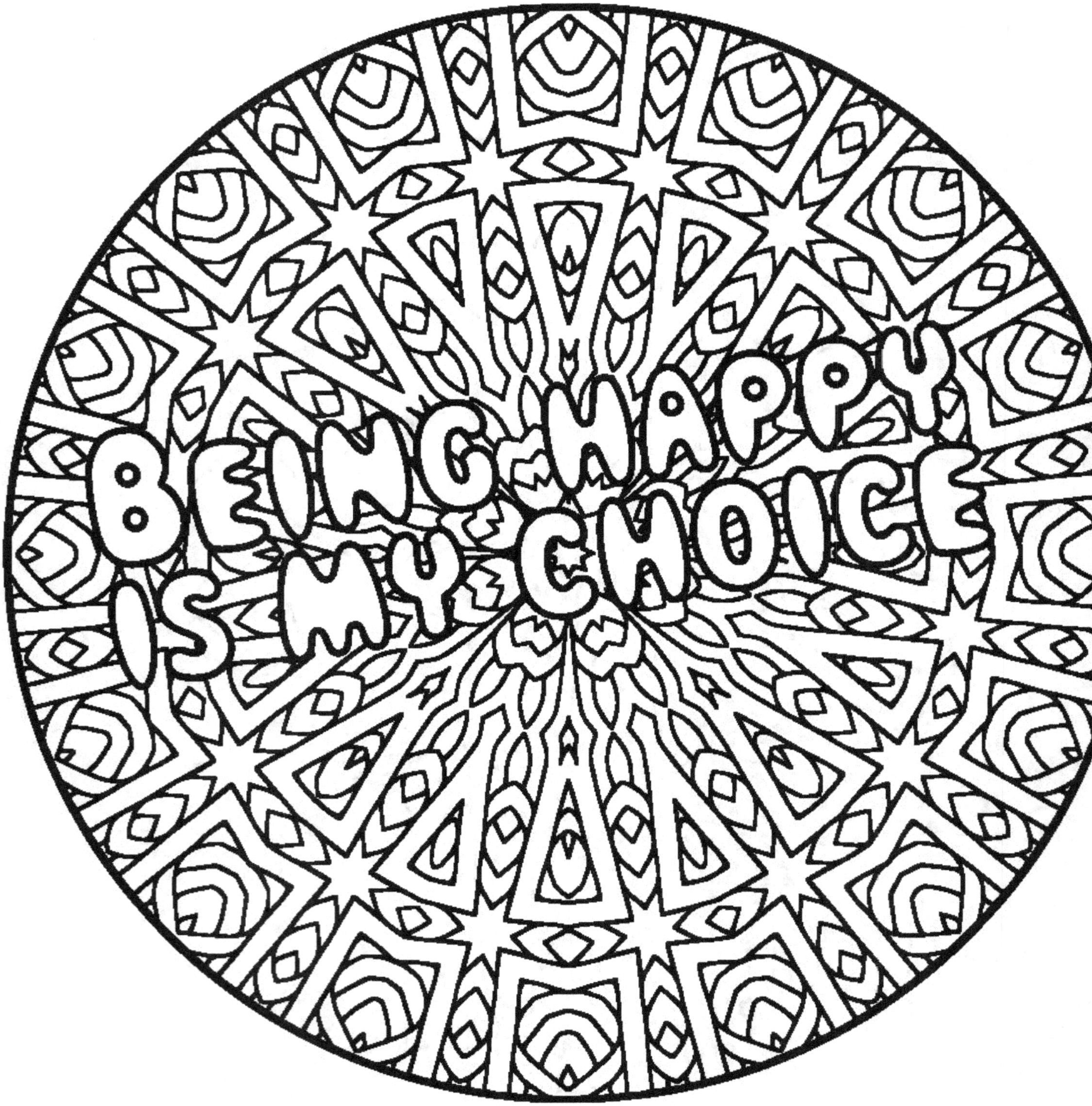
BEING HAPPY
IS MY CHOICE

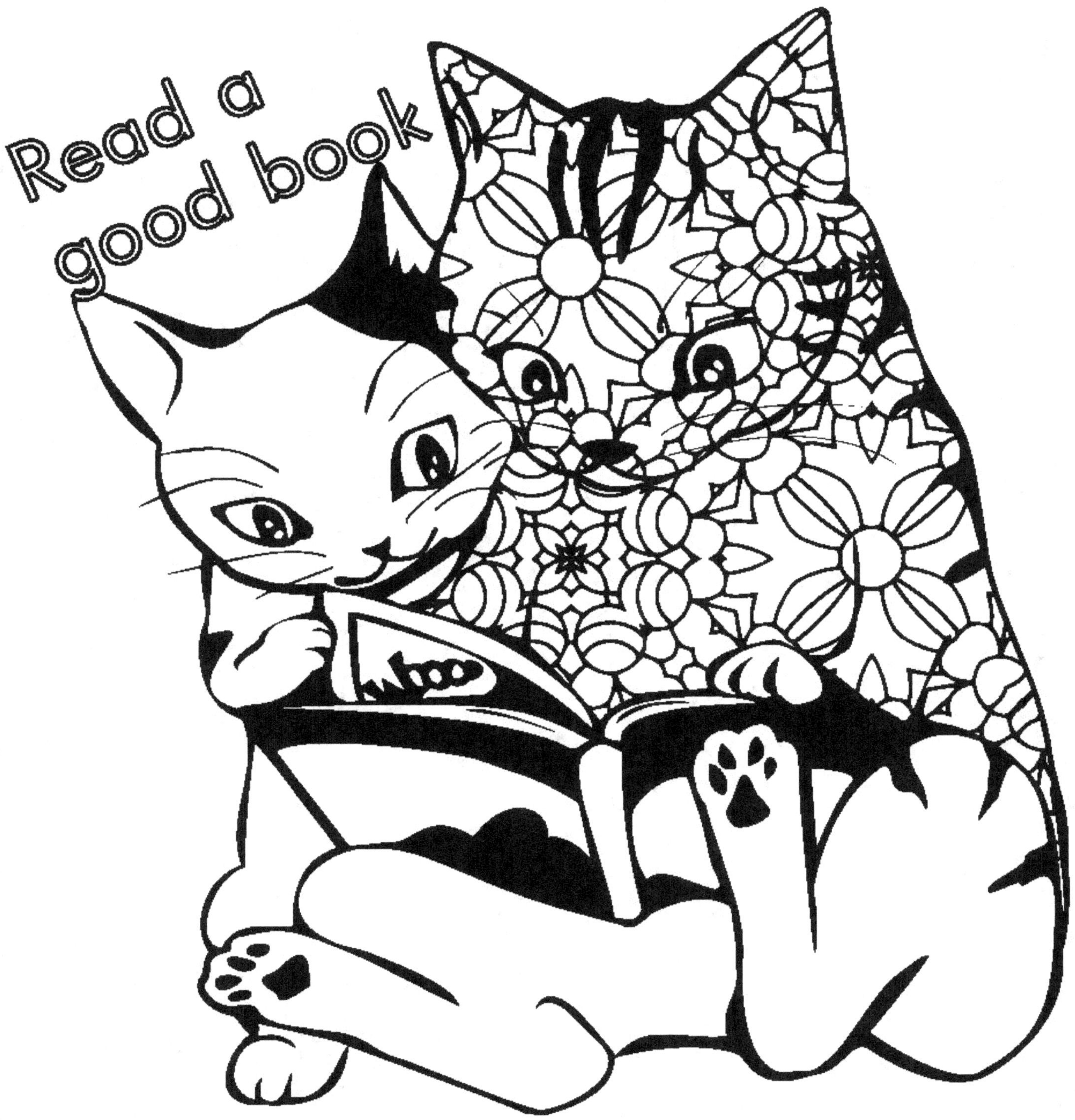
Read a
good book

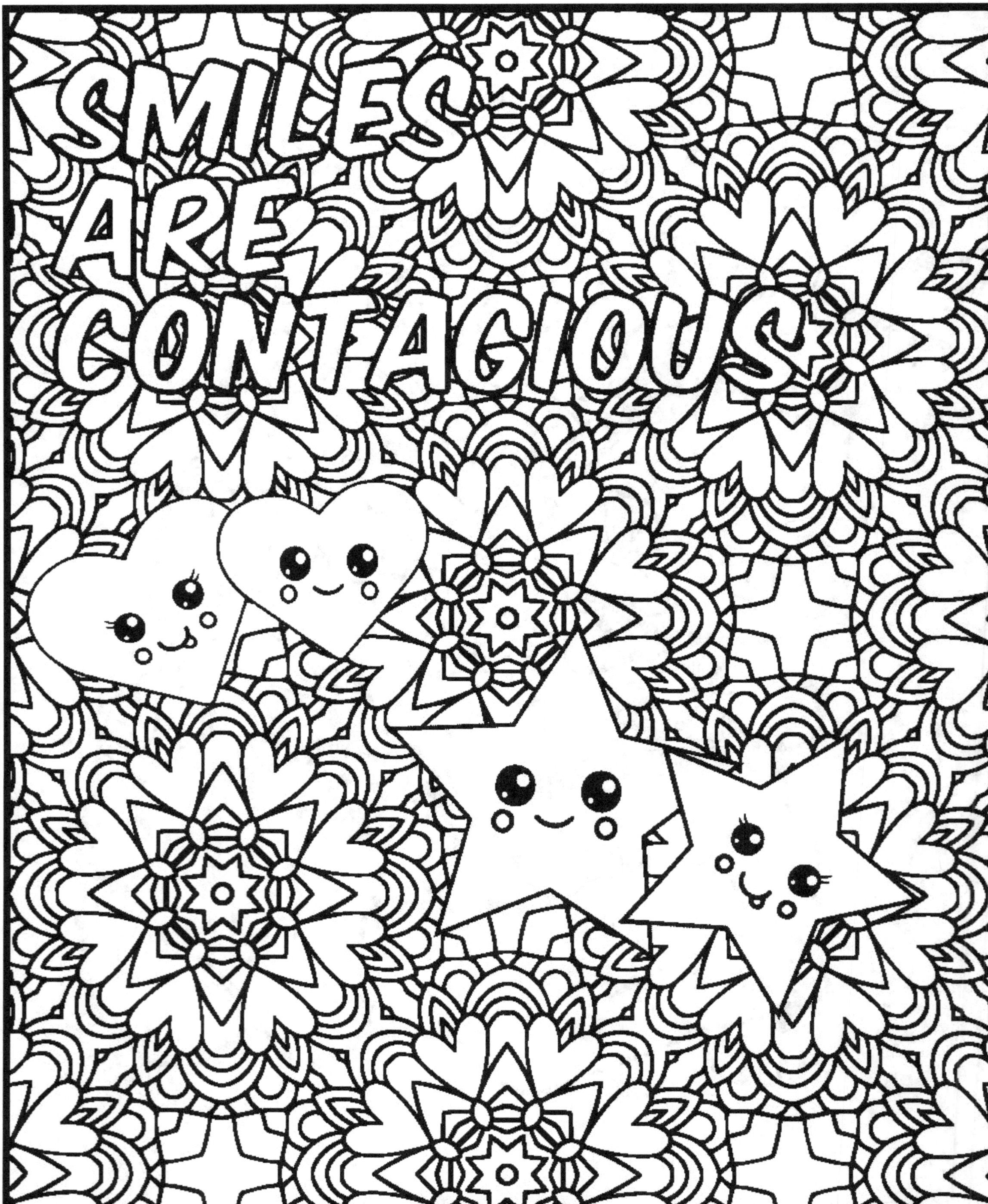
SMILES
ARE
CONTAGIOUS

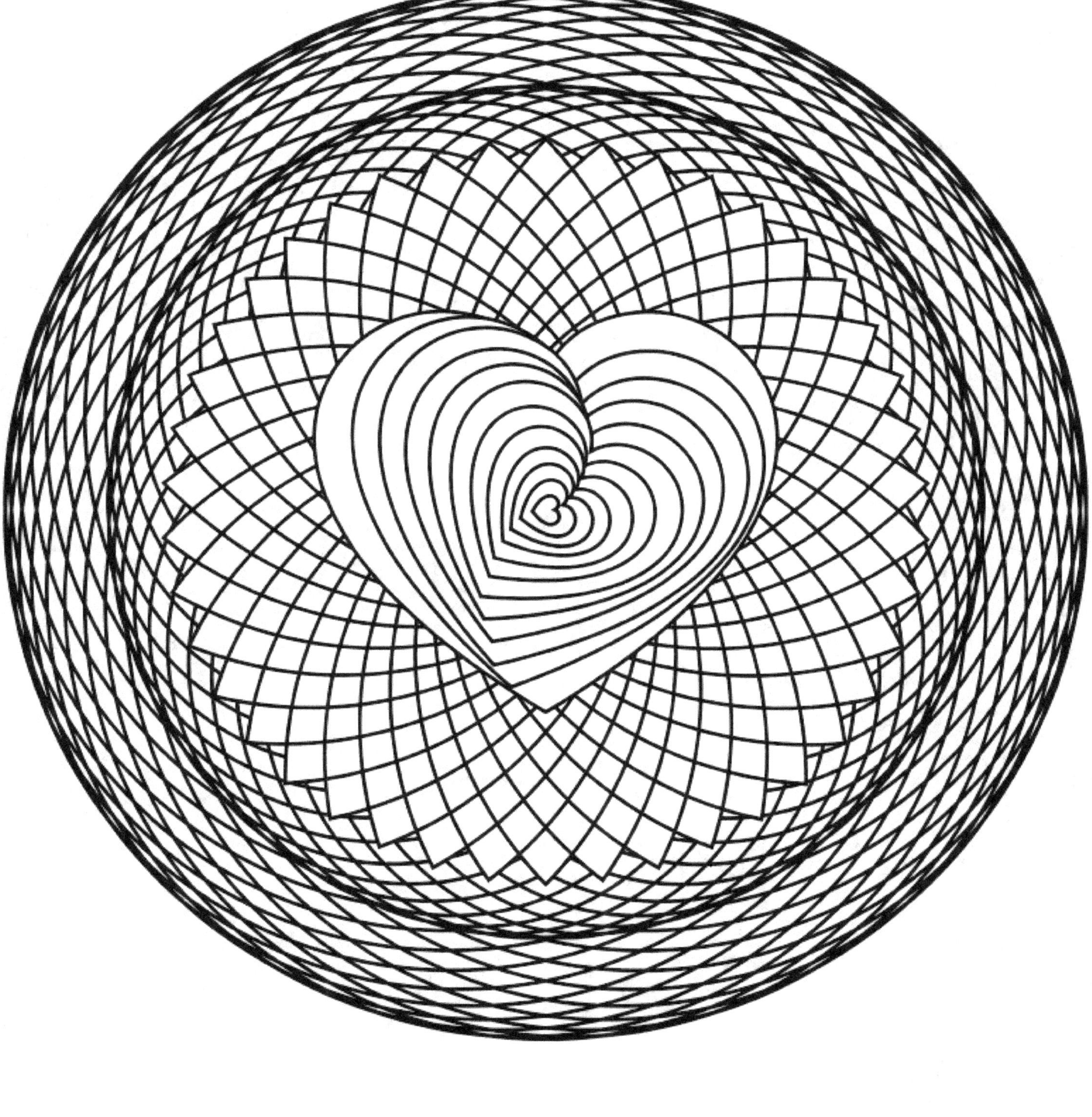

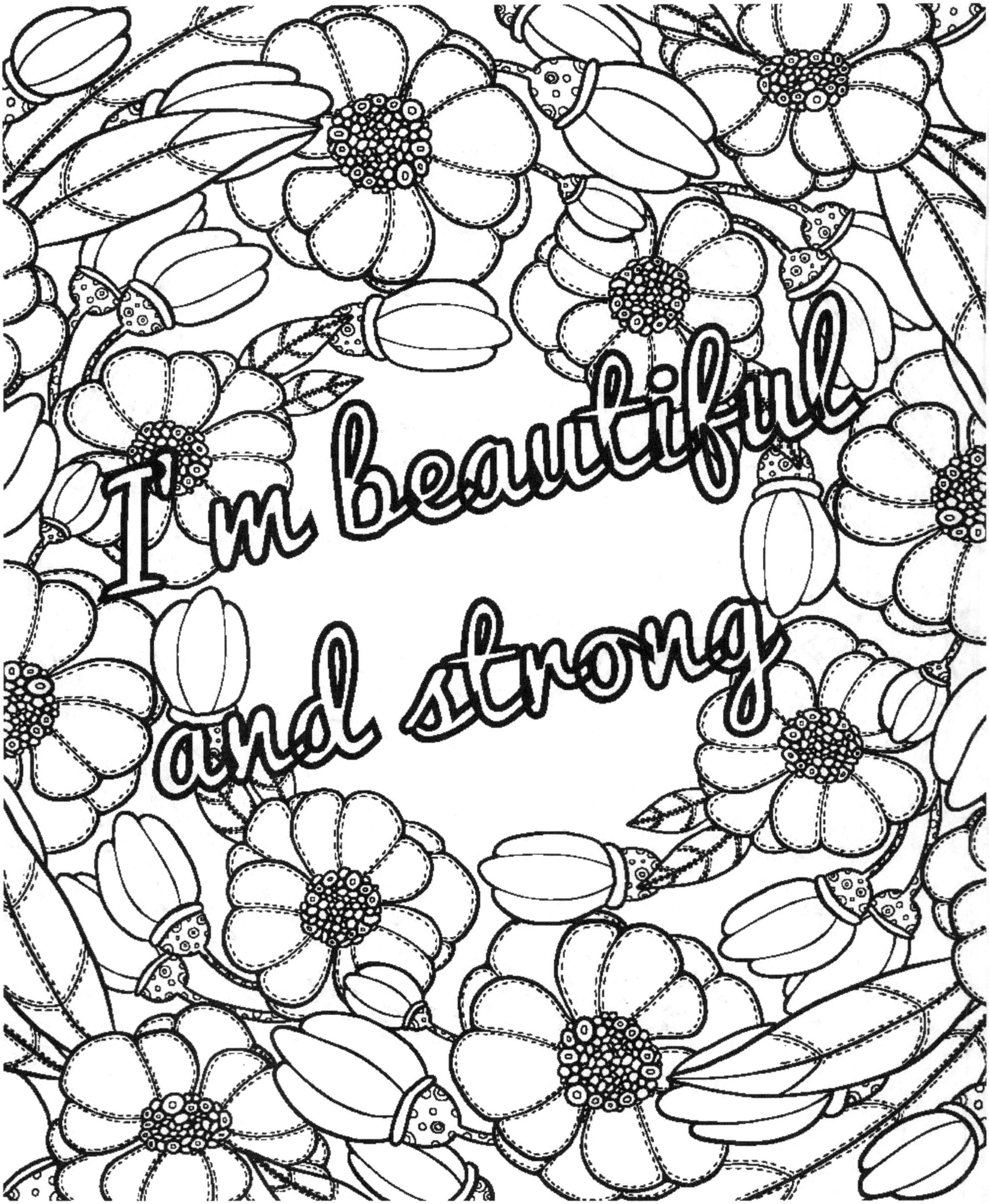
I'm beautiful
and strong

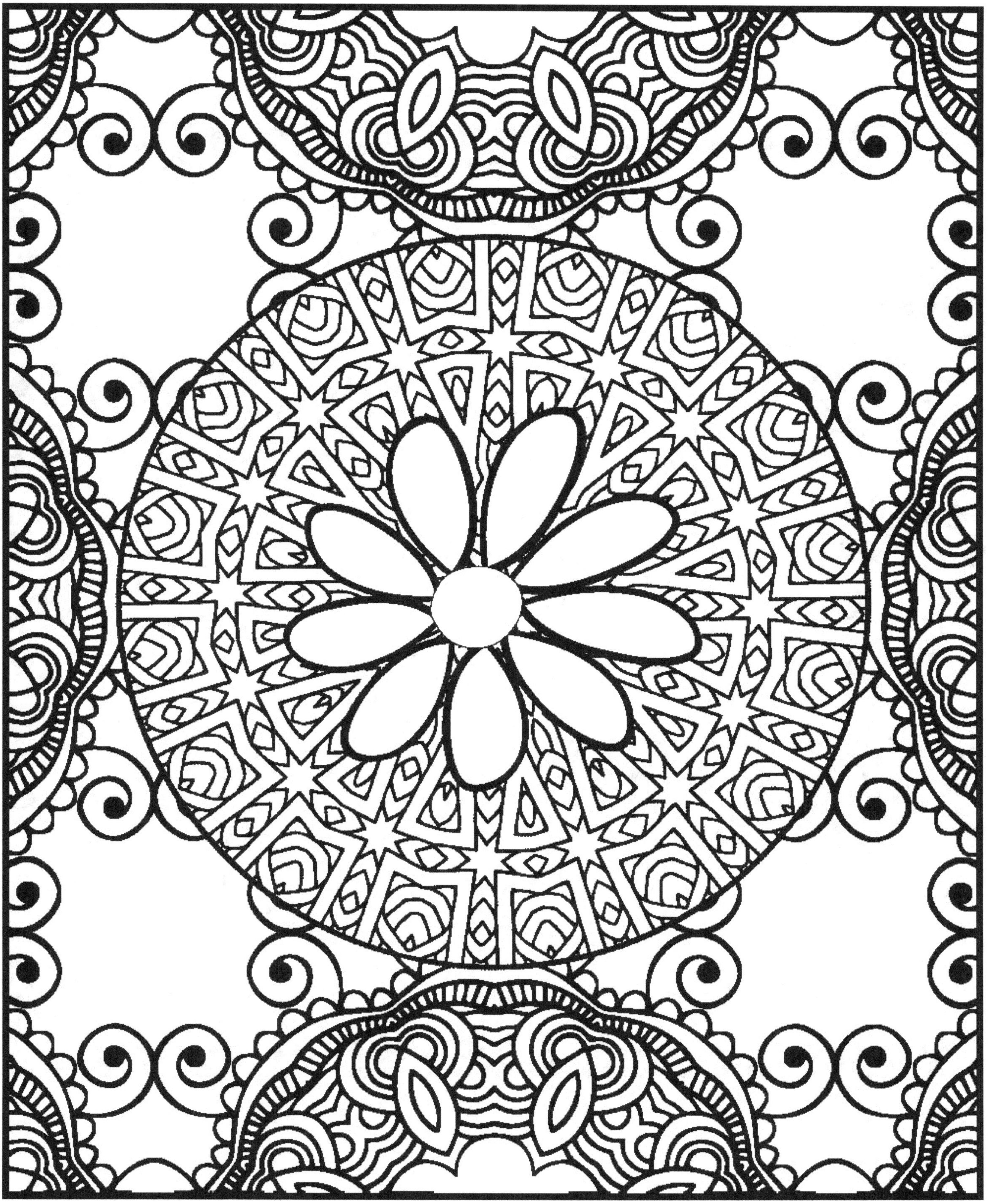

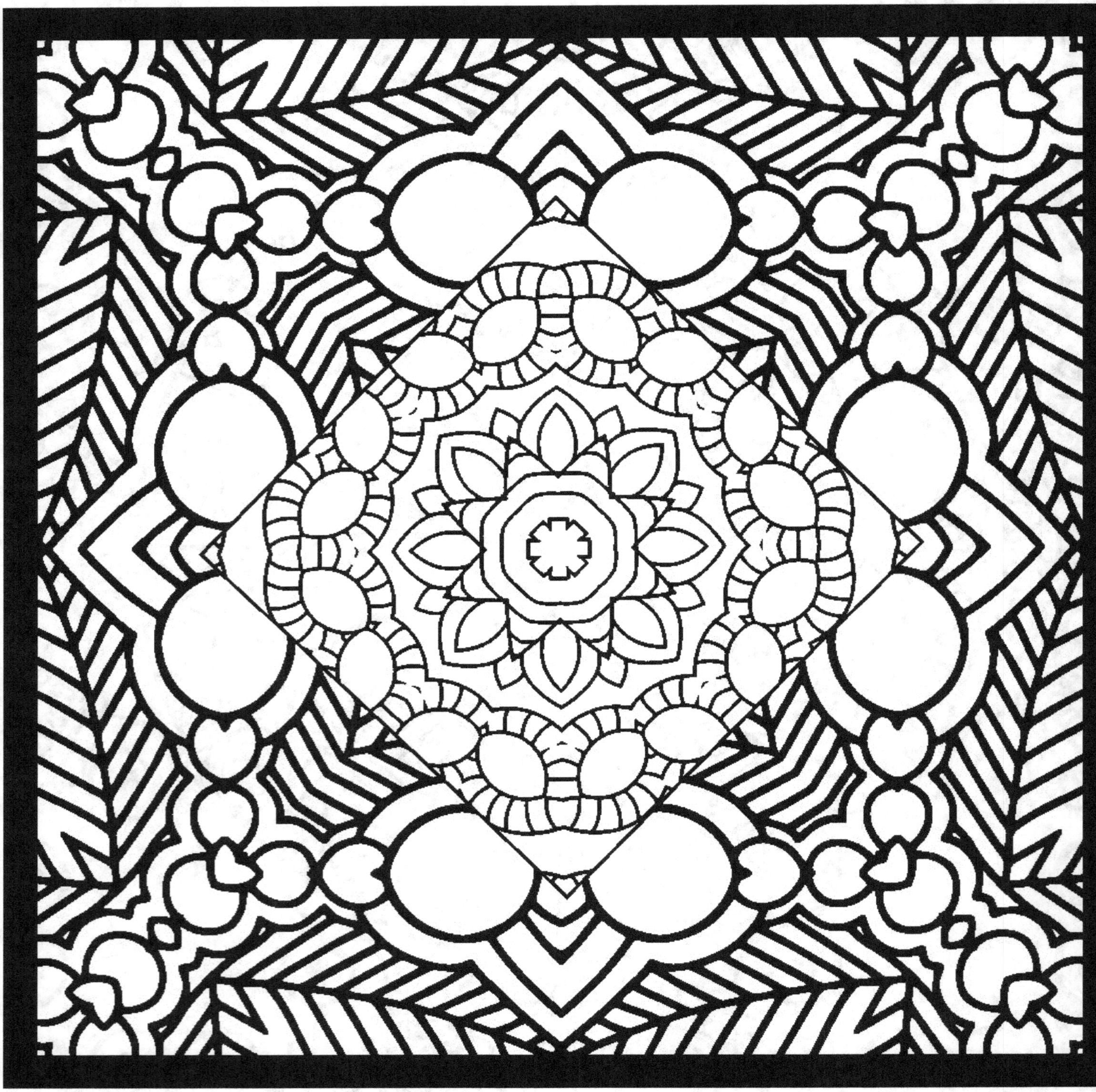

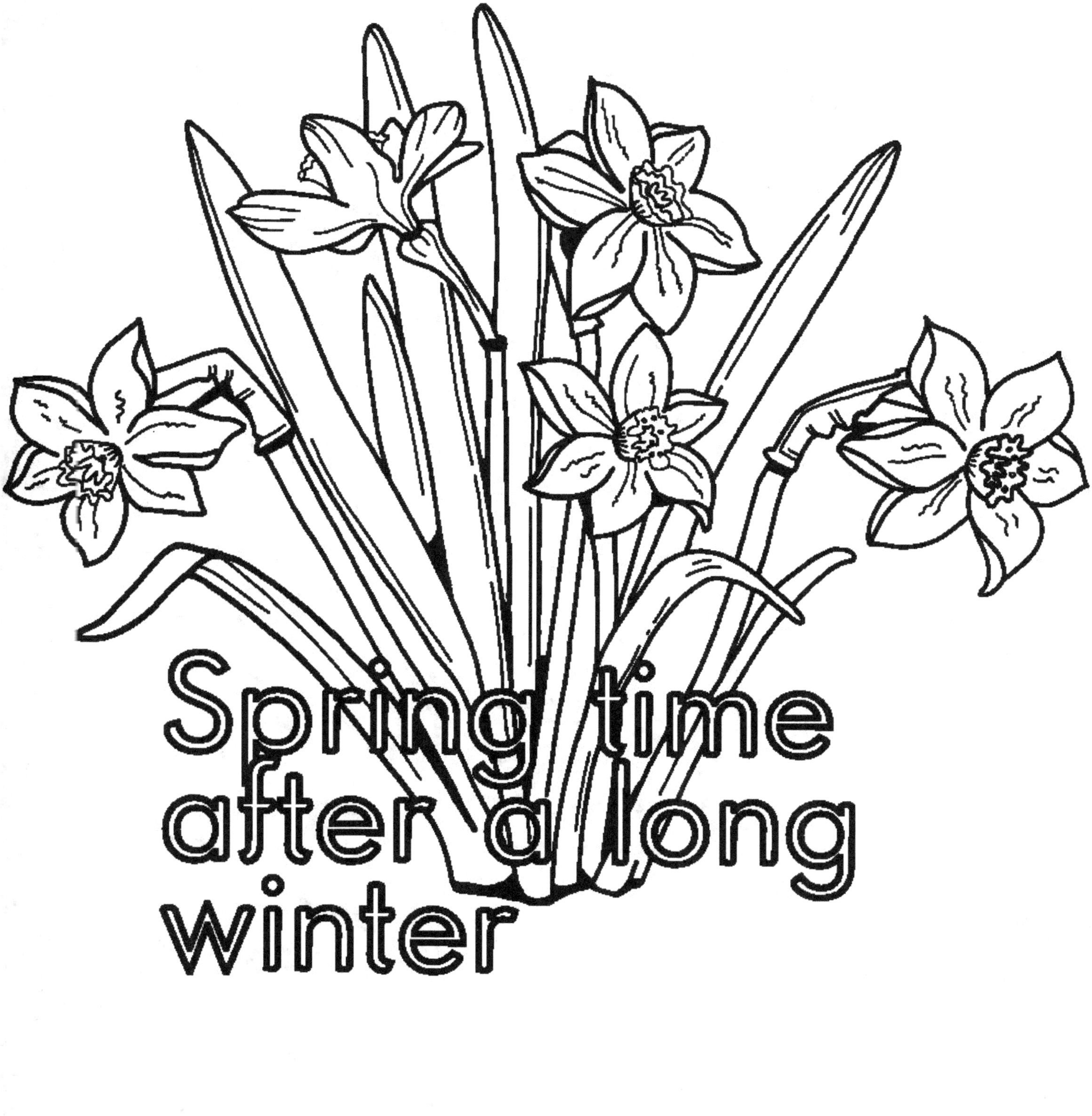
Spring time
after a long
winter

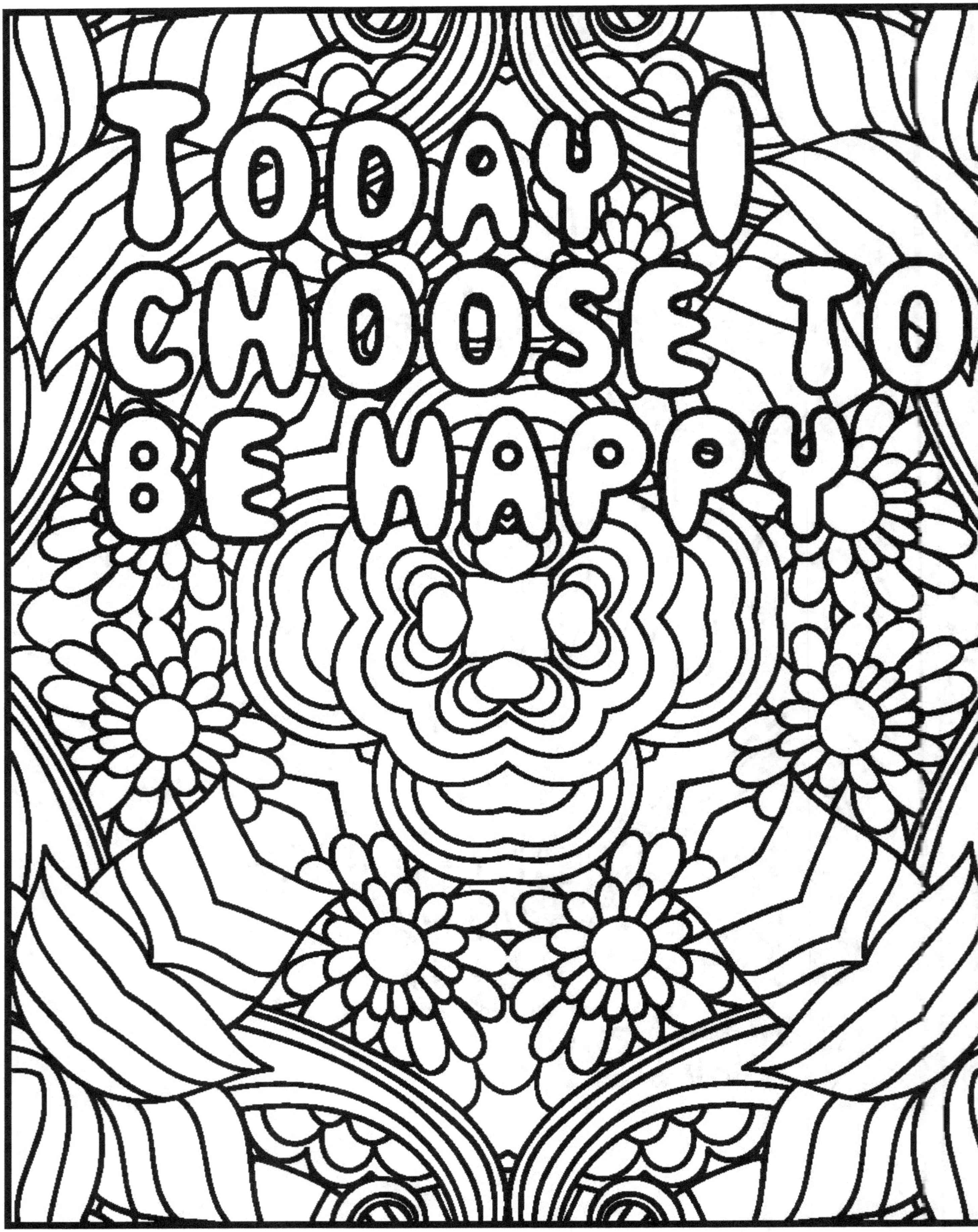
TODAY I
CHOOSE TO
BE HAPPY

www.ingramcontent.com/pod-product-compliance
Lightning Source LLC
Chambersburg PA
CBHW081520220526
45467CB00010B/2988
* 9 7 9 8 7 1 1 5 1 6 0 9 5 *